MAINE STATE LIBRARY

THE
MEANINGS AND DERIVATIONS
OF
CHRISTIAN NAMES.

WHAT IS YOUR NAME?

A POPULAR ACCOUNT OF THE

MEANINGS AND DERIVATIONS OF CHRISTIAN NAMES.

BY

Sophy Moody,

AUTHOR OF 'THE FAIRY TREE,' 'THE PALM TREE,' ETC.

Let us answer to our names.

LONDON:
RICHARD BENTLEY,
PUBLISHER IN ORDINARY TO HER MAJESTY
1863.

Republished by
GALE RESEARCH COMPANY
Book Tower • Detroit, Michigan 48226 • 1976, 1984

929.4   M817w   1984

Moody, Sophy.

What is your name? A popular
account of the meanings and
derivations of Christian...

**Library of Congress
Cataloging in Publication Data**

Moody, Sophy.
   What is your name?

   1. Names, Personal. I. Title.
CS2367.M6 1976   929.4   73-5523
ISBN 0-8103-4250-2

PREFACE.

A BOOK on the same subject * by a well-known author having lately appeared, the writer of the present work assures her readers that, anxious as she is to behold its formidable rival, she has deferred that pleasure until after the publication of her own work.

'WHAT IS YOUR NAME?' was completed by Christmas Eve 1862, but the idea of it had long before suggested itself to her,—before, indeed, she was aware of any book in any language having been written on the subject of Christian Names. From the writer's first little book she ventures to quote the *motif* of her present one:—

'She aye tell't the lassies the meanin' o' each o' their Christian names. "Aiblins," said she,

---

* 'History of Christian Names,' by the Author of 'The Heir of Redclyffe,' 1863.

"thae pretty thochts may be blessed to them. The very ca'ing o' their names wad be a reminder o' some Christian grace; for," said the leddy, "the lesson ance learned, wad Lætitia be sulky, or Amy be dour?"'*

Hinton Lodge, Bournemouth:
October 17, 1863.

---

* Scotch Margaret's Story: 'The Fairy Tree,' p. 141. Nelson: 1861.

CONTENTS.

CHAPTER I.

An Advertisement—All Christian or Individual Names are significative—Value of Names—Good or evil fortune often attending on them—Crowns won and lost through the signification of Names—Story of a Spanish Princess—Twenty Names of a Portuguese Princess, their Derivations and Significations—Numerical Value of Names—Greek and Arabian Calculations depending thereupon—Names of Power—Individual Names inalienable Property—Advantages which may be derived from our Christian Names—God the first Name-giver—Motives influencing Choice of Names in Olden Times—Destinies of Names—Value of Names as Reminders—William *the Helmet* (or defence) *of many*—George the *Sower*—Esther the *Star*—Winifred the *Winner* or *Lover of Peace*—The Promise in the Advertisement redeemed . . . . PAGE 1

CHAPTER II.

National Names more characteristic than their Proverbs—Antiquity of many Names in common use amongst ourselves—A great Vitality in Names—Religious Rites attendant on Name-giving in various Nations—Story from the Laxdæla Saga—Roman Soldiers' Names engraved on their Shields 32

CONTENTS.

CHAPTER III.

Variety of Subjects connected with the History of Names—Sovereignty in Names—Names of Ancient Dynasties—Certain Names attached to Royal and Noble Families
PAGE 62

CHAPTER IV.

An Individual Name originally sufficient. Family Names adopted—Principles of Roman Nomenclature—The Four Roman Names—Nomenclators 80

CHAPTER V.

Change of Name—Examples of Change of Name—Abraham—The Four Hebrew Captives—The North-American Indian 'Brave'—Caribs—Dacians—Greek Emperors and their Brides—Princesses marrying into Foreign Lands—Queen Dagmar of Denmark—Signification of Alexandra—Brunechilde of France—Eleanor of Austria—Popes—Literary Men, their Assumption of Greek and Latin Names—Enforced Change of Name in Ireland, Spain, and Scotland—The M'Gregors 90

CHAPTER VI.

For one's Name's sake—Heroes, Inventors, and Discoverers honoured through their Names—Sovereigns' Names stamped upon Coins—Names clinging to Old Wells—Stories of Lives contained in the Names of Individuals—Christopher Columbus—Pollio Vedius—Contrasts between Lives and Names—Misnomers—St. Felicitas—Julius Cæsar—Legends derived from Significations of Names—Semiramis—Monkish Legends, St. Lucia, St. Sophia, St. Katharine, St. Margaret—Mary Magdalene—Miriam and Mary 110

CHAPTER VII.

'Besoin de Nommer'—Name-giving a Natural Instinct—Adam's first Work in Paradise—Names of Stars—Saxon Names of Months—Names of Animals and Plants—Legend of St. Veronica . . . . PAGE 140

CHAPTER VIII.

Curiosities of History of Names—Lucky and Unlucky Names—Diocletian—St. Hippolytus, &c.—Superstitions connected with Names—Lucky and Unlucky Letters—Talismans—Moses' Rod—Solomon's Seal—Abracadabra—Alphabets of Trees and Plants—Anagrams and Acrostics—Imperial Riddle of the Vowels—Sad Story of an Anagram—Variations in a Name 154

CHAPTER IX.

Antiquity of our Baptismal Names—Bible Names the Favourites in England—Art of Name-making died out—Names connected with French and English Revolutions characteristic — English Diminutives of Names : their Love for them of ancient Date—Christian Converts clinging to old Names—Origin of the Popularity of some Names; Peter, Catherine, Paul, and Margaret—Successive Causes influencing the Adoption of Names—Our Patron Saints, Heroes and Saints, Honoured Men and Women—Romances—Names beginning with Z—Suggestions for New Names from the Spanish, &c.—Nameless Creditors—Names amongst Africans, North-American Indians, Hindus, Jews, and Arabians . . . 180

CHAPTER X.

The Four Nations from which our Christian Names are principally derived : Hebrew, Greek, Latin, and Teutonic. Dominant Note in each—Characteristics of Hebrew and

CONTENTS.

CHAPTER X.—*continued.*

Arabian Names—Characteristics of Greek Names—Characteristics of Latin Names—Characteristics of Teutonic Names; Origin of some of these last—Celtic and Gaelic Names—The undying Value of a Name—The premier Grenadier de France, La Tour d'Auvergne . PAGE 219

CHAPTER XI.

Classified List of Names classed according to their Significations—Names significative of and relating to Deity—Hebrew, Assyrian, Persian, Greek, Latin, Scandinavian, &c.—Notes 233

CHAPTER XII.

Classified List—Names signifying and significative of Abstract Qualities; Virtue, Courage, &c.—Hebrew, Greek, Latin, Teutonic, Arabic, North American Indian, &c.—Notes 242

CHAPTER XIII.

Classified List—Names signifying and significative of Personal Characteristics; Beauty, Complexion, &c.—Hebrew, Greek, Latin, Teutonic, Arabic, North American Indian, &c.—Notes 274

CHAPTER XIV.

Classified List—Names signifying and significative of Miscellaneous Subjects; Animals, Plants, Numbers, Places, &c.—Hebrew, Greek, Latin, Teutonic, Arabic, North American Indian, &c.—Notes 281

WHAT IS YOUR NAME?

CHAPTER I.

An advertisement — All Christian or individual names are significative — Value of names; good or evil fortune often attending on them — Crowns won and lost through the signification of names — Story of a Spanish princess — Twenty names of a Portuguese princess; their derivations and significations — Numerical value of names; Greek and Arabian calculations depending thereupon — Names of power — Individual names inalienable property — Advantages which may be derived from our Christian names — God the first name-giver — Motives influencing choice of names in olden times — Destinies of names — Value of a name as a *reminder* — William the Helmet of Many, George the Sower, Esther the Star, Winifred the Peace-winner — The promise of the advertisement redeemed — Individual names — Individual mottoes.

READER, whatever your name may be, I think I can scarcely be wrong in supposing that, occasionally at least, you glance your eye down the second column of the 'Times'—sorrowful, wondering, or amused as the strangely contrasted advertisements successively bring before you dark glimpses into miserable homes, dazzling gleams of sudden accessions of fortune, or oddly worded descriptions of pets strayed away, or missing articles. Our hearts are stirred by wailing cries from deserted or rifled nests: 'Charlie, boy, come back; your father has forgiven you.' 'Minnie, darling, come home, come quickly, if you would see mother alive.' Tears are yet glistening in our eyes when we are irresistibly provoked to laughter by announcements of 'a red gentleman's pocket-book' having been lost, or 'a blue lady's umbrella,' and then some tantalising accounts of 'unclaimed dividends' and 'heirs wanted.'

But little filling in would be required to manufacture from the suggestions of that wonderful column a magnificent sensation novel, for still and ever the strangest romances are to be found amongst the realities of life. I am not now about to attempt a novel, and yet it is from that same column of the 'Times' that I would take the introduction of the subject of my book. Would that the tiny volume might fly half so far and wide as do the mighty wings of the giant chronicler of the day! See, now!

IF any persons bearing the Christian names (surname in each case immaterial) of ALBERT, EDWARD, ALEXANDER, GODFREY, EDMUND, or GUY — ANNE, ELIZABETH, DOROTHY, BEATRICE, EDITH, or EMILY—will apply at Messrs.   , on the   day of   , they will hear of something to their advantage.

Do you smile, reader? Nay, if you will laugh outright, 'strike, but hear!' laugh, but listen!

Bold as it may seem, yet do I in all humility trust that to all my readers bearing such names, and to many, very many more besides,* I may make my promise good, that they *shall hear of something to their advantage.*

It may be they have heard my good news before, but good news bears twice telling; and in these days of being 'en rapport' who shall say that the kindly feeling in my heart towards my known and unknown readers may not communicate itself to theirs? Our journeyings will be over many lands, and backwards into distant ages—the skeletons of dead nations will live again for us—at the graves of the mighty we may learn precious truths—so may we also from the birds of the air and the flowers of the field. Sometimes merry, sometimes grave, always in earnest, some pleasant moments may be ours, and parting good friends we may look to meet again.

In the nineteenth century fortune is supposed to wait on *surnames* only. Their importance is universally acknowledged, and there is no lack of treatises corresponding to the interest which they excite. But is not the value of Christian names comparatively ignored, except where children are named after godfathers, godmothers,

* In a classified list at the end of the volume will be found upwards of 1,500 names and their significations. An alphabetical index will refer to all Christian names at all likely to be in use amongst ourselves. Many names omitted in lists hitherto published are here mentioned, and their derivations and meanings suggested by the writer. To such names an '*S*' is attached.

relations, or friends, either for love's sake or for prudential motives? Little Stephens and Margarets are often expected to benefit at some future time by the tie which links them to their namesakes. These hopes may or may not be fulfilled; meanwhile, are there none who remember to tell the little ones that in each pretty name of *itself* there is value untold? Lovely reminders are they of treasures surely to be won, if rightly sought, and beyond all possibility of mischance.

Little Stephens, forget not the *crowns* you may win! Sweet Margarets—*pearls* and daisies—do not discredit to the exquisite significance of your name!

In one of the volumes of the British Essayists ('The Adventurer') a pretty tale is to be found, by Dr. John Hawksworth, a friend of Dr. Johnson's. Amurath, a sultan of the East, succeeding in early youth to his father's throne, is oppressed by a sense of unfitness for his great responsibilities. He is visited by a benevolent genie, who bestows on him an invaluable counsellor and friend in the shape of a talismanic ring. This ring contains a ruby of surpassing lustre and richness of colour; but whenever, in thought, word, or deed, the young Prince is about to err, the golden circlet presses his finger, and he beholds the magic gem become dim and pale.

Do we not carry about with us, each one of us, our own especial talisman? Not mute, like the ring of Amurath, but hourly sounding in our ears its peculiar note—it may be of warning—it may be of encouragement, telling of high aims and glorious rewards.

Not here the fitting place to dwell upon the best and dearest privileges attached to all *Christian names*. One only glance at the ineffable bliss awaiting those who by such names (their angel names, as we may imagine they will be) are adopted into the family of heaven—one only glance—and then, bearing the gladsome recollection in our hearts, we will pass on to the present temporal advantages that it would seem may be derived from almost all *individual* names in common use amongst ourselves.

Why should these names, which are in many cases rich with suggestive eloquence, fall on our ears but as empty sounds?

Why should not that poor peevish discontented Lætitia (*gladness*) strive to connect with the calling of her Christian name an endeavour after the Christian grace of ' cheerfulness? ' And those undutiful children, John and Jane—causes of worry as they are to all around them—why should they not learn, and benefit by the learning, that they continually contradict the beautiful meaning of their names, signifying in Hebrew *God's gracious gift*?

Of surnames, the value of many is confessed by everyone. They are an inheritance of themselves—good fortune waits upon them. The old Roman proverb, 'Nomen et omen,' holds good in our day. There are *Læliuses* amongst ourselves of whom it may be said, not only that their names are synonymous with 'bonus augur,' and that all they foretell is certain to come to pass, but also that all they attempt is sure to succeed.

Who does not know that 'wagging of ancient pows,' cheerily *perpendicular*, whereby members of certain families are assured of success in all their undertakings; and that other 'wagging,' solemnly *horizontal*, that foredooms others—'poor Such-a-one'—to certain failure?

And why is this? Trace back the family histories, and you will find that it was no blind chance, but sterling worth, that *first* caused its current value to be stamped on the coin. Family honours are gained. 'Noblesse oblige.' Men seek to live up to their name.

There is inexpressible value in names! The prince of poets—the magician by whose wand the secrets of all hearts are laid bare—is quoted to justify a contrary belief. But in whose mouth does Shakspeare put those words: 'What's in a name?' It is the indignant protest of an impassioned girl against the wide-spread feeling (prejudice, if you will) which the very vehemence of her remonstrance showed that she knew but too well did exist.

And still, as in that Italian city of old, there are Montagues and Capulets! Against the stubborn rocks of family prejudice, ah! how many young hearts are daily wrecked? What avail fresh winds and full tide setting fair for glad havens where eager barks would be, when stony barriers uprear themselves between, which no daring, no skill can surmount? With the wrecks of gallant ships so shattered the waves of this troublesome world are strewn.

Not dreamy-eyed Romance alone, but her grave sister History, tells us strange facts as to the value of names, actually in themselves, even when unconnected with family associations. With the Romans auspicious names were ever in the ascendant. Amongst innumerable examples we need only instance here Regalianus, elected emperor by the Roman soldiers solely on account of the royalty suggested by his name. But lightly won, alas! lightly lost—he did not long wear the crown of the Cæsars. On an equally sudden impulse the troops put their newly-elected emperor to death. His name gave him a crown, but could not preserve to him his life.

A still more singular instance of a name, and a Christian name, influencing the destiny of an individual, is told by Herrera, the Spanish historian. Louis VIII. of France, surnamed 'Cœur de Lion,' desiring a Spanish princess for his bride, ambassadors were sent to the court of Madrid. The eldest and the most beautiful of the royal sisters was the one destined by her own family to share the diadem of France. But where was the wise fairy godmother who in all nursery tales presides at the naming of beautiful princesses? At the cradle of the unfortunate eldest daughter of Spain, it would seem, there was no fairy godmother, nor even an earthly sponsor gifted with musical ear or æsthetic tastes—her name Urraca, harsh in sound, was in its signification yet more objectionable, for in Spanish it signified a *magpie*.

A magpie queen, and to mate with a lionheart? Impossible! The dismayed ambassadors felt themselves compelled to reject the young beauty. Her name had deprived her of a noble husband and of a crown. The lovely Urraca saw her younger sister (less fair than herself, except in name) preferred before her, and Blanche the *Fair* of Castile was carried in triumph to France to become the honoured wife of Louis the Lionheart, and the proud mother of St. Louis.

In this singular story of so great a mishap attending an ill-chosen name we may, perhaps, find the key to the custom of an extraordinary number of names being always bestowed on princesses of Spain and the neighbouring kingdom of Portugal.

The 'Saxe-Gotha Almanack' (1862) tells us of a little Portuguese princess who has been endowed with no less than twenty names, derived from five different languages—chosen with due regard to mellifluous syllables, fortunate associations with angelic and saintly namesakes, and, with the exception of the hallowed first name, all having pleasing significations:—

Hebrew—Maria (Mary), *Bitterness.*
Hebrew—José, *One raised up.*
Latin—Beatrix, *Making blessed.*
Hebrew—Joanna (John), *God's gracious gift.*
Greek—Eulalie (*S*) (εὔλαλος), *Speaking sweetly.*
Teutonic — Leopoldina (Leopold, Leof pold), *Beloved and brave.*
Teutonic — Adelaide (Adelhilda), *Noble lady.*
Hebrew—Isabel (*Spanish form,* Elizabeth), sig. *Worshipper of God.*
Teutonic — Carlotta (Karl), *Strong, valiant.*
Hebrew—Michaela (Michael), *Who is like God?*
Hebrew—Raphaela (Raphael), *Medicine* (or *healing*) *of God.*
Hebrew—Gabriela(Gabriel), *the strength of God.*
Teutonic—Francisca (*Frank*), *Free, indomitable.*
Greek or *Latin*—Paula (de Assise e do), παῦλα (*S*), *Rest,* or paulus, *Little.*
Latin—Inez, Spanish form of Agnes. *A Lamb.*
Greek—Sophia, *Wisdom.* Arabic —Safiyeh, *Chosen.*
Hebrew—Joaquina (*S*) (Jehoiachin) *Strength of Jehovah.*
Hebrew—Theresa (*S*) (Tirzah), *Pleasant, beautiful.*
Latin—Benedicta, *Blessed.*
Teutonic—Bernarda(Bernhard), *Bear's heart,* significative of *Courage.*

We shall find when we go more fully into their history that it is scarcely possible to overstate the immense importance attached to names by all the nations of antiquity. Names were as prophecies for good or evil.

Not only were these lucky and unlucky names simply accepted as such—in some cases independent of their respective significations and associations—but a strange superstition respecting them was exalted into a science, known by the Greeks as Omantia, from ὄνομα, a *name*. It claimed Enoch as its originator and

Pythagoras as its supporter; by it destinies were foretold from the numerical value of the letters of a name. Thus it was shown that Patrocles, *a father's glory*, whose name-number amounted only to 861, was, of necessity, conquered by Hector, the value of his name being 1,225, while he in his turn, in spite of the signification of his name (*holding fast*, as an anchor), was forced to yield to Achilles, the number of whose name reached to 1,501.

Up to the present day astrological calculations are made by the Arabs, founded on the numerical value of the letters which compose the names of individuals. Amongst other discoveries supposed to be so made, the very important question is decided *before* marriage as to whether the husband and wife will agree, or, in event of disputes, with whom the supreme authority will rest. This singular enquiry, as described in Lane's Notes to the 'Arabian Nights,' resolves itself into a simple sum of arithmetic:—

'Adding together the numerical values of his or her name and that of the mother, and, if I remember right, subtracting from 12 the whole sum, if this is less than 12, or what remains after subtracting or dividing by 12. Thus is obtained the number of the sign. The twelve signs commencing with Aries correspond respectively with the elements of fire, earth, air, water—fire, earth, and so on.' *

* Vol. i. p. 431.

Should the numbers obtained indicate the same sign, a similar agreement in the dispositions of the individuals is inferred. The terrible question of supremacy in conflict depends on whether a ruling element is indicated by the number of the man or the woman. Should the sign of the man be *fire*, and that of the woman *water*, this last being the ruling element, it is believed that in the household that dreary state of affairs will ensue where the master's 'pipe is put out.' Should the signs be reversed, the power will then rest with the husband of making things equally uncomfortable by 'throwing cold water' on any pet plan of his wife's.

In all countries, whenever man or woman anticipates in marriage not a blessed bond of loving companionship and mutual dependence, but a miserable series of struggles for despotic rule, it might be as well perhaps for such calculations to be made before it be too late. When the result is unsatisfactory, another selection may be made; or if the sentence of fate be received as irrevocable, resignation may be learned, and useless conflicts be avoided.

Anagrams, or transpositions of the letters of a name, also assumed the form of prophecy. We shall find that some curious instances are recorded in the history of days when this somewhat laborious amusement was in vogue.

Amongst other extraordinary calculations connected with names, we read of a singular kind of divination resorted to by Theodotus, the Gothic King of Italy, A.D. 540. Trembling behind the walls of Rome at the approaching downfall of his power, this unworthy descendant of a race of heroes, in his superstitious terror, submitted to an ignominious expedient for enquiring into futurity which was suggested to him by a Jewish name-wizard. By his advice, given no doubt in secret mockery of the Gentile combatants, thirty hogs were for a time shut up together: ten were named by the Gothic King after his own people, to ten others were given Greek names, and to the remaining ten were assigned Roman names. The time of probation ended, of the first-named almost all were found to be dead; of the second, all were alive; of the third half were dead and half much injured. Strange to say, the ridiculous experiment was typical of the actual result of the conflict of the three nations.

Let us turn to a nobler aspect of the power of names.

In days of chivalry—ay, farther back, before the word chivalry was known—the name of a hero was ever as a standard to which all men flocked, and where its loved sound floated in the air there was victory! Drawn by its potent spell, as if inspired, men pressed forward to the thickest of the fight, where like a trumpet-call rang out on high, above the clash of spears and the hurtling of arrows, the NAMES of the leaders they loved best—'A Talbot!' 'A Percy!' or the joint names of king, country, and patron saint.

> Upon this charge
> Cry God for Harry, England, and St. George.
> *Henry V.*

Or hark to a war-cry more ancient far in the Song of Deborah, and in the Prophet Hosea, who bids cornet and trumpet sound and the war-cry of the brave Benjamites be raised: 'After thee, O Benjamin!' To and fro the tide of battle rolled, its mighty thunder following in the wake of the triumphant shoutings of those names of power.*

And those who bend a reverent ear still catch the echoes of those priceless names haunting the fields where their imperishable glory was won: names of power are they not with us yet? Our old heroic names—and they are many in our lion-hearted race †—are with us still, and to those that bear them they are a heritage more precious than lands or gold, because imperishable inalienable pledges of honour none dare gainsay.

Could a Sydney do a dishonourable act? Could a Desmond be other than brave?

---

* Names as significant of power:—
> 'Our battle is more full of *names* than yours.'
> Shakspeare's *Henry IV.*

† '... Our names
Familiar in their mouths as household words.'
Henry V.

But while some names have in them the ring of trusty metal, the true steel of a gallant warrior's sword, there are others that tinkle yet more musically in the ears of some—ay, even with the sound of silver and gold.

Amongst our princely merchants there are simple names 'good' for the ransom of kings and kingdoms. Countries on the verge of bankruptcy have been rescued by a word, when that word was a *name* known far and wide as a trustworthy 'promise to pay.'

But while I write the words '*princely merchants*,' do not my readers' hearts swell like my own with fervent gratitude to him who, some months past, in a few words of almost childish simplicity, and with all a child's exquisite purity of motive, bestowed on the poor of our metropolis the munificent gift of 150,000*l.* ?

Apicius of old devoted his enormous wealth to the pampering of his body—that body which by his own act was given, while yet in manhood's prime, to be food for worms. The names of such men pass into by-words and jests, but the name of *Peabody*, homely as its sound may be, will long be as music in the ear of England's poor. Wafted to heaven on their prayers, it will be dear to the hearts of us all, so long as those sweet words are remembered—' Inasmuch as ye have done it unto one of the least of these, my brethren, ye have done it unto me.'

But we linger too long, perhaps, on the thres-

ADVANTAGES TO BE DERIVED. 15

hold of our express theme. None deny the preciousness of honourable surnames; but they, like talents, riches, and beauty of face, are not of our own choosing, nor can they be chosen for us by those to whom we are dear. Our family names are appointed for us. We cannot at will be Sydneys, Talbots, Barings, or Rothschilds.*

But amongst Christian names parents are free to choose. Names of noblest significance are open to all, suitable to all, princes and peers. Of individual names already bestowed on us there can scarcely be one in which may not be discovered some germ of thought, which, if cherished, will surely be suggestive of some one good word or work, of some high aim, some ennobling influence.

Therefore is a small voice now lovingly raised, earnestly asking for Christian names some attention and regard from their possessors. Remembering to what a vast portion of the human race the subject appeals, is it not within probability that even so low a voice may win its way to the hearts of some? The whisperings of 'Picciola,'

---

* These lines were written before the ridiculous fashion commenced of people exchanging their real names for others of better sound, but to which they had not the slightest claim. We hope the example of Norfolk Howard, alias Bug, has been too much laughed at for it to gain many followers. When a new name is assumed, surely one may be selected out of family connections, or, better still, the Christian name of father or mother be adapted to a surname. With a little ingenuity a new form may be given to one of these names, and the original composition thus afford a pleasant feeling of ownership in the new name assumed.

the prison flower, were listened to by one who had been deaf to the teachings of wise men.

This individual right of ours, small and insignificant as it may at the first glance appear to be, should, if only in one respect, deserve some notice—it is inalienable. May we not venture to say that it is the only inalienable individual property that men, women, and children throughout wide Christendom do possess? All other properties may take to themselves wings and fly away. What earthly treasure is there beyond the power of mishap? Our fair ancestral homes, our bags of gold, our possessions of every kind—intellectual superiority, beauty of form, strength, and skill—not one of all these is inalienable. Nay, if a long life be granted to us, the infirmities of age must deprive us of all personal gifts. The clearest intellect must be obscured, the brightest eyes grow dim—the most skilful hands, the most powerful frame, be paralysed before the numbing influence of approaching death.

How closely do men resemble the time-pieces, the making of which is one of the chief triumphs of their handiwork!

Beneath the gathering dust of successive years and the moisture of the atmosphere, which is as tears, the brilliancy of the fair dial-plate is effaced, while within the once busy wheels begin to lag as the gathering rust grows over them, and the life-like springs lose their elasticity—more and more languidly the hands revolve—fainter and fainter sounds the ticking of the old clock, till at last it stops—and the warning voice of Time passing away, too little heeded perhaps by those that heard, is heard no more!

Darlings of fortune we may be, but we may lose all on which we are priding ourselves; but one thing we cannot lose—our little-regarded Christian names. Bestowed on us in our sinless infancy, they will still be ours, unchanged through all the changing scenes of life—ay! passing with us into the very portals of the grave. That first and individual name of ours, to which for good or evil we shall have responded hundreds of thousands of times—the letters of which we shall so often have traced for purposes of evil or of good—that Christian name, alas! how often desecrated in our daily, hourly use of it!—that name, a witness for us or against us, will be engraved on the door-plate of our last earthly tenement, whether our coffin be of lordly oak or pauper deal.

Companions with us through the varied scenes of our whole lives, our Christian names become an actual part of ourselves. At the sound of that name, breathed tenderly by a mother's lips, we as babes stretch forth our dimpled arms all eager with delight. It is heard by the maiden with crimsoned cheek and beating heart when it is for the first time whispered by the voice she loves best; and it is thenceforth the only name she cares to keep. Father, mother, brother, sister, friend: it is by them we are called by our Christian name, and, uttered by the lips of our dearest ones, to it is given a peculiar music of its own.

Ours inseparably! In absence or in death, at the familiar sound of our names, a familiar form starts up before the memories of all to whom we are known, clothed in the individuality of our words and deeds. Shall that undying form, thus inseparably connected with our names, be lovely or the reverse?

Names are significant of many graces. Let us *answer to our names*—so shall the answering remembrance of ourselves be clothed with its fair characteristic graces.

Can we think lightly of those names which will be ours to all eternity? Do we not hope to hear them breathed by white-robed angels—dear ones who have gone before, but who tarry yet at the golden gates: tarry for us, that theirs may be our first glad welcome to our true home?

Alas! how utterly must all recollection of the first and holiest meaning of all *Christian names* have faded from human hearts when, by those very names, men and women are summoned to the commission of crime, and pledges of baptismal vows are signed to contracts for devils' work.

From this inalienableness (if we may resume the use of an old word)—this continual companionship of our individual names—can we not derive some benefit? The power of habit is confessed by all. In the thoughts we think habitually is to be found the key-note of our lives. The little words we say, the little things we do each moment of the day—are they not as the living atoms which build up imperishable coral rocks? Do they not build up the actual representation of our individual selves as beheld by our fellow-men?

This is especially a utilitarian age. Amongst the many marvels of the day there are few greater than the ingenuity with which everything is turned to account. Refuse and rubbish are now, as to their original meaning, obsolete words. *Impossible* is a word long since ignored by great minds; and, by the appliances of modern science, the word *useless* has been consigned to the same fate.

On certain days of the week go through the poorest streets of our towns and villages: before the meanest hovels you will find a woman or a child who pass slowly on their way, trailing along huge bags, and their shrill cry is, 'Any sweepings?'

If in our material economy we have learned the great lesson, 'Let nothing be lost,' how much more should we strive to enlist all and every spiritual influence surrounding us in the service of the 'Good Master' from whose teaching that lesson came! A sound which is heard and answered by us a million times perhaps in our lives—a sound endeared to us by hallowed influences, tender recollections, and innumerable pleasant associations—oh, who will say that it is incapable of being made suggestive of richest melody? A whispered syllable has ere now unsealed hidden well-springs in human hearts. Children's natures especially, quick and impulsive, are awake to innumerable influences apparently slight. Delicately constituted scales are the hearts of our little ones—a feather's weight will sometimes turn the balance the right way or the wrong. Let us care, then, for the feather-weights.

Children generally think a great deal of their Christian names. They have few personal possessions: their individual names are amongst these few, and they are proportionably interested in them.

Try the experiment, dear reader! Go to a national school, say of girls—in a more educated class the effect would be still greater. Ask a child her Christian name. In the south of England there are many Ellens. Tell her that her pretty old Saxon name has a pretty meaning, *fruitful*, and that some of our sweetest fruits are brought forth by small plants. Beaming faces will quickly show you all the *Ellens* in the room. When months have gone by, if you return, you will find that in many a little heart the tiny incidental lesson has not been forgotten.

But are there not many, both old and young, who may be won by the charm of a subject which combines all the graces of poetry with absolute practical utility? How suggestive, how eloquent is a significant name! It is as an enchanter's wand, summoning before us visions of beauty without end—it is as a solemn voice, teaching us lessons for time and for eternity.

All names are significant. If they are not so to us, it is because we do not understand the language in which they speak. Amongst the nations of antiquity to whom, as children to their parents, we are indebted for our names, every name expressed an idea. Jehovah Himself, as the first name-giver, bestowing on the first man a name, gave to him one of deeper significance than perhaps we have been accustomed to remark. To the lord of measureless domains—to the absolute master of the whole animal world—to the possessor of all the infinity of treasures in the vegetable and mineral kingdoms—to him who, crowned with every blessing heart could desire, had his home in Eden's garden of delight—to him God gave a name which should remind him that in himself he was nothing: called into being by the hand of Omnipotence—a child of dust! Adamah, *earth*, the *red earth* of which they were made, was the name given by their Creator to man and woman on the day on which they were created.

How different from the lofty names expressive of celestial origin which in after times the followers of false gods manufactured for themselves!

Ra-meses, *Begotten of the sun*; A-mosis, *Begotten of the moon.*

But this subject, with an infinity of other subjects embraced by our theme, will more fully unfold itself in succeeding chapters. We will now, in reference to the dominant idea of the first chapter, glance hastily back to discover the motive which usually determined the choice of names. At different times and amongst different nations different motives prevailed; but, more than any other, a feeling after futurity will be traced. Hope was the name-giver which the young world most approved. Ere a child had been born to him, Adam called his wife Eve (*Heb.* Chavah, signifying *Life*): for she was *to be* 'the mother of all living.'

Sometimes, indeed, an overpowering present swallowed up the remembrance of the future. In the same family strong contrasts will be found: brothers' and sisters' names telling of successive sunshine or shadow passing over the home at the moment of their respective births.

Who does not remember the touching difference between the names of poor Rachel's first and last child? Joseph, 'He shall add'—the joyous onlooking of the mother to the glad troop of sons that should come; and then the babe named in her dying gasp Benoni, 'Son of my sorrow'—that passionate desire, 'Give me children, or I die,' fulfilled in death.

Amidst countless examples of names suggestive of parents' ambitious views, we find amongst Hebrew names one touchingly expressive of pure fatherly love. It is a picture some centuries old, but its colours are bright as if painted but yesterday. Despite the universal preference for male offspring, we see a father delightedly stretching out his arms to welcome his little daughter, hailing her by the name of Abigail, 'A father's joy!' In the original the name is yet more expressive: the word 'giyl,' affixed to abi, *father*, signifying to *dance*, to 'leap with exultation.'

This name affords a striking instance of how strangely, in the lapse of time, the origin and true meaning of words sometimes pass out of remembrance. 'An abigail' has with us grown to be almost synonymous with a maid-servant, and in this wrong but very general acceptation the real and lovely meaning of the name is lost.

This undesirable impression is doubtless to be traced to the reiterated use of the epithet 'handmaid,' as applied to herself by the Abigail of Scripture, who went even beyond, it would seem, the hyperbolical language of the East in professing herself, at the moment of receiving David's proposal to make her his wife, willing to be the 'servant of his servants.'

Strange destinies of names as of all earthly things! Lucifer, the 'Light-bearer,' shares the misconception of Abigail, 'the father's joy.' Milton, carrying out Isaiah's suggestion of fallen greatness in 'Lucifer, son of the morning,' has stamped the name as significant of pride. Fallen indeed! The herald of day—the morning-star—Lucifer, the light-bearer, is indebted for the restoration of the true meaning of his name to his tiny namesake in a match-box, the value of which is scarcely to be computed, being so small a fraction of a penny.

Amongst innumerable ancient names given prospective of future destiny we read of Seth, or Sheth, 'appointed,' or 'put in the place of'—Abel (whose name, alas! was prophetic too), a 'breath,' a 'vapour:' his young life which was soon to pass away; or 'vanity,' that is, of all earthly hopes. Noah betokened 'rest,' 'consolation;' and Solomon, 'peace.' In all nations, however remote and unconnected with each other, we trace this natural desire of parents to attach to their offspring names of good import.

Why should we lose sight of this loving custom of old? As Christian names can be chosen, why should we not choose them with reference to the future good we desire for our darlings? Why should we not be influenced by the *meaning*, not only, as now (with but few exceptions), by the *sound* of names? Both for men and women there are a goodly list of right honourable names from which to choose, and rarely are any of them unmusical.

Good names being chosen for our children, let us, when they are old enough to understand, tell them of their *meaning*, so that to individual names not only sounds but *ideas* may be attached. A child's early developed notions of individual property will secure the pretty lesson from being forgotten; and who shall say how the remembrance of it may be blessed in after years? Ah! who shall say that at the very moment of some meditated crime the old familiar sound, the old familiar look of his or her Christian name, may not bring back the recollection of the sweet lesson taught in connection with it in the sinless days of infancy? The mother's gentle voice, the father's kindly tone sounding, as it were, in their ears—the Eustace, about to yield to temptation, may 'stand firm'—and Katharine, 'the *spotless* and *pure*,' be startled from the first step towards shame.

If the wise Greek and bold Roman of other days, and all the most accomplished nations of antiquity, were so moved by the power of names that enterprises of the highest importance were undertaken or abandoned according to the suggestive significance of names, or the good or evil influence they were supposed to possess, shall this hope, which in all earnestness I suggest, be looked upon as an idle dream ? If heathen names were so mighty, shall Christian names be powerless? With their old significance restored to them—clothed with ideas made instinct with spiritual life—in continual companionship with us, with all their countless influences of real redeeming power wafted to heaven as they are on the winged prayers of those that love us, day by day and hour by hour since first we were by them enlisted as soldiers of Christ—may they not become mightier far? * .

See now that sturdy little fellow, whose crisp curly locks are of a golden brown—his sapphire eyes dancing in light—his resolute little mouth, with lips of cherry red, tell of the full vigour of health and strength and happiness. He is a noble boy; but the love of power is already developing itself in him. As yet his tiny despotism amuses, and even perhaps secretly delights, both his mother and nurse. They are proud of his

---

* God forbid that I should be supposed to feel or to advocate a superstitious belief in any real and absolute power existing in names. I write to Christians, humbly professing myself to be such also; and so I believe that, excepting 'the name óf Jesus Christ of Nazareth,' as significative of and belonging to the person of the ever-blessed Son of God, 'there is no other name under heaven given among men whereby we must be saved'—no other name by which, in its own power, any one thing can be accomplished. But who will say that with names, as identified both with persons and with ideas, there have not always been, and there may not always be, *influence*? And where influence is, there is always a greater or a less degree of power. The power of influence may be for an hour—it may be for ever.

When I plead for consideration of the influential power of names, I do it as one who longs after, and deeply feels her own need of, a continual *reminder* of the straight path she fain would keep—of the glad prize it is her heart's desire to obtain. Such a *reminder*, it seems to me, may with God's blessing be found in almost every Christian name. As I have elsewhere said, the 'fruits of the Spirit' grow in clusters—the name of one of them may bring the others to mind. Oh, why think lightly of any, even the smallest way-mark, when the path is hard to keep—when our goal is the heavenly city?

'spirit.' With looks that contradict their words, they affect to regret their inability to manage him. 'He is such a boy!' 'Naughty Willie!' or 'Master William will have his own way!' When the handsome young ruler of the nursery has all his wishes fulfilled, 'all goes merry as a marriage bell;' but let little Mary or Maude dispute his commands, or even baby Frank retain the toy which he desires to have—there is thunder in the air, and the stormy atmosphere makes itself felt throughout the whole household.

But the boy has a loving heart. Not yet can that beautiful child's breast be overgrown with the poisonous fungus Self-love, by which all that is lovely and noble in human nature is in time surely destroyed. In that little heart-garden the flowers of natural affection still bloom, though surrounded by noxious weeds, which if not rooted up will choke every blossom soon; and then the nursery tyrant will progress into the bully at school and the torment of home. When come to man's estate, if he marries, God help his unfortunate wife, his children, and all his dependents!

By those who love children devotedly—with a fond and earnest and anxious desire for their present, future, and eternal weal—no suggestion that may *possibly* help the great work will be despised. Once more, then, may the remembrance of my new talisman be whispered to you!

All who love children know that there is no

charm more potent over their fresh eager young hearts than a story well told. Put, then, your lesson to that handsome but imperious little fellow in the form of a story. Tell him of some knight of old—Bayard of France, 'sans peur et sans reproche,' fearless and faultless—or of our own Sir Philip Sidney. In the lives of those glorious men, and in countless examples besides, down to the gentle Raglan of our own day, show him how the bravest have ever the kindest hearts, for never was *steadfast unfailing* courage, mental as well as bodily, found in a tyrant's breast. Describe then the armour of a knight: the shield, the sword, and the *helmet* above all, where his ladye-love's token was carried, and his distinguishing crest and plume were borne. Tell him of all things it was necessary that the helmet should be trustworthy, for its office was not to *offend*, but to *defend*. It guarded the head. Shorn of his helmet, the strongest knight was at the mercy of his foe.

Now tell your boy the lovely meaning of his name, that he by God's help may answer to it.

Derived from the language of the old Teutonic race, Wil-helm, the *helmet* of *many*, signifies one who *protects* and *defends* many. Willi or Vili is still preserved in the German 'viel,' *many*; so too is 'helm,' with the identical meaning of old (which grew out of the word 'hilma'), to *cover*. In the Icelandic 'hialmr' is *helmet*; in the Saxon 'helan' signified to *cover*, to *protect*; in our own language, derived from those above mentioned, familiar to all is the 'plumed *helm*' of Shakspeare and all our poets.

Scarcely less beautiful is the other meaning of this doubly significant name, the Saxon 'helma' signifying the *helm* or upper part of the rudder, which is grasped by the steersman who guides the ship.

Is not our common name of William, then, a name to live up to? A *helmet of defence*, a protector; or a *helmsman*, a guide to *many*!

To those who care for the significance of names there is a delight in reading the 'Life of *William* Pitt,' at the appropriateness of the name to 'the pilot who weathered the storm.'

Amongst our simplest names there are many others full of bright meanings to be carried out in like manner.

Remind your idle little George that, as a *husbandman*, if he sows not neither shall he reap. Let Esther, the *star*, and Winifred, *winner* or *lover of peace*, learn and love the hidden beauty of their exquisite names.

Still in the unchanging East mothers hang talismans round their children's necks—a gem, a stone, a string of seeds, a written paper—they are charms to protect them from harm.

Dear English mothers, will you not try my little talismans? Necklaces and gems may be lost or stolen, but the individual names of your darlings can neither be lost nor stolen away.

Ah! would that each and all of us might associate with our every word and deed recollections of the lovely meanings of those Christian names which are hourly sounding in our ears, and which rightly belong to us only as we are in truth the adopted children of God! Why should we not marry mottoes to our individual names as noble houses have united them to their family names—both by such unions being rendered more illustrious?

Say that no eye but that of our Father in heaven beholds our hidden banner 'with strange device!' shall the time not come when in the story of our lives it may be read in characters of light by men and angels?

In the battle of life let all choose for themselves such 'mots de guerre.'

A few only are suggested here, to redeem my especial promise to those bearing certain names.

Teutonic—Albert, *altogether bright.* 'Walk as children of light' (Eph. v. 8). *
Anglo-Saxon—Edward, *keeper of happiness.* 'Finem respice.'[1] Look to the end.†
Greek—Alexander, *a brave defender* or *helper of men.* 'In trying strength comes.'

---

* It is hoped no apology is necessary for illustrating some of the names with verses from 'the Book.' Is it not strange that the most worldly men see no objection in classical authors alluding to their gods, yet many think it bad taste for any scriptural allusion to be found in works not solely of a religious character?

† The Latin originals are given, because they are more terse than any English translation can be.

[1] Motto of the Irish Earl of Darnley.

Teutonic—Godfrey, *God's peace.* 'Corde fixum.'[2] Steadfast heart.
Anglo-Saxon—Edmund, *happiness and peace.* 'Bear and Forbear.'[3]
French—Guy (*S*), *standard-bearer* (from Guidon). 'Excelsior.' Carry great ensigns, and your lives shall be great.
Hebrew—Anne, *gracious.* 'A gracious woman retaineth honour' (Prov. xi. 16).
Hebrew—Elisabeth, *a worshipper of God,* literally, 'God is her seven,' or her 'oath.' 'Worship Him in spirit and in truth' (John iv. 24).
Greek—Dorothy, *God's gift.* 'Every perfect gift is from above' (James i. 17).
Latin—Beatrice, *making blessed,* a *joy-giver.* 'Essayez.'[4] Try.
Greek—Emily (*S*), *winsome* (from αἱμυλία). 'Willows are weak, but they bind strong woods' (*Herbert*).
Anglo-Saxon—Edith, *blessed or perfect happiness.* 'Deo, non fortuna.'[5] From God, not fortune.

Dear reader, have I not kept my word?

[2] Motto of the family of *Godfrey* of Hurst.
[3] Motto of the Irish Baron Langford.
[4] Motto of the English Baron Dundas.
[5] Motto of the English Earl Digby.

CHAPTER II.

National names more characteristic than their proverbs — Antiquity of many names in common use amongst ourselves — A great vitality in names — Religious rites attendant on name-giving in various nations — Story from the 'Laxdaela Saga' — Roman soldiers' names engraved on their shields.

HAVING now, I trust, won to my side some willing companions, I would fain show them as rapidly as may be how wide a field of interest the history of names embraces.

A name falls on our ear. It is not a mere sound: besides its peculiar message to him or her to whom it belongs, every name has its story, and some are of exceeding interest. A history of names is as a world of voices. Not only human beings, but bright stars overhead and tiny flowers at our feet, all bearing names, would each have its tale to tell, but that the volume then might grow too heavy in your hands. We will but glance at such things. Do you love romances? In how many names thrilling and real romances are contained! Do you care for history? How many a revelation of the past is unfolded in names! Strange legends, too, over which we have wondered and doubted—the signification of a name reveals all their hidden mystery.

The proverbs of nations have, in all times, been considered of exceeding interest, but a far more certain key to national characteristics will be found in the names which were invented by nations, and which became naturalised amongst them.

Significant as they are for the most part of gifts and graces, the names of nations tell us, at a glance, what gifts and graces they most prized.

When once we accept them, as in truth they are, as expressions of abstract qualities or personal characteristics, are not the names of a people an absolute record of their feelings and tastes—a moral census, as it were—the more trustworthy because each household furnished its information unconsciously? It was no written chronicle, 'by order,' of preferences for this virtue or for that; names of children in families were freely chosen, and with no thought that in after-times a preponderance of certain names, or a deficiency of others, would be as an engraved portrait of themselves—here a succession of small strokes thickly coming together, and there a few lines faint and far apart—is it not thus that the true representation of a face is given by the engraver?

The castle of Sidon stands on a '*Tel*,'* a large

---

* May one venture to connect with a play on this Arabic word 'Tel,' or 'Tell,' a *heap*, a home lesson too? How the little proportion of which consists of bits of broken purpura, small in themselves, but their collected numbers formed great heaps which, to this day, recall the chief pursuit of this ancient city—the manufacture of purple dye.

The smell of the morning and evening sacrifice comes to us in the names of the Jewish people. Chosen out of all the nations of the earth to be the keepers of the sacred oracles—the revelations of the Most High God's purposes towards mankind—we find in Hebrew names, and in the kindred Arabian, constant repetitions of the Holy Name.

The clash of swords and the whirring of spears are heard in the names of the warlike Teuton and dauntless Gael.

In the delicate word-painting of Greek names are revealed the æsthetic tastes of the most accomplished people of all times; while in the short, descriptive Roman names, for the most part simply suggested by personal peculiarities, we behold the practical nature of those who cared more for the achievements of material power than for the sublimer triumphs of the intellect.

There is a strange vitality in names. Nations pass away, their language becomes dead, but as

unthought-of acts, continually adding up day after day, do in our lives become a great *tell*!—*tell*ing for or against us, a witness—such as we read these heaps are considered in all lands—of some act performed, some engagement entered into at that spot!

in our home-fields now and again we stumble against some fossil which suddenly carries us back to some far-distant period of time, so with the sweet, familiar names which are hourly sounding in our ears, if we do but track them to their original birthplace, the skeletons of dead nations will rise up and live before our eyes.

Hark! At that cottage door an English labourer is calling to his rosy-cheeked daughter, 'Esther! Esther!' The name has come to us through our bibles, where the English poor love best to find names for their children; but we must go farther back than to the tents of Israel to catch the first echoes of that pretty name.

For twenty-two centuries, flocks and herds had roved over fields on the banks of the Tigris, where grassy mounds were seen, to some of which the Moslem had given the name of 'Tombs'—to one of them the name of Nebbi Yunus, '*the Tomb of Jonah*,' signifying *the Dove*. These green mounds encircling the city of Mosul, were indeed the upheavings of a mighty grave, in which lay buried the 'exceeding great city' Nineveh, called after its builder Ninus, signifying *Beautiful*. In singular connection with the name of the Hebrew prophet who foretold the city's destruction, was the name of its beautiful, far-famed queen, Semiramis, which in Syriac also signifies a *Dove*.

We must with Layard build up again those walls of sculptured alabaster, those gorgeously painted ceilings, and with eagle-headed human figures and winged bulls of gigantic size on either side, we shall, in one of Assyria's magnificent palaces, be where the name of Esther was first heard in its original formation, Sitareh, *the Star*. It was no doubt bestowed on some lustrous-eyed Assyrian princess privileged by her birth to claim relationship with the heavenly bodies.

Adopted by the Persians, the name of Sitareh (in the Hebrew Ester) was given by Artaxerxes (Ahasuerus) to his beautiful Jewish captive, instead of her original name Hadassah, signifying a *Myrtle*.

Of some names, significations and derivations can only be suggested, but of by far the greater number they may be confidently affirmed, although they may have been deciphered with difficulty, owing to the extraordinary variations of spelling through successive generations. Those only who have gone into the subject of Christian names or surnames, or are lovers of genealogical or heraldic researches, can imagine how numerous are such variations.

Without going farther than our own English tongue for examples, we find Dr. Chandler speaking of seventeen modes of spelling Waynflete; while, according to Dugdale, Mainwaring has been spelled in one hundred and thirty different ways.

But, even as the antiquarian can determine the history of the battered coin from what seems to uninitiated eyes a series of confused and random strokes, so the patient name-hunter makes his pleasant discoveries, guided by way-marks of various kinds, trusty, though sometimes so slight as to be overlooked by the casual observer.

The immense importance attached to names by the great nations of antiquity can scarcely, as we shall see, be overstated.

In the meditations of the philosopher, in the song of the poet, in the laws of senates, we find the absolute and intrinsic value of names directly or indirectly proved.

It is in Socrates' mouth that Plato has placed the words that 'the giving of names is no small matter, nor should it be left to chance or to persons of mean abilities.' It is the prince of poets, Homer, who has embalmed the memories of the beautiful and the brave in names of such exquisite significance that they have passed into epithets. It was a law of Athens that forbade the names of the youths Harmodius and Aristogeiton ever being given to slaves.

Dying as they did in the endeavour to rescue their country from a tyrant's grasp, their countrymen proclaimed them martyrs, and, in thus ennobling their names, crowned them with undying homage; for of such homage no after ingratitude can deprive great men. Name and fame is a union which is indissoluble.

Triumphal arches, statues, and purses of gold decreed by grateful lands to those who have done good service—all these may perish and pass away; nay, the tear-blotted pages of history tell of outrage sometimes succeeding to applause; but the *name* which the statesman, the warrior, the poet, or the sage have themselves rendered illustrious is out of the reach of the corroding touch of envy or caprice; it is lifted into a purer air, and placed by Omnipotence beyond the power of Time itself to destroy.

The first of Rome's victorious sons distinguished by a name of honour lived to recognise in it an unchanging joy, the only one of which his enemies could not deprive him. The early services of Caius Marius were forgotten by his ungrateful country, but Rome herself could not rob her banished general of the name conferred on him by acclamation when, flushed with triumph, he was received by her as the Victor of Corioli; and still as Coriolanus the dead hero is known to successive generations. His name of honour has outlived the base calumnies by which he was hounded to death.

Themistocles, Leonidas, Curtius, Regulus, and Arria, brave wife! your bones have long since mingled with the common dust; yet still, in lands which were barbarian when you lived your immortal lives and died your glorious deaths, let but your names be breathed even in the sobering precincts of a school-room, and the red colour springs to the cheeks and the sparkling light to the eyes of all true-hearted boys and girls.

A sacredness in names has been almost universally acknowledged, even when in foreign tongues their signification was not understood.

Psellus, the counsellor of successive Greek emperors in the eleventh century, was warned by Chaldaic oracles that misfortune followed on all attempts to change the names of the stranger. Pagan priests in their religious ceremonies frequently invoked strange names of which they knew not the meaning, using them as acceptable sounds in the ears of the gods of the nations from whom they had been learned.

History affords us striking instances where the conqueror's strong arm laying fenced cities even with the ground, and blotting out whole peoples from the book of nations, had yet failed permanently to impose on particular spots names different from those given by their original possessors.

That city of many sieges from the time of the Crusaders to our own day, termed by Napoleon the Key of Palestine, impatiently bore under Greek and Roman rulers the name of Ptolemaïs. With many another Syrian town, it has long since resumed its old name; such original names being for the most part founded on local definitions. Accho, signifying '*heated, sandy,*'* exactly describes the tract on which this city of romantic interest is built.

The history of nations will show us that, with

---

* Stanley's Sinai and Palestine.

scarcely an exception, men have always considered the giving of a name to their offspring as an important act, worthy to be consecrated by religious rites.

Nor can we wonder that such feelings should be instinctive, and therefore to be found amongst the most untaught children of nature, when we read in the Holy Scriptures that the Great Creator of all men preceded His giving a name to our first parents by giving to them His 'blessing.'*

To Adam, as to God's vicegerent upon earth, was assigned the honour of naming all the then created beings. It was the first act which God called on him to perform, and therefore it has been rightly said, 'Of all arts that which was first practised was the art of giving names.'†
To name being to define, wisdom to do so rightly was, we may be sure, inspired by God Himself.

In the after history of God's chosen people we trace the value attached to names, in that the Most High honoured His servants by giving or altering their names according to their express signification; with some, as with our Lord Jesus, the name being appointed prophetically before the Holy Infant's birth.

St. Jerome discovered in the Scriptures ten names by which the Almighty was Himself dis-

---

* Genesis v. 2.
† Léon Scott, 'Art de Nommer.'

tinguished. One of these names, written in four letters, was incommunicable. It was not to be pronounced except in the holy precincts of the Temple. Once in seven years the Jews of old time repeated it with great solemnity to their children, but after the death of the aged Simeon, it was never more uttered, not even in the sanctuary. Familiar to all must be that solemn scene when out of the burning bush went forth the Almighty's voice. Moses, the chosen ambassador charged with a message to the children of Israel from 'the God of their fathers,' besought to know the name of Him that sent. And God said unto Moses, 'I am that I am.'

Combinations and transpositions of the sacred name and sacred attributes constitute a remarkable feature in Hebrew names; more than a thousand are said to have been compounded from the titles of Jehovah.

A beautiful example of this ready adaptation was given by Moses, when with prophetic wisdom he distinguished the bravest of his warriors by changing his name Hoshea, signifying *Help*, or salvation, into Joshua, signifying *God's Help* or salvation, or more properly *Jehovah's Help*.*

A wisdom surpassing man's bestowed on zealous, impulsive, but too often faint-hearted Simon, the name of Peter, signifying a *Rock*. How gloriously in trials and in death did the

* The various contractions of the sacred name will be given in a subsequent chapter.

unshaken fortitude of the faithful disciple fulfil the divinely-appointed name!

The Church of Christ in all lands* sanctifies the giving of names by uniting with it the holy rite of baptism. In our own day touching instances are known of heathen converts asking that the name of their missionary teacher should be the one bestowed on them in baptism, as a continual remembrance that through him they had been called to a new life.

Familiar to all Christian readers, as recorded in Scripture, is the Jewish rite of circumcision, by which on the eighth day all male descendants of the Father of the Faithful were admitted to the privileges of God's chosen people. Modern Jews require ten witnesses to this solemn act; the name being given to the infant between the first and second benediction. With girls, the bestowing a name with prayers and blessing does not take place till the infant is six weeks old. The cradle, adorned with more or less magnificence, according to the wealth of the parents, is upheld by young maidens, one of whom performs the corresponding office of a godmother with us. Amongst German Jews a cup of wine is lifted in the air at the moment of pronouncing the girl's name.

Jews in England generally attach a Hebrew name to each child in addition to that by which

---

* It is said that Quakers and Baptists are the only exceptions to this rule.

they are commonly known; the derivation of this last being immaterial. A singular custom prevails amongst this people of changing a child's name in cases of extreme illness. When all remedies have failed, as a last expedient they resort to this.

In giving a new name to the child they would seem to discover a hope of renewing its being; or this practice may have arisen from a fear that misfortune attached to the former name. As it not unfrequently happens, from the well-known tenacity of life in early youth, that their darlings are restored to them as if from the very jaws of death, such recoveries are, of course, attributed to the fortunate change of name. In Livonia it is a common custom to change an infant's name if at six weeks old it is at all sickly.

Another peculiar Jewish custom connected with the individual name is the name-verse. A verse in the Psalms being discovered the first and last letter of which correspond with the initial and final letter of the name, it is carefully written out, committed to memory, and repeated every night at the conclusion of prayer. Those versed in Cabalistic mysteries assert that after death an angel descends to demand from the dead its name. A good Jew or Jewess will remember and repeat the sacred verse, upon which they will be left in peace; but all memory of the holy words will have passed from the minds of those whose lives have been evil, and they will accordingly be tormented by the avenging angel. With the ancient Greeks, the act of naming their children, called Onomasteria, was kept as a high festival. The seventh day from the infant's birth was selected, from the mysterious value which in all times and in all places has been attached to that number. Sacrifices were offered up to their gods, and a banquet given to all the relations and friends of the family. These festivals were also called Amphidromia, from the principal ceremony performed: the nurses and women attending on the mother *ran* round the *fire*, one of them carrying the child in her arms. By this act the newly-born babe was supposed to be placed under the protection of the household gods, to whom the pagan's hearth was always consecrated. During the ceremonies of the naming day, an olive garland or a fleece of wool was suspended from the door. Both were significant: the olive, symbolical of agricultural labour, denoted that the child was a boy; while a girl was typified by the fleece of wool, expressive of the womanly arts of spinning and making raiment.

The names of the paternal and maternal grandfathers were usually bestowed respectively on the first and second son; those too of illustrious ancestors were given, and sometimes the important matter was decided by chance, or, as they would have expressed it, by the Fates. Different names were attached to a certain number of wax tapers, and the name was chosen from the taper which burned the longest, supposing that it would insure the longest life.

Amongst other relics of paganism, this superstition lingered long amongst the early Christians. In vain was it denounced by St. Chrysostom, the *golden-mouthed* (significant of eloquence), for still in the thirteenth century we find that the Greek Emperor Andronicus (Paleologus) publicly employed this method of determining the name of his daughter. The names of the twelve Apostles were those selected, and chance decided for the princess the name of Simonides, from Simon, signifying in Hebrew *obedient.*

In Greece and Rome the original custom had been to name an infant at the moment of its birth; when laid at its father's feet, the act of his lifting the babe from the ground was looked upon as an acknowledgment of the child, and an engagement to perform a parent's part in bringing it up according to its station in life. From the Latin word 'tollere,' to *raise* or *lift up*, was derived the name of Tullius. The original Tullus was, we may suppose, a particularly fine baby, and by this significant name the father expressed his peculiar satisfaction in *lifting him up*.

The Romans afterwards kept the festival of Nominalia, on the ninth day for a boy, and on the eighth for a girl. They adopted the Grecian ceremony of Amphidromia. In the Latin name Arabella, signifying *Fair Altar*, we may find a reminiscence of this custom. This name is also noticeable as amongst the few originally feminine names which we have derived from the Latin, by far the greatest number being only feminised forms of names originally designed for men.

Mighty conquerors as they were, the inferiority of the Romans to the accomplished Greeks in so many of the refinements of life is recalled to our minds by this particular, incidentally betrayed by the history of names.

Such names as Areta, *virtue*, Arsinoë, *elevation of mind*, Eulalia, one who *speaks sweetly*, Aspasia, *winning*, Eucharis, signifying *excelling in grace, altogether lovely*, with countless others, remain to show us that in Greece the especial graces of womanhood were not ignored.

Alas for the lack of chivalry in the early days of Rome, when we read that two letters reversed were considered sufficient to represent womankind! C and M *reversed* (as if to point the insult!) signified Caia and Marcia. By these tokens were women once designated by a people whose history was to be illumined by the lives of Lucretia, Portia, and Cornelia the mother of the Gracchi.

As time went on, the women of Rome, gaining continually increasing respect, won for themselves individual and appropriate names, till at last we find amongst those of Latin derivation one of the most beautiful names a woman can bear, Beatrice, the Joy-giver, *one who makes blessed.*

The first step was to distinguish daughters by a feminised form of the name of their house, which, as in the case of the tenderly beloved daughter of Tullius Cicero, was sometimes softened into a diminutive, Tulliola. But if more than one daughter was born in a family, they were designated as major and minor; if more than two, by numbers. The sisters of Brutus were known as Junia major, Junia minor, and Junia tertia. The names of Secundilla, Quartilla, &c., remain to show us that, in some names at least, attempts were made to soften the chilly sense of such disembodied names as numerals appear to be. An English huntsman would take shame to himself were he unable to suggest a suitable name for each individual hound in his pack.

Rome's scant courtesy to her daughters finds no parallel in the history of names, except amongst the Chinese. The owners of the distorted feet known as 'golden lilies' were at one time also known in their father's house simply as 1, 2, and 3.

Look backwards now to the time when the human race consisted of but a few families, ere, for the wickedness of man, 'the fountains of the great deep were broken up,' so that while from 'the windows of heaven' cleansing waters passed over the face of the earth, huge masses of its framework should be disjointed below, to remain for ever witnesses of the overwhelming might of

God when sin persisted in provokes His wrath. Contrast the supposed perfection of civilisation of the conceited Chinese with those earliest days of all, when men took delight in distinguishing their women by names of pleasing significance. We read that Lamech's wives were called Adah, *Ornament*, significative of great beauty; and Zillah, *Shadow*, in a hot country a word of delight, and significant of a gentle nature, where would be found refreshment and rest.

From ancient Assyria came, as we have seen, Esther, *the Star*, and from thence also came Susan, the *Lily*.

The followers of Mohammed,[*] even while they deny to women a place in the paradise to come, do honour here to those on whom their earthly happiness depends, by seeking their names from amongst flowers and gems, and even from the firmament of heaven itself. The Arabic Jullanar, in Persian Gulnàr, signifies the brilliant *pomegranate blossom*; Yasemeen is the *fragrant jasmine*; Zumurrud is an *emerald*; Shejeret-el-Durr is a *tree of pearls*, and plural also to denote the extreme of excellence which no single object could portray; Budoor signifies *Full Moons*.

Shall we turn to savage tribes? A brave from amongst the North American Indians, though his tones are those of a master who must be obeyed, yet summons his docile squaw to his

[*] The writer's suggestion to be afterwards set forth.

side by a name which at least indirectly proves his real appreciation of her charms, recalling as it does some lovely aspect of nature, or some familiar object of grace. Her musical voice, perhaps, has gained for her the name of Minne-ha-ha, or *laughing water*; Tah-mi-roo, or the *startled fawn*, expresses the soft shyness of her beautiful eyes; O-li-ti-pa identifies her with the pretty *prairie-bird*; Mong-shong-shaw, the *bending willow*, describes her graceful form; and Hu-la'h-dee, the *pure fountain*, tells of the dearest and most lasting of all charms, a pure, true heart.

Some of the sweetest of our women's names in present use amongst ourselves were originally the gift of the fiery Celt and fierce Teuton, or his descendants, the Norseman and Anglo-Saxon.

Gwendaline, in the Celtic Guenddolen, signifies '*the lady of the white bow.*' If the Arabs prefer the *full moon*, it would seem our ancestors loved best the crescent or young moon.

Or, as the crescent form tells alike of age and of early youth, let us—rather than do any possible injustice to a Celtic lover—see in this musical name the key-note of that sweet song in the Irish Melodies —

Believe me, if all those endearing young charms.

Why should not Ango, the *Undeviating*, when he breathed the name of Guenddolen, have meant all that his descendant, Thomas Moore, did say in after years?—

> Let thy loveliness fade as it will,
>   Around the dear ruin each wish of my heart
> Would entwine itself verdantly (*lovingly*) still.

The Teuton Adel-hild (Adelaide) tells us of the *noble maiden* or *lady*, Bertha of the *shining one*, and Gertrude of *her* who is *trusted and true*; Scandinavian Val-borg signifies the *chosen tower*, i. e. the stronghold of happiness; and Saxon Ead-eath (Edith) signifies *happiness that is blessed*; and Mildred means one that is *gentle of speech*.

Some names there are now fallen into disuse, which, if we regard the rude times in which they were first invented and used, claim for the hardy sons of the North especial honour from the gentler sex, showing as they do with what tenderness the strong regarded the weak.

Looking as they did upon woman in the lovely light in which she is *first* represented in Paradise, a 'help meet' for man, we find the Celtic Cwenborg, '*a woman who is a Helper*,' and the Saxon El gifa, the *Help-giver*.

As a woman—the manner of Romans and Chinese distinguishing women by 1, 2, 3, as only convicts are distinguished now, excited such warm indignation, that to the east and west, north and south, I hastened to do instant homage to the worthy champions of my sex—may I be pardoned for having so interrupted the account of the ceremonies which, in various nations, have attended the act of name-giving?

It is singular to read how, for many years before the light of Christianity dawned on the kingdoms of the North, a kind of infant baptism prevailed. The Eddaic poems make mention of it, and in the Chronicle of Snorro Sturleson we see a Norwegian nobleman in the reign of Harold Harfagra pouring water over the head of his new-born babe, calling him Hakron after his father.*

In the Laxdaela Saga, which embraces a period of time between the ninth and eleventh centuries, this ceremony is also alluded to, and a strange story is told in connection with the child who was so baptised by the name of Olaf or Aulaff, signifying the *Olive*—a name singularly inappropriate to the infant, who was by no means a bringer of peace.

Höskuld, a merchant from Iceland, visiting Norway for business purposes, was tempted by a Russian trader to invest in a far more dangerous purchase than the logs of timber which we may suppose were the articles in which he principally dealt. Höskuld purchased from the Russian a lovely slave. One element, however, in which a woman's power of mischief principally resides, was wanting: so far as the mighty

* Mallet's Northern Antiquities.

engine of the tongue was concerned, the beautiful girl was harmless, for she was deaf and dumb.

Carried by the merchant to his Icelandic home, the fair captive became to him the second and inferior wife, which the laws of the island allowed. The original Mrs. Höskuld—Jorumna, as she was called—found some consolation in the infirmities of her rival: beautiful as she was, her silent empire could scarcely, she thought, be a lasting one; and so they lived together in tolerable amity.

But the dumb wife became a mother, and, wonderful to relate, her transports of joy were not speechless! Thinking herself alone, the young mother was overheard one day lavishing on her babe a thousand expressions of joy and tenderness. Gaily she sang while the little one laughed, and when his violet eyes grew dim, she softly murmured a lullaby. Her words were not understood, for she spoke in a foreign language, but beyond all doubt they were words, and thus was the fact revealed that her deafness and dumbness had been assumed.

By degrees, she made her story known. Melkorka, daughter of Mirkjarten, an Irish king, had been taken captive, at eleven years old, by one of the Scandinavian sea-rovers, who were the terror of the coast of Ireland. Sold to a Russian trader, the resolute child determined that the voice of a daughter of kings should never be heard from the lips of a slave. For years her vow had been kept inviolate, but the cooing of her little one had proved irresistible, and had won from her a reply, and then—the long-pent-up stream of melody had impetuously gushed forth in never-ceasing fountains of tenderness.

To us the tale is poetry—to how many a woman's breast has the touch of her first baby's hand been as a divining wand, beneath which a spring of eloquence, vocal with delight, hitherto unknown and undreamed of, has leaped into life!

But poor Jorumna naturally saw things in a different light. Only on account of her supposed infirmities had the fair slave been excused the service she, as inferior wife, was bound to render to her superior; but this right Jorumna now enforced, and the story ends in anything but a poetical manner.

We may be sure the Irish princess brought no willing mind to the task of waiting on her Icelandic mistress. One day Melkorka dropped the stockings she was handing to Jorumna; the stockings were flung at the Irish girl's head; her Celtic blood was up, and she avenged the insult with a blow. Höskuld, becoming convinced that happiness and two wives were incompatible, sent Melkorka away to a distant part of the country. When her son Olaf was grown up, he visited Ireland, and became acquainted with his royal grandfather. A series of romantic adventures, duly related by the Saga, terminates with the fortunate youth taking the name of 'Pa' or 'Pafugl,' a *peacock*, from an old gentleman who made him his heir.

Amongst the Mohammedans of Turkey, Arabia, Persia, and Hindustan, infants are sometimes named when only three hours old, but more commonly on the seventh day. Their Prophet left particular directions to guide them in their choice of names. Abd-Allah, *Servant of God*, and Abd-el-Rahman, *Servant of the Compassionate*, are amongst those which are most approved. His especial blessing was promised to those who, for love for him, were named Ahmed, *praised*, and Mohammed, *greatly to be praised*; this blessing was even extended to all assemblies where men bearing such names were present.

Astrologers, too, are frequently consulted in the selection of names. It is also a common custom to write five names on separate papers, which are placed together within the leaves of the Koran; the first chapter of the book having been read, one of these papers is drawn out at hazard, and the name so pointed out is given to the child. Although the injunction is frequently neglected, a sacrifice is solemnly prescribed to be offered up on the naming day, a ram or a goat, of which 'not a bone is to be broken.'*

Amongst the Parsees or Fire-worshippers the newly-born babe is purified in holy water, and

---

* Notes to Lane's Arabian Nights.

made to drink of a consecrated liquor; after which a name is bestowed.

The most ancient laws of the Hindus (and they are amongst the most ancient in the world) contain special directions for the solemnities attending the imposition of names. On the tenth or eleventh day after the infant's birth, according as the day of the week and aspect of the stars were propitious, the child was to receive from its father a name suitable to the caste to which he or she belonged. If a Brahmin's son, the ears being pierced at the moment of pronouncing the name, the boy's name was to be expressive of *favour*; if a warrior's son, of *power*; cultivators of the ground and merchants were to bestow names denoting *riches*; and those of the lowest caste such as expressed *dependence*. The names of women were to be easy of pronunciation— soft, melodious, pleasant, and of good augury— terminating in vowels, and *sounding* like *words of benediction*.*

As the ancient Greek, and at times the early Christian also, were wont by lighted tapers to determine the choice of names, the Hindu of to-day resorts to burning lamps. Two lamps are placed over two names, and the one over which the lamp burns brightest is the chosen name. A second name is often added, that of the planet ruling at the time of the child's birth.

* F. Schlegel.

The names having been chosen, the parents sit on the ground, the infant being in its mother's arms; the father writes the two names on a plate of raw rice, which is handed to him by the officiating Brahmin, and the first name is repeated three times.

In Ceylon the ceremony is full of poetry. The mother carries her child to the temple, and with it an offering to the god. She also takes three flowers; to each of them a name is attached, the initial letter, in all alike, being that of the constellation which was in the ascendant when the child was born. The offering is first presented; the Brahmin next presents with prayer the flowers to the idol, and then returns one of them to the mother. The names being unknown to the priest, it is believed that his unconscious selection of one is directed by the god or goddess; so that the name is received as if directly from them.*

In Thibet infants are bathed, and, after prayers have been recited over them, two names are given: one, the name of a divinity, is selected by the priest, and is to be used only in religious ceremonies; the other, by which he is to be commonly known, is chosen by the family.

The Japanese are said to take new names at four different periods of life: the name given to a child is succeeded by one adapted for a youth, which is again exchanged for that of a full-grown

---

* Rev. F. de Ward's India and the Hindoos.

man, and followed by another suitable to an old man.*

Princes of Japan bear the names of their territorial possessions in addition to those of their family and their individual appellations. Our late interesting and intelligent visitors the Japanese ambassadors were known as Také No Ouchi Shimodzukéne Kami, Matsudairu Twamino Kami, and Kiogoku Notono Kami. Kami appears to be a title, but it is left to more learned enquirers to afford the signification of these names.

In China changes of names are frequent; a man has sometimes six names given to him at different periods of his life. Great ceremony attends the bestowing of the first three names. The 'milk name' is given when the infant is a month old; it is introduced by its mother to assembled friends, the father pronouncing its name aloud; prayers and sacrifices are then offered up. On a boy's first entering school the 'book name' is given; the accompanying ceremony is significative of a religious and moral obligation. The master, kneeling before a paper on which is inscribed the name of a sage, a follower of Confucius, or Koong-foo-tsi, prays for his favourable influence on the boy, mentioning him by his new name. The master then seats himself, and his new scholar pays homage to him by the Chinese act of prostration. On a man's marriage

* Noël's Dictionnaire Historique.

he receives a new name from his father; an entertainment is given, and the ancestors of the family are worshipped. Every man adds two characters or syllables to his individual name on the marriage of his eldest son, his family name remaining the same. 'I beg to enquire your lofty surname and great name?' is a common address in China.*

Some of the Tartar tribes do not name their children till they are six months old. A particular day is then appointed, and the child receives the name of the person who first accidentally passes by its side.

In parts of Guinea infants are named by their mothers at the time of their birth, after a secret consultation with their fetishes.

In other parts of Western Africa a feast is given in honour of the newly born. The babe of shining blackness—a little image, as it were, in jet—is placed upon a palm-leaf, and palm-wine (the beloved 'mimbo') is drunk by the parents, their cups being lifted above the child so that some drops may fall upon its face. At the first cry uttered, a name is discovered supposed to resemble it in sound; so that African babies enjoy the peculiar privilege of naming themselves.

From this singular origin is said to be derived the name so widely bestowed on the negro race, Quaco, which otherwise might have been supposed to claim kindred with the *Duck* language.

* Davis's Sketches of China.

It is, with regret, found to be impossible even to suggest a signification.

A negro tribe on the Ivory coast are known by the name of the Quaquas or Quacas. Quamina (?) is a favourite name amongst the Ashantees; it figures amongst their list of kings, and may often be heard in negro villages in the West Indies.

Forty days' feasting, with sacrifices, celebrate amongst the Abyssinians the name-day of their children.

Significant names, and some of them of great beauty, belong, as is well known, to the Indians of North America; but the ceremony of a youth's receiving a name is attended by solemn and mysterious rites concealed from European eyes. It is left to their braves to gain subsequently for themselves names of greater distinction, expressive of their individual prowess and skill in war or the chase.

In Mexico and Brazil the names of the natives are also significant, and the giving of them is attended by feasting and religious rites.

What boundless fields for reflection and research do we thus glance at while we speak of but the first use of names! Unconscious babes are by them enrolled under their respective standards of faith, varying from the sublimity of doctrine and purity of precept professed by the followers of Christ, down to the degrading practices of the avowed devil-worshippers.

But the Prince of Darkness rejoices in the services of many who are not his avowed followers. In all lands there are enemies—more or less openly so—of the light.

May all who in earnest love the 'Good Master' hold fast to *His* name, and its signification as united to their own names in holy bonds—Christians, and therefore *anointed* 'priests and kings,' bound to live pure and noble lives!

But we are soldiers too. The contest of good and evil goes on continually, without and within. Do we seek to overcome? Let us take a lesson from earthly conquerors.

The nation from whom we have derived the noble name of Vincent, he who *overcomes*, or the *invincible*, and Victoria, the auspicious name which needs no translation, was above all others a conquering nation. It was not by inheritance, not by good fortune, not by wise policy, that Rome became the mistress of the world, but by the dauntless bravery of her troops.

Amongst her laws we find one that is strangely suggestive. It was permitted to various classes to change their names on certain occasions: slaves on becoming freedmen, plebeians passing into the patrician order, assumed names of higher import; but Rome's soldiers—those on whose indomitable valour the existence of her empire depended—to them it was forbidden to change their names.

On each man's buckler his name was engraved;

had it not a voice as it went before him to battle? His *name* going before him—who dared be a coward then? An abandoned shield proclaimed aloud the infamy of its owner; the runaway's name was lost—and for ever!

See now, too, the ensigns which go before the respective troops. Those glittering eagles of silver and gold, consecrated by prayer, rarely dishonoured by defeat—on them you may read the number of the legion, and its leader's *name*!

CHAPTER III.

Infinite variety of subjects connected with the history of names — Sovereignty in names — Names attached to ancient dynasties; also to royal and noble families.

IN the history of names there is indeed 'l'embarras des richesses;' the difficulty throughout is not ' what can one say ? ' but what one must leave unsaid.

From the moment we are awakened to the value and power of names, to that when, a great list lying before us, we shall look on the names of many nations, classed according to their significations, we shall find innumerable by-paths opening out on either side.

Which of these shall we enter? Which must we pass by?

We have learned the burden of the song, *Let us answer to our names*; we have glanced at the strange power possessed by names, and at the various solemn rites by which various nations have consecrated, and still do consecrate, the act of name-giving; let us again take wing — or, if you like the image better, let us together mount the library steps, and, reaching down some dusty old tomes, see what we can gather in ancient histories about names.

The theme is too wide to be fully set forth in a sketch like this; but we could not pass by the interesting subject of the nature of the names which monarchs assumed in the earliest periods of the world's history. They are all of striking significance, especially those which were adopted as being in themselves expressive of sovereignty. Such names passed on, with crown and sceptre and royal robes, from dead kings to their successors.

It can scarcely be doubted that this practice originated in the belief of metempsychosis. In its supposed transmigration through various bodies, the royal soul, thus retaining its name, carried out the idea as expressed in later days: 'Le Roi ne meurt pas. Le Roi est mort. Vive le Roi!'

Well might the mass of the people in those far-off days have believed in undying kings, when by one unchanging name the laws of successive generations were enforced. The names so invested with perpetual sovereignty, in those remote times, were also so grand, and of such wide significance, that in them the individuality of their temporary wearers might well be lost. Royal names for the most part signified a god or a conqueror.

The appellations of ancient Assyrian monarchs, successors of Belus, builder of Babylon, repeat in various combinations the name of Bel or Baal, the Sun-god, whose worship under different names was so widely spread throughout the glowing climes of the East. Egyptian monarchs also claimed to be emanations from the Deity.

The names of Pharaoh and Rameses are both derived from the Sun-god, the tutelary divinity of the land. Ra-messu signified the *sun-begotten*, and Pharaoh was from Ph *the*, Ré *sun*; Potiphe-ra signified *consecrated to the sun*. One of the Pharaohs assumed the additional name of A-mosis, signifying *sprung from*, or *son of the moon*.

In the Syriac tongue Pharaoh included the meanings of both a *king* and a *crocodile*, the hideous monarch of the muddy waters of the Nile.

The name of Ptolemy, which in later days was borne by many kings of Egypt and Macedonia, was derived from the Greek, and signified a *warrior*. There was much meaning in the name, for in many instances the crown was won by the sword.

In the battle-field of Persia unbroken lines of kings are not to be found, but names of exactly similar import to the Pharaohs and Ptolemies of Egypt alternate as the appellations of the monarchs of Iran.

Kouresh (the Cyrus of Greek and Latin historians), signifying the sun, was in the ancient Pehlevi dialect still more expressive—Kor-shid, *the splendour of the sun*; the old name still sounding in our ears in Khor-assan, *Sun-land*, and

Kour-distan. As a sun, indeed, in its bright rising, its glorious noon, its crimson setting, was the life of Cyrus, the Persian hero of so many romantic tales. Hoping to shield him from the cruel designs of his grandfather, who mistrusted a child of whom such great things were predicted, his friends attempted in vain to rear the son of the royal Mandane in a herdsman's family. The instincts of race shone forth in the superiority instinctively claimed by him over his boyish companions, and which they as instinctively ceded. The young Khor-dad, signifying *Gift of the Sun*, chosen in sport as their king, as a king in earnest enforced his authority, and through some rebellion in his mimic court the secret of his royal birth became known.

It was when, the prophecy fulfilled, he united in himself the throne of the Medes and Persians, that Kor·shid, the *Splendour of the Sun*, assumed his resplendent name, so singularly appropriate to the vicissitudes of his fortunes. In the dawn of life clouds had obscured his horizon, but suddenly they were all dispelled. The glory of his manhood's prime was as the splendour of the noontide sun, and in his death the figurative expression for the red sunsets of eastern climes— 'the sun setting as in a sea of blood'—also became, through the cruel Scythian queen, Tomyris, a terrible reality. Cyrus, when taken prisoner by her, was beheaded, and his head was thrown into a huge leathern bottle filled with blood, the savage queen exclaiming, 'You have thirsted for blood—now satisfy your thirst.'

The name of Kouresh, or Korshid, as expressive of an emanation of deity, was ere long succeeded by that of Xerxes, a name so translated by the Greeks, and said by Herodotus to signify a *Conqueror*. The Greek Xerxes, Median Cyaxares, Hebrew Ahasuerus, and the Kh-sh-yarsha of ancient monuments, has in later days been translated by 'the *Lion King*,' a natural Oriental figure for a conqueror. Xerxes, if derived from the Zend word Ksathra, Sanscrit Khsathra, signifies a *King*. Artaxerxes, a name borne by many successive Persian monarchs, signifies 'the *Honoured* King;' the prefix, Persian Ar, Sanscrit Arya, signifying '*Honoured*.' From the same root sprang modern Iran's old name of Ariana.

In the ancient kingdom of the fire-worshippers, where, in the city of Yezd, or Izad (the Holy Name), it is said that the heaven-descended fire still burns unquenched since the days of Zoroaster, the old name of their tutelary god constantly returned in various combinations as their sovereign's name. Hormuz, or Orosmades, signified *Pure Light*, and Khosru, the *Sun*. Mithra, another name for the sun-god of Persia, gave to kings of Armenia and Pontus the name of Mithridad, translated by the Greeks Mithridates, a synonyme of Khor-dad, *Gift of the Sun*.

In later days the 'Sophis of Persia' again proclaimed how in Ariana, the 'honoured' land, the religious element indissolubly combined itself with the principle of sovereignty. The royal title, when it ceased to claim the name of deity, assumed that of its ministers.

The sun and fire, chosen as objects of veneration by these descendants of Shem, were typical of their religious history. The clouds of superstition and the smouldering darkness of human corruption again and again threatened to quench the light of the true faith, but its glory was never wholly obscured. Amongst idolaters (allowing that they were so) the fire-worshippers, as they have been called, have always been distinguished by the comparative purity of their doctrines and lives.

Christians may well lay to heart some of the noble precepts of the Zend-Avesta, or '*Living Word*,' given to the Persians by the great Zoroaster, the Greek rendering of whose Persian name, Zerdusht, signifies a *Pure* or *Living Star*. Some learned writers read the name as Ziru Ishtar, 'The seed of the goddess Ishtar;' the Assyrian name for the planet Venus. The Magian philosopher's name was suggestive indeed, for *star*-like amidst the gloomy fatalism of a Pagan world must have shone forth such words as these:—'In your afflictions offer to God your patience; in your joy render to Him *acts* of thanksgiving.' Do not the trees of our orchards, the blackberry bushes of our hedge-rows, repeat the same lesson to us? See how they silently bend beneath the chill weight of winter's oppressive snows; see, again, how at the first breath of spring they hasten to put forth their green leaves and fair blossoms. The summer sunshine falls not on ungrateful objects there, for behold in autumn their good fruits.

But the Persians of old had another teacher besides Zoroaster, and another holy book besides the Zend-Avesta. The Sofh, or 'Persian Bible,' as it has been called, is said by some writers to have derived its name from the Greek σοφία, *wisdom*. How may this be, if indeed this venerated book be of such antiquity as to claim for its author Abraham? Shall we not rather suppose that the Greeks themselves adopted this word, as they *did* adopt other words, and the whole tangled maze of their mythology, from the fertile East? Must we not look to the Sanscrit paradêsa if we would know where the Greeks found their paradeisos—our paradise, or *garden of delight*?

Sophi, or Sofi, is said by Bochart to mean, in the original Persian, one '*Pure in Faith*,' 'devoted to God.'* The significations of the Greek and the Persian words Sophia and Sofi, *Wisdom* and *Purity*, are in the Inspired Word united. ' The wisdom

---

* The books of the Muslim darweeshes (dervishes) of the order of Soofees are called ' Ta sow wuf,' that is, *of spiritual life*. D'Herbelot, Bibliothèque Orientale: quoted by Lane, Arabian Nights, vol. ii. p. 240.

that is from above' is there said to be '*first pure.*' Do not our own hearts tell us also that only by the 'pure in heart,' who *see* God, can true wisdom be found? The Hebrew word Zophim, explained as '*Seers,*'* carries out this idea, confirmed by the Hebrew prophet Zephaniah's name, which (translated by the French Sophonie, and Italian Sofonia) is said to signify '*The Secret of Jehovah.*'

The Greek Sophia, though cruelly misused by the so-called sophists of the schools, did still so retain its original holy signification, that it was at one time used by the early Christian Church to express the Incarnate Word as the '*Wisdom*' of God. It was then considered too sacred to be used commonly as an individual name.†

This name, of Eastern origin (as I believe), once held in such especial honour, will be found amongst the heroic names of Arabian conquerors of old—Sofian, and Abu Sofian. In its feminine form, it becomes in Arabic Safiyeh.

In Turkish it is Sofiyeh, as a woman's name, and signifies *Chosen*.

In the magnificent mosque of Santa Sophia—the name of which has been preserved by the Turks, though the city is called Stamboul—once a Christian church, and which Moslems themselves believe will become so again one day, eight of the great columns were brought from the

* Stanley's Jewish Church, p. 403.
† 'Therefore some godly men do dislike it as irreligious that it should be communicated to any other.'—Camden's *Remains,* &c.

Temple of the *Sun* at Baalbec, and eight from the Temple of Diana (the *Moon*) at Ephesus.* Do not these superb spoils of the false gods of Assyria and Greece, thus consecrated to Divine Wisdom, seem to say—

> Th' unwearied sun from day to day
> Does his Creator's praise display.
>
> Soon as the evening shades prevail,
> The moon takes up the wond'rous tale.

History tells us how the word Sofi was disgraced by cruel Persian kings who bore the name, and yet more by the horrible doctrine subsequently taught under the name of Soofeism. Our ancestors brought back to us from the Crusades a new and terrible word, *Assassin*: it was used to designate the red-handed followers of Hassan, the mountain-chief of Alamoot, signifying the *Vulture's Nest*. Assassin, once supposed to have come from Hassan, was really derived from Hashish, a kind of hemp, by means of which the Fedavee, or *Devoted*, were intoxicated, when it suited the purposes of their wicked chief.

We will now see how the name Sofi was crowned with sovereignty and became that of a royal dynasty. A race of sheiks long dwelling

* The long-lost quarries of Rosso and Verde Antico, which were rediscovered about two years ago by the German sculptor Herr Siegel, contain an inscription saying that from them were taken the columns for the temples of Baalbec and Ephesus, which now adorn St. Sophia's at Constantinople. Bremer's Greece, vol. i. p. 97.

THE SOPHIS OF PERSIA.

at Erdebel, had successively passed their lives in mystic contemplation of this sacred book—the Sofh—containing doctrines called by them 'Kish Abraham.' In the fourteenth century a member of this family rose into eminence as Sophi-ed-Deen, signifying *One Pure* or *Wise in the Faith*. By his descendant, the warlike though cruel Ismael, was the dynasty of the Sophis, Sefés, or Suffavees (in Shakspeare's time called 'the Sophys of Persia') established, which lasted for upwards of two hundred years. The followers of Sophi-ed-Deen were distinguished by a cap of crimson wool, and the Mohammedans, who so often fled in terror before these Kussilbashes, or red-caps, even while themselves cherishing the name of Sophian, have attempted to cast ridicule on the title of Sophi by pointing to the woollen cap as its origin, 'Souf' being the Arabian word for *wool*.

As a religious order, the Sophis still exist—the reigning Shah of Persia being considered the grand master of the order. The first convent of the order, in Egypt, was founded by the chivalrous opponent of our Cœur-de-Lion, Salah-ed-Deen, signifying the *Goodness of the Religion*, or the *Faith*.

Looking to ancient India, we find in Porus the Greek form of the name of a brave monarch—of one whose noble nature, kindred with his native palm-tree, no weight of misfortune could depress; discrowned, but still a king, commanding the respect and admiration of his conqueror

Alexander. Porus has been said to signify a 'Prince,' but, traced to its original Sanscrit, it has a nobler and far more appropriate meaning, Paurusha signifying a *Hero*.

Names significant of sovereign power were common in the East, such as Archelaus, signifying in Greek *Ruler of the People*; and they had their synonymes amongst the Teuton princes of the West, who themselves claimed to be of Asiatic origin.

In that word of infinite significance, thu, *to do*, the words Teut, signifying *God, Father, Ruler*, and Thiudans, signifying the *People*, alike had their root. Thence arose the grand name of Theod-o-ric, which signifies a *Chief*, who is *Father of the People*. Grandly was the name carried out by the mighty monarch of the Ostrogoths, whom history and song have delighted to honour.

Æthiopia claimed the sun as her father and her king; but the dark-skinned race were ruled by women, their queens successively bearing the name of Candace, which is said to signify 'pure possession.'*

The 'Brothers of the Sun and Moon,' who rule the celestial kingdom, called by barbarians China, not content with their heavenly designation, affect also such earthly appellations as may strike terror into the hearts of their foes. From B.C. 49 to A.D. 1832, Lûng, a *Dragon*,

---

* Cruden.

has been a favourite cognomen in 'the Flowery Land,' having been assumed not only by lawful sovereigns, but also by rebel leaders. Hwâng Lûng, *Yellow Dragon*, Tsing Lûng, *Azure Dragon*, figure amongst their chronicle of kings; yellow and blue being the colours most affected by the Chinese, considered by them as typical — the yellow of earth, the blue of heaven.

Chaou-kin Lûng, the *Golden Dragon* of 1832, is said by Sir John Davis to have always worn, as significant of his name, a yellow dress.

In the far West, where Pizarro and his followers sought not for undying fame, but for perishable gold, they found, in the Incas of Peru, misused by them so cruelly, another royal race, who claimed to be children of the sun— descendants of the heavenly visitants, Manco Capac and Manca Ocolla his wife.

From the fifteenth century the emperors of Morocco and their descendants have successively borne the name, or more properly the title, of Mouley, signifying *Lord* and *Master*.

Zay, or Saï, was the general title of the Ashantee kings.

The Negro kings of Loanga have adopted the prefix of Manna, which answers to the Spanish title of Don. Their names most frequently represent their most cherished article of property. Manna Gangala signifies Don *Shield*; Manna Belle, Don *Knife*.*

* Noël's Dictionnaire Historique.

The Princes of Mingrelia selected the noble name of Dadyan, signifying the *Just*. The Emperors of China and Japan are known after death by different names from those which they bore when living. By these new names they are worshipped by their people as divinities.

So, too, in Rome, their deified heroes sometimes received fresh appellations. To Romulus, whose name signified *Strength*, was given that of Quirinus, the name of an ancient Sabine divinity.

The reckless claimers of supernatural descent, so numerous in remote ages, grew less frequent as the strong arm of military power was found to be the more certain element of success. As time rolls on, we find the simple family name of a successful general deemed of sufficient value to express in itself the idea of sovereignty.

When Rome's invincible soldiers clashed together their brazen shields, and with a mighty shout hailed some comrade by the name of *Cæsar*, he was straightway invested with the purple. To Cæsar Augustus the imperial diadem itself belonged, and with it dominion over all the known regions of the world.

This name, surpassing all human names in celebrity, and which, up to the present day, is synonymous with empire—for emperors of Austria still affect to claim the title of 'the Cæsar'—may well have engaged much attention as to its derivation.

But, in itself, the name was nothing, its signification was as nought. It was from its wearer, from the Cæsar himself, that the mighty name derived its subsequently mighty significance.

To Julius Cæsar—of whom it has been said that, as general, statesman, lawgiver, poet, orator, and historian, he achieved such excellence that the distinction he gained in each character would separately have made any man remarkable—was rendered the most superb homage ever rendered to man.[*]

We shudder to read of Pedro the Cruel's ill-advised homage to the unhappy Inez de Castro—her fleshless brows marked by the glitter of a jewelled crown—but the honour paid by Rome to her slaughtered son was nobler far than any imaginable outward demonstration could have been. Unmatched in ancient and modern times is the spiritual grandeur of the investiture of the dead hero's *name*—himself uncrowned—with the insignia of royalty. To be a Cæsar was henceforth to be a King. Alas for the monsters that in Rome's later days disgraced the name!

The Cæsar would seem to have adopted the Punic signification of his name, by having an *elephant* engraved on the coinage of Rome while he was in power, it being contrary to law for the name of a man to be stamped on the money of a commonwealth.

[*] Smith's Classical Biography.

But the most generally received derivation of this mighty name is from the Latin *cæsaries*, *hair*. Such a name, bestowed on an infant who was born with much hair, accorded with the ordinary Roman custom of deriving names from personal characteristics. It only becomes singular when regarded as the distinctive name of a family of the *Julia* gens, *iulus* being derived from the Greek ἴουλος, signifying *downy*, or the soft hair of early youth; this name having been, it is said, first assumed by Ascanius of the royal house of Troy, on the occasion of a successful combat while yet the early down of manhood was upon his lip.

The name of Augustus is in our own language sufficiently suggestive. Derived from the Latin verb Augeo, to *honour*, it was first bestowed on Octavianus, the nephew and adopted son of Julius Cæsar, its Greek synonyme being found in Sebastos, signifying to be *reverenced* and honoured. As the name of the first emperor, and in itself expressive of rulership, it was, when joined to the name of Cæsar, indicative of supreme authority. Augusta was the title given to the empress.

But it is not only in ages past, and amongst such high and mighty personages as Egyptian Pharaohs and Roman Cæsars, that certain names have been attached to certain dignities.

In both the communions into which the Syrian Church is divided, the custom prevails of transmitting from prelate to prelate the same name.

The head of the Jacobite Church, who claims the title of the Patriarch of Antioch, is always called Ignatius (from the Latin), signifying to *kindle* or *inflame*. It was a name worthy to be remembered as that of the first Bishop of Antioch, once called the 'City of God,' where the followers of Christ were first called by His name. St. Ignatius, martyred in the emperor Trajan's reign, torn to pieces by lions in the amphitheatre of Rome, is said to have been the blessed child taken to the Saviour's arms when He spoke the words, 'Of such is the kingdom of heaven.'

The Maronite dwellers in Mount Lebanon, who from the twelfth century have been distinguished from the rest of the Eastern Church by their professed allegiance to the Church of Rome, always give to their spiritual head the name of Peter.

The beautiful names of Victor Amadeus and Victor Emmanuel are hereditary in the royal house of Savoy; Victor signifying in Latin a *Conqueror*, Amadeus (Latin), a *Lover of God*, and Emmanuel (Hebrew) signifying 'God with us.'

Lords of Lusignan have chosen the name of Geoffrey, said to have been of Teutonic origin, signifying '*Joyful*.'

Simon, in Hebrew signifying *Obedient*, has been attached to the house of De Montfort; and Anne, a woman's Hebrew name, signifying *Gracious*, to the house of De Montmorenci, Premier

Baron of Christendom. The name was first introduced into the family by Anne of Bretagne, who gave it to her godson. Henry, derived from the Scandinavian Eoric or Eric, signifying a *Great Lord*, is so identified with the German Princes of Reuss, that the Saxe-Gotha Almanack of 1862 chronicles Prince Henry the Seventy-fourth.

In a curious old French book (1681) on the origin of names, by Messire Gilles André de la Roque, we may see how Guy, Baron de Laval, fourteenth of the name, obtained from Pope Pascal II. permission for all his heirs in perpetuity to bear the Christian name of Guy. It was to preserve the memory of services rendered to the Church by the Baron and his brother, while serving in the Holy Land under Godfrey de Bouillon. This privilege was confirmed by letters from Philip I. of France. By the will of a succeeding baron, the lordship of Laval was made inseparable from the name of Guy. None could succeed to the honours of the house who was not of that name; in the event of an heiress, whoever she married was bound to assume it.

This beautiful name has been by some writers simply translated from the French Gui, *Mistletoe*; others have derived it from the dwarf Guion of Celtic mythology, connecting him with the sacred plant of the Druids. But such stringent directions for the preservation of the name, as perpetuating the recollection of some military service, would seem to show that the lords of

Laval, time-honoured owners of the name, did themselves derive it from guyer, guier, guidon (old French), signifying to *guide*, to *direct*, whence our word *guide*, identical with the French, though differently pronounced. Chaucer uses the word 'gie' in the same sense, to conduct, and almost the same idea is expressed in the Icelandic 'gae,' to *take heed*, a necessary qualification in a guide.

In connection with this derivation is preserved the beautiful signification of a *standard-bearer*, one who goes before, carrying the guidon or broad pendant. The proper name is in fact frequently so spelt, 'Guidon' in old French books.

We may be sure that the first Guy de Laval won his beautiful name by some gallant deed as a *guide*, or a *standard-bearer*, or as both. If Messire de la Roque, living nearer those times, had but sought out its origin, and not told us only of its preservation!

CHAPTER IV.

One individual name originally sufficient — Family names adopted — Principles of Roman nomenclature — The four Roman names — Nomenclators, &c.

IT would be impossible in a history of names strictly to divide the subjects of individual and family names. The one or the other may be the principal theme, but one cannot pass either entirely by. The most superficial glance will at once show how closely they are interwoven with each other, being, indeed, convertible, the individual names of one generation becoming the family names of another. William is said to form the basis of no less than twenty-nine surnames in England.*

In the early history of the world one name was sufficient to distinguish individuals, but, as these multiplied, it was not only becoming but necessary for family names to be added. By these second names were distinguished the various branches of the one original stock, while individuals were still marked out by distinctive and significative personal appellations.

It is singular to remark how at different times

---

* Lower on Surnames.

and under different circumstances honour and dishonour are attached to the same particular.

In the history of Rome we find her great men priding themselves on two, three, four, and sometimes six names, while slaves were forbidden to use more than one. In our own history we read that in the twelfth century a wealthy heiress objected to marry Robert, natural son of Henry I., on the plea that

> It were to me a great shame
> To have a lord withouten his *twa* name.

Yet two centuries before, in Domesday Book, that ancient register of the landed proprietors in England, we find that the comites or counts, the men of highest rank, were simply distinguished as Comes Hugo, Count Hugh—Comes Rogerus, Count Roger—thereby assimilating themselves to royalty: in all lands the special distinction being conceded to sovereigns and their immediate families of using their individual names only, from their exalted rank no surname being required to distinguish them.

Christians in the house of God are carried back as it were to the infant days of history. Surnames are not acknowledged there. When, as individuals, we stand before the Lord and Maker of all, the conventionalities of the world are lost sight of, and we are known only by our individual names.

Tokens of our worldly position must surround us perforce, but unheard are the names of power by which we claim precedence amongst our fellow-men. By the cambric robe or the cotton frock the rich man's or the pauper's babe may be told, even as the dress of costly lace or cheap print betokens the respective stations of the brides; but only as individuals known by individual names, the children of one Father, the servants of one Master, take their place at the font and the altar. Alike in this—only by their baptismal names— our sweet Princess Alice Maude Mary pledged her faith to Prince Frederic William Louis of Hesse, and poor Mary Ann, the lodging-house girl, promised to be true to her John.

Family names are said to have originated with the Etruscans;* adopted by the Sabines, through them they passed to the Romans on the occasion of their treaty of alliance. To cement this union more closely, it was required that every Roman should add to his own name the name of a Sabine, while in like manner each Sabine should take a Roman name.

Instinctively thus regarding the person in the name, the red Indian of the far West also exchanges names with the white man whom he adopts as a brother.

To our word surname two distinct derivations have been assigned:—Sire-name, the father's

* Salverte.

name, and Surnom (French), Sopra nome (Italian), from the original custom of placing the second or family name *above*, not, as now, *after*, the baptismal name.

The early history of the Greeks affords occasional examples of individuals bearing two names. In some instances this second name was a patronymic (derived from the father), and occasionally it superseded the personal name. This was still more frequently the case when the added name was commemorative either of some victory gained, or of some peculiar grace of body or mind.

Tyrtamus, the favourite disciple of Aristotle, was by him first named Euphrastes, signifying *one who speaks well*; but it is only by the still more flattering name which his admiring master subsequently bestowed—Theophrastes, signifying *he who speaks as one inspired*, or the *god-like speaker*—that Tyrtamus is commonly known.

Plato was originally named after his grandfather Aristocles, signifying the *better glory*, or the *glory of that which is good*; but the name by which he is known in all lands—Plato, signifying *large*—was given to him on account of the breadth of his chest and forehead; and also, it is supposed by some, as significative of the largeness and fullness of his eloquence.

But sometimes those additional names were the reverse of complimentary. Amongst the witty Greeks nicknames were common. Doson, which expressed the *future* of the verb *to give*, was a name bestowed on a king of Macedonia who was liberal in promises, but sparing in actual gifts.

Amongst the Arabs we also find some of these names which were bestowed in ridicule. Abu-Horeirah, '*Father of the Cat*,' was so named by Mohammed in consequence of his excessive fondness for a cat, and in the nickname so universally adopted the man's real name has been wholly lost. And at this day, in the streets of Oriental towns, the 'gamins' of the East use this prefix in the composition of names of ridicule. Dr. Thomson, an American missionary, tells us, in 'The Land and the Book,' that the Syrian boys called after him 'Abu-Tangera'—*father of a saucepan*—because they fancied his hat resembled one in shape. Abu 'sh Shámát—*father of moles*—is given by Lane as an actual Arabian name, and as moles are considered lucky it would be a name of good omen. The south-west wind is called the *father of rain*.

The prefix refers to the universal custom so long prevailing amongst the Arabs, and also to be found amongst the Hebrews, of reversing the European practice of sons deriving their names from their fathers, as illustrated in our English, Scotch, and Irish names, Fitz-William, Mac-Donald, O'Connor. A father in the East relinquishes his own name and adopts that of his child, with the prefix Abu, *father*. We read that in

Syria this custom is so universal that men without children, and even children themselves, are called by courtesy Abu ——, after an imaginary son. Abu-Bekr, a well-known name in the history of Mohammedanism, was the father of Ayesha, the prophet's favourite wife: in honour of her the name was assumed, which signifies *father of the girl*.

Women, in like manner, assume the name of their first-born, with the prefix Em. Sometimes it is a daughter's name that is taken, and as these are generally highly poetical, even amongst the lower classes, one's washerwoman may answer to some such resplendent name as Em el Bedr el Kebeer, *mother of the great full moon*.

The compliment is extended to Europeans. The wife of the English Consul at Jerusalem is always addressed by the natives as Om (or Em) Iskender, her eldest boy's name being Alexander, the child himself being spoken of as Abou Jacobi.* James being the father's name, it follows in the East that his son's son should be called after him. An unbroken chain of loving remembrance is thus kept up from father to son.

The addition of one or more syllables was frequently used in both Hebrew and Greek names, as an indication of increased greatness in the individual. For the most part, short names were

* Beaufort's Syrian Shrines.

in Greece confined to slaves, while men of rank rejoiced in the rolling melody of four and five syllables.

In Greece and Rome certain names were set apart, and could only be given according as they were assigned respectively to citizens or slaves. It was, however, permitted to freedmen to add to their own names the 'nomen' or 'prænomen' (that is to say, the family or personal names) of their master. In Rome, therefore, as amongst the Highland clans, a preponderance of certain names betokened the larger following of those houses. The Cornelia gens was one of the most distinguished in Rome: from it sprang more illustrious men than from any other Roman house. All its great families were of the patrician order, but it also included many that were plebeian. The Dictator Sulla bestowed the Roman franchise on 10,000 slaves, calling them Cornelii, after his own name, so that he might always reckon on supporters amongst the people.

The four names usually borne by men of rank in Rome were—

1. The *Nomen*, the family name, or race-name as it may be called, answering to the Greek patronymic. This preceded, not followed as with us, the personal name. For a considerable period but eighteen of such names were in much repute, so that it sufficed to use their initial letters only.

2. The *Prænomen*, or personal name, was

used to distinguish the various individuals of a family.

3. The *Cognomen*, or surname, which distinguished the several branches or families descended from the same stock.

4. The *Agnomen*, which somewhat resembled the cognomen; but in that it was frequently a title of honour, it partook more of personal character.

All these names were significative. The two first were for the most part simply descriptive of personal characteristics, such as Flavus and its derivative Flavius, signifying *yellow-haired*. The two last were usually honourable distinctions.

We may find an example of these four names in Publius Cornelius Scipio Africanus, one of the most illustrious of the sons of Rome, were it not for the shadow cast upon his fame by the tragic story of the Carthaginian Princess Sophonisba.

In this instance the prænomen preceded the nomen.

Publius was a name of good augury, signifying one *honoured by the people*.

Cornelius, the name of this distinguished race, was also a name of good augury. It might be said to have a threefold significance. If derived from the Latin cornu, a *horn*, it suggested cornucopia, signifying a *horn* of *plenty*, abundance; or as a *cornet*, a trumpet, it might have seemed prophetic of the far sounding of the name. If derived from the Greek (korone), it signifies a *rook*, a bird of good omen.

Scipio signifies a *staff*. This was a name of honour won by a Cornelius, founder of the family of the Scipios, who had been as a *staff* daily to support and guide a blind father.

Africanus was a title of honour conferred by acclamation when the conquerors of the Carthaginians returned in triumph to Rome. In connection with the subject of names a noble answer of this hero is recorded in history.

The talent for remembering names has been called a 'royal gift,' but in republican Rome it was so necessary for the candidates for public favour to remember the names of their fellow-citizens that certain slaves called nomenclators were in constant attendance on the great men of the city. It was their duty to make themselves acquainted with the names of the citizens, and in a low voice repeat to their masters that of each individual as he drew near. Some men prided themselves on not requiring the services of a nomenclator. On Appius Claudius vaunting himself on this accomplishment, Scipio Africanus replied that 'his greater care had been to make his own name known to his countrymen, than to become acquainted with all theirs.'

Wonderful tales are told of the gift of remembering names. Cyrus and Mithridates are said to have known by name each soldier in their armies. Cynias, ambassador from Pyrrhus, saluted each member of the Roman senate by name. The Emperor Hadrian used to correct the mistakes of his nomenclator.

CHAPTER V.

Change of name—Various scenes and stories connected with such change—Abraham—The four Hebrew captives—The North American Indian brave—Caribs—Dacians—Greek emperors and their brides—Princesses marrying into foreign lands—Queen Dagmar of Denmark—Signification of Alexandra—Old Danish ballad—Brunechilde of France—Eleanor of Austria—Popes—Literary men: their assumption of Greek and Latin names—Enforced changes of name—Ireland—Spain—Scotland.

THE subject of Change of Name claims a chapter to itself. It might fill a volume. I may only give it here a few pages.

It has been said, ' Notre nom propre c'est nous-mêmes.'* It would seem to have been instinctively so felt, if we compare the capricious fancies which have occasionally led to a change of surname† with the grave and earnest occasions on which alone, even before the days of Christianity, new personal names have been adopted.

The assumption of a new individual name has always supposed the assuming a new manner of life, or at least the entering into some new and important phase of life.

---

* Salverte.

† The ridiculous fancy lately sprung up in England of changing ugly surnames for those of prettier sound, without right or title to them, will surely soon die out again.

But the Church of England has always considered Christian names inalienable; and in England, even before the Reformation, we read of severe penance being inflicted on a woman who had changed her son's baptismal name of Edward for that of Henry. We change our surnames or family names, but our individual, or ' font-names,' as they were once called, are ours unchangeably—ours by the grace of God. Let us seek to have them written by the finger of God—where none can blot them out—in the Book of Life.

Innumerable pictures rise before us as our minds rest on those words, *Change of Name*. We may but glance at a few of them.

We see the princely patriarch of old—who was called forth from his birth-place Ur (of the Chaldees), signifying *Light*—so that the light of his faith should penetrate the darkness of heathenism, and that from his chosen seed should arise a Light ' to lighten the whole world,' even the glorious ' Sun of Righteousness.' We see this chief of a great following—men servants and maid servants, with many herds, and with much silver and gold—bowed with his face upon the ground, for ' God talked with him.' From the High and Holy One Himself, the Father of the Faithful received the charge ' to walk before Him, and be perfect;' and in making His solemn covenant with him God changed his name from Ab-ram, the *lofty father*, to Ab-raham, the *father of multitudes*.

The name which Persian tradition affirms was the patriarch's original name, Zerwan, the *wealthy*, was it not significant also? Was he not made rich indeed to whom was given the title of 'the Friend of God:' the modern town of Hebron, we are told, being now called in memory of its illustrious first occupant, El Khalil, the *friend* ?*

Our next picture of far-away times is a very different one. It is in sorrow, not in joy, that this change of name takes place. The new name is not as a pledge of favour from a gracious God, but it is as a heavy chain pressing about a prisoner's neck—it is as an act of sacrilege abhorrent to a heart that is devout. By their new names the four Hebrew youths, captive to the King of Babylon, were dedicated to their conqueror's false gods. Daniel, signifying *God is my judge*, was exchanged for Belteshazzar, *Bel has formed a prophet* or *wise man*; Hananiah, signifying *the gracious gift of Jehovah* (a synonyme with John), was exchanged for Shadrach, signifying *royal, king's own*, or *belonging to the king*; Mishael or Michael, *the strength of God*, for Meshach, *belonging to Sheschach*, an Assyrian goddess; and Azariah, *the help of Jehovah*, for Abed Nego, *servant* of Nego or Nebo, the god or planet Mercury.

We behold monarchs of all the various empires

* Stanley's Jewish Church.

of the East, on ascending the steps of a throne, crowning themselves, as it were, with new names significative of empire. And lo! beside them there are conquerors, of haughty mien and strong-handed, writing their new names in fire and blood on scathed and devastated lands.

And see, in other lands, hands that were up-raised in enmity are now clasped in brotherhood, and new names are given and received. The form and the feeling are alike, though the great ocean and the sea of time rolls between the Sabine and Roman of other days, and the red Indian and his white brother of to-day.

Look again to the Western world, with its sea-like lakes and primæval forests, where year by year on the unkindly bosom of the North the lodges of her red children grow fewer and farther apart, and their graves draw closer and increase in number. It is on the shores of the Mississippi, a village of the tall Osages, the young braves are returning from a fierce encounter with their deadly enemies the Pawnees. There is joy amongst those who go to meet them. The old chiefs and the women rejoice, for the scalp-locks of the war party are many; but the ghastly face of one lad reflects not the general joy, for the shadow of death is there. He has only strength to stagger to the door of his father's lodge. He will never rise up again, for the gaping wound in his breast is beyond the most skilful medicine-man's power to heal. But, hark! his companions hasten to recount on all sides his gallant deeds, and the great chief draws near to Shinga-wossa, signifying *the handsome bird*. He takes from his own head his crest of deer's hair and eagle-quills, and lays it upon the dying boy's head as he gives him the new name of Mun-ne-pus-kee, signifying *he who is not afraid*. A flash of joy lightens o'er his face: it tells better than words how precious to that brave lad is his new name of honour, that he once hears—once only—now for the first and for the last time.

In the islands of the West let us look on a scene which involves a change of name. It is amongst the almost extinct race of the Caribs—those courteous savages who welcomed the discoverer of the New World with offerings of palm branches. It is a bridal day, and the lovers with skins of bronze, but with hearts as loving as those of white men and women, exchange names as a pledge of perfect union.

In those 'rude huts on the Danube,' where of old the Dacian wives and mothers wept while afar off in triumphant Rome the death-struggles of their loved ones made sport for their barbarous conquerors—it was there also the custom for men and women on their marriage-day to receive from each other new names.

We have seen an Indian brave purchasing with his heart's blood a new name; and so, too, did many of the early converts from paganism to Christianity, but their new names opened to them the gates of everlasting life. Amongst such changes of name there is one example in two names which have in their keeping a story more impressive than many homilies.

A captain of the guards to the Emperor Trajan—young and noble and rich, in the enjoyment of all this world could give of happiness, blessed with a loving wife and two beautiful boys—answered to the name of Placidus, the *calm*, the *easy-tempered*. But he was meant for higher things than this world's peace alone. Converted to Christianity, the brave soldier made choice of the noble name of *Eustace*. Trials, he knew, must be his: he was willing to meet them *steadfast* in the faith. Despoiled for a time of wife, children, and wealth, they were suddenly and strangely restored to him, but only for a time. Resolutely refusing to comply with the Emperor Hadrian's command that he should burn incense before the false gods of Rome, Eustace, his wife, and children, were shut up together in a brazen bull, and a fire was kindled beneath — a death of torment followed by an eternity of bliss.

From the seventh to the end of the eleventh century bishops frequently changed their names on ordination;* and from the eleventh century it became an established custom for Popes to

* In the East the practice is continued. The Syrian patriarch Mar Gregorius, now dwelling at Jerusalem, originally bore a name of Moslem invention, Nour-ed-Deen, signifying *the Light of Religion*.

take new names on assuming the tiara. John XII., formerly Octavian, was the first, it is said, to set the example, A.D. 955. Various reasons have been assigned* for this practice, the most probable being a desire to imitate the examples of St. Peter and St. Paul. Once only has this custom been infringed, in spite of universal prognostications of evil—Cardinal Marcellus Cervin insisted on retaining the name of Marcellus, and died on the twentieth day of his pontificate.†

It is permitted to Roman Catholics to change their names on confirmation, and monks and nuns almost invariably assume new names on entering the cloister.

We find one touching exception to this rule in the instance of the unhappy Louise de la Vallière, mistress to Louis XIV. Unlike the bold bad women of her day, who gloried in their shame, soon after her fall she fled to the cloister, there by a life of penance to seek reconciliation with her God, and to weep over, though she could never recall, the irrevocable past. She willingly abandoned the pleasures of the world and all the attractions of power and wealth. She had really

---

* Noël's Dictionnaire Historique.

† Once more the writer would beg of her readers not to imagine that she shares in the superstitious fancies which she relates. History tells of these incidents, and history records the effect which they produced. Let us, who live in these enlightened days, rejoice to feel assured that joy and sorrow, life and death, depend on the ordering of a gracious Providence, and not upon the observance of any superstitious practice whatsoever.

loved her betrayer; but she closed between him and herself the iron grating of a convent. One only thing she took with her into that living tomb—her Christian name she could not part with, for was it not also *his* name whom she had loved? 'Louise de la Miséricorde' was the convent name of La Duchesse de la Vallière.

The women of ancient Greece frequently changed their personal name on their marriage. In later days Greek emperors often took to themselves new names on their coronations, and they always required of their brides to be baptised and with new names.

Pyrisca, daughter of Ladislas, king of Hungary, became the Empress Irene on her marriage with John Comnena; and Agnes, daughter of Louis VII. of France, as the wife of Alexis Comnena, was known as the Empress Anne.

Emperors of Russia, as belonging to the Greek Church, still claim this compliance from their brides.

In their turn Greek princesses sometimes surrendered their baptismal names on their marriage with foreign princes. In the sixth century the beautiful daughter of the Greek emperor Maurice married Khosru Purviz, son of Hormuz, king of Persia, who, fleeing from an usurper, had taken refuge in the court of Constantinople, and had there become a convert to Christianity. His bride's name Irene, signifying *Peace*, was prophetic, for he was soon after restored to the throne of his ancestors—a throne of such magnificence that it was supported on 40,000 columns of silver.

The exquisite beauty and graces of Khosru's Grecian queen, still celebrated in Eastern song, won for her in her adopted land the Persian name of Shereen, signifying *Sweet*—in sound and signification somewhat resembling her own; and in Persia to this day the 'Loves of Khosru and Shireen' are sung.

The story of an ancestress of our fair Princess of Wales illustrates the practice in a Northern land. Margrethe (Margaret), the *pearl* of Bohemia, who was born about the year 1186, was wooed and won by Waldemar the Victorious, of Denmark. She, too, gained all hearts in her adopted land, and the beautiful and significant name bestowed on her by the Danes has come down to us, not only in the history of the country, but also in its old ballads (in German Volkslied), which are as the cradle songs of nations, and have ever therefore a peculiar sweetness of their own.

In one of these we are told that the sweet lady, whose memory is cherished as that of a saint, held the good of her people so near to her heart that on the day succeeding her marriage,

> Early in the morning,
> Before the risen sun,*

---

* 'Wooing and Wedding of Queen Dagmar,' translated by Mary Howitt, in *Good Words* for May 1863.

she besought from her lord, as a boon to herself, that the peasantry should be relieved from the plough tax, and that all prison doors should be opened; and upon her dying bed, she again renewed her kindly petitions.

The name given by the loving Danes to Margrethe of Bohemia was Dagmar, signifying *Mother of day*, expressive of the beauty and brightness of early morn. It was figurative of her fresh young beauty, and also of the gladness which, from her gracious nature, ever radiated from her presence.

A bright picture to be followed by one as dark!

Bruna, daughter of Atanagilda, king of the Visigoths, A. D. 562, on her marriage with Sigebert, king of Austrasia, was honoured, not by a new name, but by the addition of some syllables to her old name. In these syllables there was much meaning. In one letter, which was a contraction, there was the most meaning of all. Bruna, or Brenna, signifying *Brown*, dark, dark-haired, dark-eyed, dark-complexioned, or a combination of all three—a peasant girl might have borne the name, but no maiden of low birth would have dared to call herself by the name which was given to the Queen, Brunechilda; Hilda, derived from the war-goddess of the Teutons, signifying both a *lady of rank* and simply a *maiden*; but the *c* that preceded it was a sign of royalty, being a contraction of the

Teutonic cuning or cyning, German könig, a *king*. The Celts or Gaels had a somewhat similar word expressive of royalty—Conan, a *prince*.

Darkness and light expressed by their respective names do not afford a stronger contrast than do the stories of the Queens Dagmar and Brunechilda. The history of the dark beauty, from her royal cradle in the sunny south amidst the olive branches of Spain, to her death of shame and agony in a Burgundian camp, reads like a romance in the early pages of the history of France.

Her many crimes were odious, but how terrible was her expiation of these! The daughter, wife, and mother of kings, at seventy years of age—at the command of a nephew, blood-guilty as herself—exposed to the scoffs of a rude soldiery, as for three days she was paraded through the camp, covered with filthy rags, and bound on the back of an old camel. Even her frightful death was a relief—tied to the tail of a wild horse, her skull was fractured, and her body torn limb from limb.

Strange contrast to the peaceful (?) death-bed of her rival, the far more infamous Fredegonde!

The terrible hatred which existed between Brunechilda (or Brunehaut, the French form of her name) and her sister-in-law, and subsequently step-mother-in-law, Fredegonde, has passed into a proverb amongst the French. But it should not be forgotten that Brunechilda saw in Fredegonde the murderer of her sister, the Princess Galsuinda, and of her husband, Sigebert. The latter days of the Spanish Princess were indeed stained with crime; but in her earlier days her name had been associated with many excellent works. The high roads she gave to France are still called 'Chaussées de Brunehaut.'* But Fredegonde was a monster from her youth. As waiting-maid to Andovere, first wife of Chilperic, she displaced her mistress in her husband's affections, becoming first his mistress and afterwards his wife; and then with cowardly cruelty, when eighteen years had gone by, she sought out her unhappy victim in the quiet asylum of a convent: the unoffending Andovere was strangled by her orders, and her young daughter, Basim, subjected to horrible treatment. But the pages of Fredegonde's life are too black for any eye to desire to look upon them.

Our English history affords an example of a foreign princess taking as a bride a new Christian name from her new home. The Norman Princess Emma, on coming to England as the wife of Ethelred (A. D. 1001), took the Saxon name of Elgiva, the *noble help-giver*—a name of exquisite significance both as a wife and a queen.

We may hail as of good augury the Christian name of the 'Rose of Denmark,' now joyously

---

* Anquetil's Histoire de France.

grafted on the stem of England's royal rose. Almost a synonyme with Saxon (or Teutonic) Elgiva is the Greek Alexandra—the feminine form of Alexander—signifying a *brave helper*— Alexis signifying help, or *defence,* and Andreios *courageous.* Our own beloved Queen Victoria has, as a second name, its diminutive Alexandrina.

As a bridal gift from the King of Denmark, the Princess of Wales possesses a facsimile of the now well-known Dagmar cross. Would that it could whisper her, in an English voice, two verses from the old ballad already quoted!—

>   Now listen, my handsome lady!
>   Rejoice, and give God the praise,
>   You will never repent {'this'/your} voyage
>   To the latest of your days.
>   And as long as my life endureth
>   I will be your servant true,
>   And all the {'nobles of Denmark'/people of England}
>   Will love and honour you too.

At one time empresses of Austria changed their names on their marriage and coronation.* In the fifteenth century Eleanor of Portugal, married to Frederic III. of Austria, took the name of Helena. In the seventeenth century the saintly daughter of Philip-William, first Elector Palatine of the branch of Newburgh,

---

* Coxe's House of Austria.

married to Leopold I., changed her name of Magdalen Theresa to that of Eleonore.

The simple inscription which she chose for her coffin—

Eléonore,
Pauvre Pécheresse.
Morte le 19 janvier
1720—

was in perfect keeping with her holy life. One cannot but regret those mistaken ideas of a God whose name is Love which made the life of the royal Eleonore a painful succession of acts of mortification, pilgrimages with bare and bleeding feet, frugal fare, and adornments not of gold and precious stones, but bracelets with sharp iron spikes lacerating her tender arms; but, at the same time, who would not hold in high honour one who in all sincerity thus sought to obtain subjugation of self?

Her ardent desire was in all things to fulfil the Divine command, 'Be ye perfect.' As the member of a church which esteemed such acts of penance, she was unwearied in performing them; as an empress and a wife, she was equally in earnest to do that which was right. Her public duties were never neglected for the sake of her private wishes. For a time the reins of government were in her hands: they were held with admirable discretion and wisdom. To please her husband she alike attended public entertainments and prepared with her own hands delicacies for his table at home. An exquisite musician and perfect linguist, she cultivated her talents for the enjoyment of others. During the last illness of her husband she was a tender and devoted nurse, taking no rest by night or day.

Amongst holy women whose lives may be as lessons for us, let us not forget Eleonore or Magdalen Theresa of Austria.

We have already seen how in Japan and China men take new names at different periods of their lives, and how Arab fathers and mothers both delight to lose as it were their own identity in that of their first-born—giving up their own names to share the one which they have bestowed on their child.

A fancy once existed amongst literary men of assuming classical names. This was especially the case in Italy and during the fifteenth century. They claimed as their precedent an academy founded by Charlemagne, where all the members, including the emperor, were designated by ancient Greek and Roman names.

Pope Paul II., suspicious and cruel, sought by imprisonment and torture to drag from some of these unhappy men avowals of heretical motives for such changes of names. Unadvisable as the practice was, it had, however, simply arisen from an overstrained admiration of classical authors. Platina, the historian of the Popes, whose real name was Sacci, suffered a year's imprisonment.

Sometimes these enthusiastic admirers of

ASSUMPTION OF GREEK AND LATIN NAMES. 105

Greece and Rome contented themselves with translating their own names into Latin and Greek. By this means also traces of the native country and the parentage of many writers are lost to the general reader; and in some cases they have been almost, if not altogether, swept away even from the student.

But some men are from their greatness recognised by all through any disguises. Of Syrian extraction and of Greek birth and education was the Latin-named Longinus—the philosopher, chief counsellor, and friend of Zenobia, queen of Palmyra. On the taking of the city the Emperor Aurelian covered himself with disgrace by ungenerously putting to death this faithful servant to the conquered queen.

The Greek name of Longinus's disciple, Porphyry, had a double significance. Porphura, *purple*, in that it was the 'Tyrian dye,' recalled his native town Tyre; and in that it was the royal colour, it was a figurative rendering of his original Arabic name Malek, signifying a *king*.

Said Ibn Batric, a celebrated historian and physician of the ninth century, born in Egypt, translated his Arabic name Said, signifying *happy*, into its Greek synonyme Eutychius.

The still more celebrated Arabian physician of the following century, Avicenna, called by Hebrew writers Abou Sina, might well be spoken of by a shorter name than that which properly belongs to him:—

Al-Sheikh Al-Rayis Abu-Ali Al-Hossein Ben Abd-Allah Ben Sina. Al-Sheikh signifying a title of respect especially belonging to saintly or learned men, and Al Rayis signifying the *chief*.*

It could not be said of this learned Arabian as it was of some Frenchman in later days—that, possessor of many names while alive, dying he left no name behind.

Before Avicenna had attained his twenty-first year he had written a cyclopædia, the Arabic title of which, Kilât el Mainu, literally means ' the *book* of the *sum total.*' In his work is to be found the earliest mention of oranges, which our crusading forefathers, on first beholding them in Palestine, believed to be the golden apples of the Hesperides.

The Swiss reformer, Philip Schwartserdt, *black earth*, is scarcely known to us except by the Greek version of his name, Melancthon. Unrecognised as his by the Pope, some of his writings appeared under the name of Ippofilo (Philip reversed) da Terra.

The Dutchman, Van der Beken, signifying *streams*, called himself by a Latin name Torrentius, signifying *torrents.* We have preserved the word *beck* from our Saxon forefathers. Westmoreland and Cumberland each have a river Troutbeck, or trout *stream*, the word itself being

* We read in all Eastern travels of the *Reis* as the chief or head man, the captain of the ship or boat, &c.

commonly used in the north of England for small streams.

An enforced change of name has been amongst the engines of cruelty employed by tyrants to make their subjects miserable. In 1465 Edward IV. of England commanded his Irish subjects to take for themselves and their children English surnames, on pain of annual forfeiture of their goods until the law was obeyed.

In 1568, the bigot Philip II. of Spain, hoping to denationalise the remnant of the Moors still lingering in the land they had so enriched and beautified, ordered them to abandon both their individual and family names, compelled them to be baptised, and to adopt Spanish designations.* His law was perforce obeyed, but all the more closely would an outraged people cling in secret to their ancient faith. Amongst Mohammedan Moors now dwelling in Africa are therefore to be found such names as Perez, from Peter, and Santiago, or St. James! †

An Act of 1603 forbade on pain of death the Highland clan of MacGregor to call themselves by their name. To this terrible decree a thrilling ballad of Sir Walter Scott alludes, ' The MacGregors' Gathering:'—

> The moon's on the lake, and the mist's on the brae,
> And the clan has a name which is nameless by day,
> Then gather, gather, gather, Grigalach!

---

* Watson's History of Philip II.
† Salverte.

The hatred and terror which were at that time inspired by the outlawed clan are said to have originated in the ferocity displayed by Ciar Mohr, the *great mouse-coloured* man (an ancestor of Rob Roy's), during a contest with the Colquhouns, in Glen Fruin, the *vale of sorrow*.

But by their loyalty the MacGregors nobly regained their name. Enrolled as Murrays and Buchanans under the banners of the Earl of Athole and the Laird of Buchanan, they gallantly fought for Charles even while his edict against them was in force. Their name was proscribed, but their armorial bearings remained, and to them these brave men responded.

The MacGregors bear a pine-tree crossed saltier-wise with a naked sword, the point of which supports a royal crown. The sword of the MacGregors has been tried in a fire from the heat of which none but a well-tempered blade could have come forth unscathed. It was a cruel edict, confounding the innocent with the guilty.

At the Restoration Charles II. annulled the various edicts against them, and restored to them their name, in gratitude for the loyalty they had shown.

The deprivation of name is a punishment fitted only for the prison and the hulks. In those gloomy precincts to which their crimes have conducted them, it is a felon's well-merited disgrace to have his name taken from him. So long as he is undergoing his sentence it is well for him to feel, as he answers to his *number* only, that he has for a time lost all right to honour and respect from his fellow-men. But to take altogether away from man or woman their proper names is to take from them, so long as one sparkle of right feeling remains, one of the strongest incentives to well-doing.

CHAPTER VI.

For one's name's sake — Heroes, inventors, discoverers honoured through their names—Sovereigns' names stamped upon coins — Names clinging to mossy wells and beetling cliffs — Stories of lives in the names of individuals — Christopher Columbus — Pollio Vedius — Contrasts between names and lives, and misnomers — St. Felicitas and Julius Cæsar — Legends derived from significations of names — Semiramis — Monkish legends growing out of old pictures — Pictures suggested by significant names — St. Lucia — St. Sophia — St. Katharine: her legend and meaning of her name — St. Margaret — Mary Magdalene — Mary and Miriam.

'FOR Thy *Name's* sake' is a solemn adjuration which we find in the Holy Scriptures addressed to the Most High God as one of the most urgent and powerful of appeals.

How many a path of glory has been trod by human beings with these trumpet-like words going before—for their *names'* sake!—for their *forefathers' names'* sake!

'A peerage or Westminster Abbey!' is one of the many well-remembered sayings of the greatest of England's naval heroes: either way it was his yearning desire to do honour to his name. *Nelson* should take its place in England's roll of peerless peers, or *Nelson* should be engraven on an honoured tomb! Some conquerors have taken names from their conquests; but Nelson, with a truer pride, placed a coronet on his own.

It is almost instinctively felt that the highest homage inventors and discoverers can receive is that the precious things bestowed by them on their fellow-men should be known by their names.

Inspired by this hope, the chemist, with calm courage, silent and alone in his laboratory, surrounds himself with an atmosphere of death—his life too often the forfeit of his daring experiments.

So, too, the adventurous sailor! He fearlessly thrusts his ship's prow through heaped-up barriers of ice: his grave may be yawning beyond—but what matter? He deems himself overpaid for hourly hand-to-hand struggles with death if but some day his name be suffered to rest upon one icy peak, one barren rock, in those far-off untrodden desolate realms.

So, too, in the region of art. We read of two wealthy men, accomplished sculptors and architects, who, caring nought for money in comparison with fame, erected at their own cost a magnificent temple at Rome, hoping that the law which there forbade men to inscribe their names on their works might be relaxed in their favour. But it was not so; and, as their only resource, Batrachus and Saurus carved on the fluting of the column of their temple *frogs* and *lizards*, such being the signification of their Greek names.

In some of our English cathedrals we see such compliments paid to bishops and benefactors. In Winchester Cathedral, on the exquisite pulpit of carved oak black as ebony, a skein of silk is represented in the carving, as an allusion to Bishop Silkstede.

Knights of old often carried their names before them on their shields, like the soldiers of Rome, but in pictured form. The heraldic bearing of the Dundases, a family as ancient as the period when Gaelic was spoken in Mid-Lothian, is the English translation of their name, a 'hill with a tuft of wood.' * A lion is attempting to push through; the motto is a challenge, 'Essayez' (Try). A Swedish family, Guyllenstern, bear the beautiful device of a golden star of seven rays, displayed on a field azure. Amongst the heraldic bearings of old families in England and on the Continent many such illustrations may be found.

One of the most ancient and most jealously guarded prerogatives of rulership, whether residing in sovereigns or senates, has ever been the power of impressing a name on the coins of a country.

On the money of Rome Julius Cæsar dared only to stamp a figurative allusion to his name,

* Stewart's Sketches of Highland Clans.

an *elephant*, which in the Punic language was the signification of Cæsar. Coins have sometimes become so identified with the sovereign's name which they bore as to be known only by that name—the Darics (from Darius) of Persia, the English Jacobus, and French Louis d'or and Napoleons, are examples.

Coins would seem in their turn to have suggested human names. From Stater, a Persian gold coin of great antiquity, is it not probable that Statira (the Greek form of), a common name amongst Persian queens and princesses, was derived? It would be significant of preciousness, as in the Arabic a woman's name, Denaneer, which signifies *pieces of gold*.

But not only have distinguished men inscribed their names on banners of fame and weapons of war, and on great works of art and science, but kindly acts of women have given to their names also a long and strangely enduring power.

The trickling waters of mossy wells throughout the land repeat in silvery tones the names of saintly maids, whose uneventful but holy lives are best cherished by those pure springs—a cup of cold water given in the name of their Lord. But hark! on rock-bound coasts, in the midst of the storm, wild winds and waters mutter wrathfully woman's soft names; for lo! the beacon-light, or the landmark, or church-tower, called after them, has saved the ship, and their prey is snatched from them.

To the north of Bude, near the magnificent headland of Hennacliff, or the Raven's Craig, there are beautiful cliffs known by the name of Morwen Stowe. In a poor village hard by, in strange contrast to its poverty, is a splendid old church. Cliffs, and village, and church, are all known by the same name, Morwen Stowe, or the station of Mor-well. Leland tells how in the ninth century the fair and virtuous and wise daughter of Breachen, a Celtic king, and Gladys, his wife, gained from the Saxon king Ethelwulph a piece of ground on that bold headland. There Morwen (signifying *lady of the sea*) built a house of God, that mariners outward-bound or home-returning, may kneel to Him who 'holds the waters in the hollow of His hand,' asking for His safe guidance, or returning Him thanks for the same.

Christian names, and even their affectionate diminutives, have been given in honour of men to inanimate things. Killingworth colliers, rough 'sons of night' as they are, call the safety lamp invented for them by the great and good Stephenson, the '*Geordie Lamp.*'

A glorious incentive to noble lives to feel that when our mortal bodies have crumbled into dust our NAMES will yet live in the loving recollection of successive generations—the very sound of them be as an inspiration—as a trumpet-call going before to victory—as the lark's song high in the air, lifting men's thoughts heavenwards!

SEBASTIAN CABOT.

But ah! these very types are themselves of earth: they, too, must have an end. The trumpet-note is the breath of man, and so it must die away. The lark, 'singing at heaven's gate,' builds her nest low on the ground, Time's cruel plough-share must pass over it.

> He builds too low who builds beneath the skies.

The fair superstructure of good deeds must have a surer foundation than the longed-for gratitude of our fellow-men. All know that the devil is a bad paymaster; but the world, is it not dishonest too?

In the history of names we catch delightedly here and there some that have been greatly honoured, shining like stars gloriously from out the grey mist of past times; but too many there are that we sorrowfully search for in vain. How many benefactors to their race have gone down in sadness and disappointment to their nameless graves—still century after century going by, and yet the injustice done to them is not rolled away!

The whole life of Sebastian* Cabot, the daring mariner who first saw North America, was, till some thirty years ago, lost in obscurity; and even now the place of his death and his grave is unknown. Even at the very moment of his discovery his name was overlooked. Let us read

---

* A sad misnomer: Sebastian sig. to be *reverenced*. Where is the *reverence* and honour that was his due?

an entry in Henry VII.'s privy-purse expenses: '10th August, 1497 : to *hym* that found the New Isle, 10*l*. !'

Romulus lives in the name of Rome, and in the city of the Cæsars the good and evil fame of her emperors is preserved. But he whose matchless enterprise gave to his fellow-men a New World, how has his name been honoured? A province here, a district there, a town elsewhere, at far-off intervals, faintly repeat the name which should have rested on the whole vast continent.

Christopher Columbus left the recording of his name to others, and how has the charge been fulfilled? The only spot, a tiny island in the Caribbees, to which the discoverer did give his own name, his Christian name, is, curiously enough, called only by its abbreviation, St. Kitt's.

But this name, so strangely overlooked, is in itself a marvel.

Reader, look with me now on a West Indian conch-shell, with its rough-looking outside and polished lining on the inside. Some of it is like a door-panel of tortoiseshell. As it lies before us there, it is as the door of an empty house, for not a sound is heard from within. But take it up, put it close to your ear, and listen! The shell has a voice—has it not told you its story? The cradle song that the great waves of ocean sang to it when it was a baby shell has never been forgotten, and the booming voice of its native sea is for ever sounding in the deep heart of the wanderer; and those who listen to the shell will hear it also.

Will you think me over-fanciful if I say that to me many names are even as the conch-shell? Voiceless they may seem to many, but if you will listen to them they will tell you the story of many a life.

The names of the great discoverer are especially remarkable. What do they signify, those names, Christopher Columbus? *The Christ-bearing Dove.* Ah! now you see what I mean!

Darkly and gloomily heaved the great sea of wrath over the drowned world, but over its angry face a sweet bird flew fearlessly, for afar off she espied a speck of land—the cleansed world was again looking forth from the waters of its baptism. It was a dove that first saw the old world renewed, for she it was who brought back the first green leaf.

Far off, and unknown to the dominant race, lay a large portion of man's inheritance, for stormy and trackless waters lay between it and them. A brave adventurer stood on the brink of that measureless sea, while, on the very beach where he stood, chill land-streams of indifference, black pools of envy and mistrust, surged up about his feet. But the wings of faith were given to him, and the bright clear eyes of hope; and Columbus, *the dove*, over-passed the great sea, and brought back green leaves—the first palms from the West. Palm-branches are alike for a conqueror's and for a martyr's grave.

And his other name, Christopher?

Was the Church's old legend of the Canaanitish giant, St. Christopher of the fourth century, prophetic of the Christopher Columbus of the fifteenth century?—the strong man battling with the troubled stream, carrying the Holy Child across. Was not the brave sailor as a giant strong in faith? Strong in his mental and spiritual convictions, he breasted rough waters indeed—patiently, for he had the nature of the dove; powerfully, because he was the Christ-bearer.

To pagan Rome belong the dazzling pages of a Cæsar's life; but the Christian world claims the precious lessons contained in the story of Christopher Columbus, significant in all its striking features.

In the commencement see the guiding chart laid to heart, and the seafaring life embraced; then come the speaking contrasts of his after-life. One day, a foot-sore traveller, he begs at a convent's gate for bread and water for his hungry child; another day a queen casts her jewels at his feet. Now wearied with procrastination, wasted with disappointment, yet patiently, perseveringly pressing onward still, combating objections and ignoring scoffs. Undaunted now and resolute, one man against a mutinous crew, he overrules them all. Success is trembling in the balance. And now the magnificent dream is fulfilled; the hopes of a lifetime are achieved. Does he meet his triumph proudly as one that has conquered?

Behold him on his knees, tearful, and kissing the ground. He rises, holding his drawn sword the while—it is to plant the cross on the land which he names San Salvador! Was he not rightly named Christopher, *the Christ-bearer*?

Yet two more scenes ere the end!

Welcomed as a prince and a conqueror, the woolcomber's son sits in the presence of royalty. And now for the sixth time recrossing those seas—which his invincible courage had made a highway for the nations—see him in his tiny cabin, a prisoner and in chains!

But not for long: the child's hard lessons were learned at last, so his Father bade him come home.

And now on the one side of Columbus dying of a broken heart, behold the pomp of a splendid funeral, and on his tomb a superb epitaph—such is earth's *payment*. On the other side, see the messenger, whose voice the easterns say is the sweetest of all the angels of God, the angel of death, Azrael (i. e. *the help of God*)—his whisper is joyfully obeyed, and the storm-tossed mariner is wafted to the haven of eternal rest—such is Heaven's *gift*.

But must that personal appeal, those momentous words, *for your name's sake*, be heard only in paths where glory and distinction may be won?

Our *Christian names* are oftenest heard within home-walls, and in ' the trivial round the common task ' there may often be found much meaning in those words ' for your name's sake'—ay, and influence and *power*, too, if we will but accept them as *reminders* of especial graces. And, be it remembered, Christian graces, 'fruits of the spirit,' have a distinguishing characteristic. ' Trees of righteousness ' are not like the trees of our orchard, where upon each tree only one kind of fruit may be found. The fruits of the spirit grow in fair clusters, combining various kinds. On every tree one fruit may be found more developed than the rest—but be sure that where 'love' is, there too will be 'joy' and 'peace.' ' Meekness and long-suffering ' may be of slower growth; but be not discouraged—they will surely put forth ere the ripened tree is transplanted above.

The especial use of *reminders* is to counteract *habits*. Most habits begin in early youth. Their name is legion; but amongst them there are few so little regarded, and yet so destructive of happiness to individuals and to those surrounding them, as a habit of wrangling and contradiction.

My little talisman, which consists in a recollection of the signification of our name, has been offered to Willie in the nursery—will Alfred and Edward accept it in the playground?

Some dispute has arisen—disputants soon grow warm. In the midst of that rapid interchange of angry words, think you that six words of advice could make their way? For my experiment I ask only room for two, and those no third person shall say. Each boy shall say, one to the other, their names—Alfred! Edward!

Alfred, *all-peace,* or the grander signification given by some to our great Saxon king's name, Aelf-fred, the *genius of peace*; Edward, Eadward, the keeper, the *guardian of happiness.*

Are the little quarrellers girls? Rachel, the *lamb,* significant of gentleness; Effie or Euphemia, the *pleasant-spoken*: my children, for your *names'* sake, remember how *a soft answer turneth away wrath.*

In our own day we see some living up to their beautiful names.

On rare occasions only may one allude to living characters, but lives overflowing with good deeds must in a measure become public, and names that are uttered with countless blessings must echo beyond the home-walls where Englishwomen best love their names to be inscribed.

To how many sick, sorrowful, and in need, has *Angela* Burdett Coutts been as the actual reality of her lovely Greek name, signifying *a messenger from God*! Florence Nightingale's surname is translated by Philo-mela, lover of song, but Philo-mena reads both as a 'lover of courage' and as one of a *loving mind,* and therefore as one *beloved.* This name she has won for herself—Longfellow's lovely lines to St. Filomena, as the 'Lady with the Lamp,' have bestowed it on her.

This name may remind us how monkish legends and countless fables of many kinds have grown out of the signification of names: although in this instance the ingenuity was still greater, the name itself being first constructed out of some detached words.

In 1802, in the catacombs of Rome, a sepulchre was discovered which contained the skeleton of a young girl. Rudely painted on the exterior of this long-hidden tomb was beheld an anchor, an olive-branch (hope and peace), a scourge (suffering), two arrows and a javelin (death); of a half-effaced inscription only these words, *lumena pax te cum fi*, remained. They were sufficient to *suggest* the story of the life and death and name of a Christian martyr; and the 'glorious St. Filomena' is said to have become within the last twenty years 'one of the most fashionable saints in Italy.' *

But ere we turn to this new matter of interest in names, we should perhaps, as a shadow to heighten the bright lights above—of Christians *living up* to their names—see how terribly sometimes the Dark Master, to whom pagans frequently dedicated their children, claimed and received—as it were, in right of their names—their services.

Come with me, then, to Pozzuoli, ancient Puteoli. Its name was doubly significant,

---

* Mrs. Jameson's Sacred and Legendary Art.

whether derived from its *wells* of sulphureous waters, or from their unpleasant smell. It is the very spot where holy Paul afterwards landed, bearing to Rome the banner of the Cross. The fish-ponds of Pollio Vedius—*evil god* (under that name the Romans worshipped the Prince of Darkness)—are filled up. Centuries have passed since their foul mists darkened the angry sky. But could those crimson-streaked waters flow again, they would shudderingly tell how living bodies of wretched slaves were flung into them, so that lampreys, fattened on those poor quivering limbs, might furnish daintier dishes to the monster whom they had served. A cracked goblet was sufficient excuse for 'a slave to be flung to the fishes.' At a banquet given to Augustus— a Cæsar worthy of his name—such an order was given by Pollio Vedius, giver of the feast. The emperor pleaded for the slave, but in vain. The cruel glutton was inexorable; and the indignant Cæsar ordered on the instant the ponds to be filled up, and every crystal goblet his host possessed to be broken before his face.

Though the burden of my song be *Let us answer to our names*, I must not pass by misnomers. There have been, there ever will be, inappropriate names; but if we look well into their meanings we may find it more possible to live up to many of these than we may at first suppose, or even their very contrariety may be made eloquent by us.

St. Felicitas and Julius Cæsar shall be our teachers in this.

Those saintly men and women of old, are they not as 'a cloud of witnesses?' Of earth, indeed, as vapours and exhalations, nothing in themselves, but in that, *feeling their own emptiness*, they have been lifted up into a purer atmosphere, they become more and more beautiful as they draw closer and reflect more vividly light—emanating from the Source of Light. 'Clouds'—exquisite in their varied shape and hues—lifted above this toiling world, as we gaze on them are we not in thought lifted heavenwards, even as we hope in a purified state ourselves to pass into that glorious 'cloud of witnesses?'

St. Felicitas, the *happy* one, a Roman widow (A.D. 173), beheld her seven sons tortured and put to death before her eyes. Scourged with thongs, beaten with clubs, flung from a rock, and beheaded—such were the cruel forms of death that a tender mother beheld her darlings undergo. But her heroic spirit never quailed. She bade her brave boys 'be strong of heart, and look to the heaven where Christ and His saints awaited their coming.' For herself, 'she blessed God that she had borne seven sons worthy to be saints in Paradise.' When her own day of martyrdom came, compared to what her soul's agony had been, her bodily sufferings were as nothing. Tortured and thrown into boiling oil, she was 'faithful unto death.' Felicitas, in another world, as a bright angel near the throne of God, listening to the harpings of her sons, answers to her name of the *happy one.*

In Julius Cæsar the curious combination of two names, both significant of *hair*, the one shaggy and the other soft, is the more striking, as the appellation of one who, as his medals and busts have sufficiently made known, was bald. The privilege accorded to the Roman hero of always wearing a laurel wreath was, it is said, peculiarly acceptable, not so much as a reminder of the glory he had won as for the green garland itself, which should conceal his baldness, which amongst the ancients was considered a disgrace. We may wonder that a man who had attained such dazzling preeminence could have attached any importance to so small a defect, his personal appearance being in all other respects most admirable. But instead of a silly sneer at the weaknesses of great minds, may we not try to turn the notice to good account for ourselves?

Julius Cæsar had neither the *soft down* of the one name, nor the *abundant hair* of the other; but was not the undying wreath that he won well worth them both?

Have any of us misnomers?

How many a Patrick is there in humble life! Patrick, derived from the Latin, signifies *nobility*, but nobility of mind is confined to no station. True nobility of heart and life may be attained by all who seek it at the hand of the King of kings. All know that 'the Crown is the fountain of honour.'

A weak and sickly lad may answer to the name of Charles, derived from the old Teutonic name of Karl, which signifies a *strong man* and *a valiant*. Be not cast down, dear boy; the more fragile and transparent the lamp, the more brightly the flame may shine through. To covet distinction is an instinct with men—to be brave is to be beloved; but the weak body has no power to daunt the brave soul—no physical strength had the hero of Trafalgar. And yet higher than earthly fame, remember that 'he that ruleth his spirit is greater than he that taketh a kingdom.'

Amongst my sisters, too, there may be some misnamed. One of the prettiest and most ancient of names, for it was that of the daughter-in-law of Methuselah, is Adah, signifying *ornament*, and figuratively expressive of great beauty. There may be Adas to whom a name significant of beauty would be inapplicable; but let us take its exact meaning, and then, sweet sisters, see if it be not in your own power, while answering to your names, to acquire a far more lasting *adornment* and charm than personal beauty by itself can bestow. In the same Holy Book which tells us of the first Adah, we are also told of the '*ornament* of a meek and quiet spirit.' Eunices, too, unknown to fame, ye may in your peaceful homes carry out the meaning of your grand Greek name, as day by day ye achieve *fair victories*.

In one widely celebrated name we find a link between the subjects of misnomers and names out of the signification of which legendary tales have arisen. The exquisite music of Rossini, superbly rendered by Giulietta Grisi, has made the name of Semiramide more familiar to our ears than perhaps that of any other heroine of antiquity.

Her actual story is like an Eastern romance, though it begins and ends with a legend suggested by the signification of her name—Semiramis signifying in Syriac *a dove*. The gentle and innocent dove was, however, no fit name for the Assyrian queen, at once warlike and voluptuous; nor was it given to her as a characteristic appellation. Yet to her (in whom many learned writers behold the original of the Syrian goddess, Astarte, adopted by the Greeks as Aphrodite, and by the Latins as Venus) doves were especially consecrated. The car of the goddess of love and beauty is always represented as drawn by them, and in honour of her doves were themselves worshipped in many parts of the East.

The Syrian town of Askelon, devoted to the worship of Astarte, was remarkable for its innumerable flocks of pigeons and doves, for it was there considered sacrilege for one of these birds to be killed. Near Askelon, in the ancient little village of Hamami, which signifies a *Dove*, we find at once the birth-place of the renowned Semiramis and the derivation of her name. Of such obscure birth was the magnificent queen, that to conceal the reality a fable was invented, assigning to her a celestial origin and a supernatural bringing up. Overshadowed by the wings of doves, she was said to have been also fed by them with milk brought in their beaks from the neighbouring village.

But the future queen of Assyria was, in truth, a child of shame, abandoned by her mother. The helpless little one was found by a compassionate shepherd of Hamami, who carried her to his humble home. There she grew up, gifted with remarkable beauty and talent, the name given to her having been compounded from that of her foster father, Simma, and Hamami, her native village. Married in early youth to the governor of Syria, Semiramis was taken by her husband to the Assyrian court, or rather to the camp, where Ninus the king carried on in person the siege of Bactria. Hitherto the besiegers had been unsuccessful; but it is said that the baffled generals were taught a lesson in their own art by the beautiful stranger, who not only planned the attack, but herself led the inspired troops to victory.

Transported with wonder and admiration at so marvellous a creation as a lovely woman who in courage equalled the bravest, in skill surpassed the wisest of his warriors, Ninus commanded Onnes to give up his wife to him. The unfortunate husband, reluctant to obey, was put to death, and the Assyrian monarch hastened to crown Semiramis as his queen. Devoted to her through life, Ninus at his death left to her the government of his kingdom, in which, after a splendid reign of forty-two years, she was succeeded by their son Ninyas.

There is no need to linger on her world-wide fame, her surpassing beauty, and marvellous achievements in peace and war; but her name and story form a striking illustration of the fact, that in the signification of names a key is often to be found to the strange wild legends of other times. In Semiramis, the *Dove*, is revealed the secret of her supposed supernatural nursing mothers, and her imaginary translation to heaven after death in the form of a dove.

The story of *Wolf*-fed Romulus is explained by Lupa, his nurse's name; and many like fables may be found to have sprung from like sources. Monkish chronicles are full of similar fanciful tales. The legend of St. René, who was said to have risen from the grave seven days after his burial, originated in his name, which, derived from the Latin Renatus, signifies *born again*. This name, adopted in the early Church as significant of a new spiritual life, suggested to credulous miracle-seekers in after times the marvel of St. René rising to a new bodily life.

To St. Athanasius, whose Greek name signifies *Immortality*, the Greek Church attributes the miraculous power of having caused a wolf to act as his obedient messenger—the simple fact being, that Athanasius sent to a monastery some herbs gathered with his own hands, and he chose for his messenger an individual bearing the name of Lycos, in Greek signifying a *Wolf*. Of this celebrated Patriarch of Alexandria, the 'Father of Orthodoxy,' as he has been called, it was said in the sixth century, 'Whenever you meet with a sentence of Athanasius, and have not paper at hand, write it down on your clothes.'*

In a work on Popular Superstitions, by M. de la Mothe A. Vayer, a long list is given of saints, the signification of whose names has led to a belief in supernatural powers possessed by them in connection with subjects corresponding to such signification.

The lame address their prayers for relief from their infirmity to St. Claude, Bishop of Besançon A.D. 581, his name being derived from the Latin Claudius, signifying *lame*.

With greater plausibility the blind seek assistance from the martyred saints of the fourth century—St. Clair, derived from the Latin, signifying *clear, bright*; and St. Lucia, also from the Latin, signifying *light*. From this signification is said to have also arisen the legend of St. Lucia's having being deprived of her eyes, of which we find no mention in the early history of the Christian Church.

* Stanley's Eastern Church.

The story grew out of the pictured representations of this fair girl, a native of Syracuse—one of the many martyrs in Diocletian's reign. Old painters, delighting in symbols and devices, introduced into their pictures of St. Lucia an eye, or eyes, as significant of her name. As time went on, a story grew, till the imaginary legend was coarsely rendered by the saint's carrying her eyes on a plate, while her other hand displayed the awl with which they were supposed to have been bored out.

A nobler, truer reading of her name was Dante's Santa Lucia, as the type of celestial light or wisdom: as such she is beautifully represented bearing a shining lamp.*

Some of these superstitions connected with the names of saints have neither a foundation of truth nor poetical imagery to plead for them. It is supposed in France to be unlucky for grain to be sown on St. Leger's day (October 2)—the martyred Bishop's name, signifying *light, wanting in weight*, is thought to affect the growth of the plant and make it *light* in the ear.

The shoemaker's choice of a patron is said by some to have simply arisen from his name Crispin, derived from the Latin *crepis* (borrowed from the Greek), signifying a *slipper*. But it would seem certain that the brothers Crispin and Crispianus, who were born at Rome, and travelled

---

* Mrs. Jameson's Sacred and Legendary Art.

to Soissons to preach the Gospel, did really follow in that town the trade of shoemaking—the two names rendered by them so illustrious being perhaps taken from their employment.

These saintly men carried out St. Paul's example and precepts in all their fullness, working with their hands the thing which was good: they also gave to them that needed, supplying shoes to the poor without payment. The good that they did lived after them, for in the name of these martyred brothers of the third century brotherhoods of charity were formed, the members of which paid the produce of their voluntary labours into a common stock for charitable purposes.

In an old romance a prince of the name of Crispin is made to exercise, in honour of his name, the trade of shoemaking, from whence, it is said, arose the epithet of the 'gentle craft.'* The name of Crispin was at one time a common nickname for a shoemaker, and at this moment in France shoemakers call the bag in which they carry the tools of their trade ' un saint-Crépin.'

In our Reformed Calendar one of the holy brothers' names is still preserved. St. Crispin's day (October 25) was one of our most venerated holy days in former times. Old England's long, long roll of victories also records that day as the anniversary of Agincourt. Shakspeare's glorious

---

* Brady's Clavis Calendaria.

speech of Henry V. before the battle commemorates both brothers' names:—

> And Crispin Crispian shall ne'er go by,
> From this day to the ending of the world,
> But we in it shall be remembered.

And when 439 years should have passed away, again was St. Crispin's day wreathed with laurel and cypress for England's heroes.

BALAKLAVA!

Frenchmen may criticise and Englishmen dispute as to who said what; but no Englishwoman will ever hear that name without glowing cheeks and brimming eyes—without thanksgiving to God that English mothers bear such sons.

Noble Curtius leaped into the gaping earth, for an oracle had said that only thus could Rome be saved; but at a breath, ere the half-uttered words were spoken, the confused order made plain—so madly jealous were they of their country's fame—England's 'gallant six hundred' rode into a gulf of fire, into the valley of death.

Peculiar interest attaches itself to the origin of all legendary tales. With much that is objectionable, there is also much to charm, much to profit, even in the *legendary* lives of saints. There seems little doubt but that, at the first, many of these legends were simply allegories, clothed with impressive language by meditative monks, hoping to affect the heart, and next, by the eager painter's hand, clothed in yet more gorgeous colouring to attract the eye. But much of the delicacy and beauty of these lessons, whether real or imaginative, has been lost by the coarse handling they received in the progress of time.

May we not win back some of their charm if we search for the fountain-head of these once clear streams? Where the old painters and poets sought and found inspiration, we too, if we seek, may find many sweet lessons for ourselves, and for every day.

We have seen how St. Lucia's legend and her pictured representation alike sprang from the signification of her lovely name, Lucia, *light*, celestial light, a never-dying lamp, making darkness light before her.

So, too, with St. Sophia—the name which we find in ancient Persia linked with faith. Adopted throughout the East, we find it in the Hebrew form in the prophet Zephaniah's name (translated by the French Sophonie, by the Italians Sofonia), signifying the *secret* or *word of Jehovah*, almost a synonyme with the Greek Sibyl, *counsel of God*. St. Sophia is represented with a martyr's crown, encircling with loving arms her three fair children, the offspring of heavenly Wisdom being Faith, Hope, and Charity.

So, too, the legend and picture of the strong man battling with the troubled stream, the holy child seated on his shoulders. Did not both grow out of the beautiful meaning conveyed by the name of Christopher, the *Christ-bearer*—a name doubtless first given to one who, bearing the name of Christian, bore also the image of his master Christ?

We must take very much away from the legend of St. Katharine ere we can look upon it with pleasure even as an allegory. The tale of the Egyptian princess has no claim on our reverence on the point of antiquity. Katharine of Alexandria, said to have lived at the very beginning of the fourth century, was not heard of even in the East till the eighth century, nor did her marvellous story reach Europe till the crusaders brought it back with them in the eleventh century.*

Full as it was of the elements of romance—a young queen of marvellous beauty, matchless wisdom, and exquisite purity of life, persecuted by a cruel tyrant, and with unshaken courage going forth to meet death in a hideous and hitherto unheard-of form—no wonder that the tale seized on the imaginations of all. St. Katharine was at once adopted as a popular saint. Wild though it was, the legend carried out the scriptural lesson of human imperfection. In a dream the *spotless* Katharine hears Christ say that ' she is not fair enough for Him.' Purified by suffering, made perfect through faith, she died for the truth, and her glorified spirit in heaven *first* hears

---

* Mrs. Jameson's Sacred and Legendary Art.

the welcome words, 'she is fair enough' to be Christ's.

In the fifteenth century, doubts having arisen as to the authenticity of her legend, and even the fact of her existence being questioned, her festival was suppressed by many prelates in France and Germany; yet never has the affection for her name passed away. St. Katharine still stands in our Reformed Calendar (her day being the 25th of November), her name still rests on many a house of God, charitable institutions are called after her, and ancient abbeys and ruined priories repeat her time-honoured name throughout the land.

One would fain believe that the reverence of so many simple hearts—carried though it was, alas! to so mischievous a height—has not been all given to a myth. Some foundation *may* have existed for the tale that the monks of Mount Sinai are said to have sent forth to the world, though no proofs can be given, and no assertions can be made. But if we simply look to St. Katharine as a wise and holy maiden, who sealed her faith in Christ with her blood, may we not in the meaning of her name discern a spiritual truth of great beauty?

'Aikatrina, *pure and undefiled*,' derived from Katharos, *spotless* and *pure*—does it not remind us of the sacred promise that 'the *pure* in heart shall *see* God?'

Yet one more sainted name demands our notice,

from the strange contrast which it affords to the story of her who bore it.

We look not now to one whose chronicle has come forth from the scriptorium of dreamy monks, for Holy Scripture records the name of Mary Magdalene. We absolutely know that in the deep abasement of an awakened conscience a penitent woman sought and found pardon and peace at the Saviour's feet.

What was her name?*—she who with hair unbound (a sign of sorrow in the East), the gold of her tresses dimmed by her falling tears, knelt silently, bowing down in her shame and anguish of heart. Magdalene (so called from the place of her birth), the *Magnificent*.

Is there no lesson in her name?

In the pride of her beauty—for the power of

---

* This question, it is well known, is open to discussion; but where Origen and Chrysostom have ranged themselves on one side, and St. Clement and St. Gregory on the other, who may dare to affirm anything positively? One can only in this, as in all other cases, speak to the best of one's belief. I fully believe, with the Eastern Church, that Mary of Bethany was a virtuous woman, and a distinct person from Mary Magdalene; or why, in her home of Bethany and in connection with Martha and Lazarus, should Mary never be called Mary Magdalene? We know that out of Mary Magdalene were cast seven devils, but whether she was indeed the woman who was a 'sinner,' I do not think Scripture has made so plain. But I would say, as one has said who carefully studied the subject: 'The woman who under the name of Mary Magdalene—whether her name be rightfully or wrongfully bestowed—stands before us sanctified in the imagination and in the faith of the people in her combined character of sinner and saint, is a reality, and not a fiction. Even if we would, we cannot do away with the associations inseparably connected with her *name* and her image.'
—Mrs. Jameson's *Sacred and Legendary Art*, vol. i. p. 333.

beauty is very great—Magdalene might once have gloried in her name — *Magnificent* as a stately *tower*.* But the tower whose foundations are on the shifting sands of time, shall it not crumble away? The magnificence which is of earth, shall it not yield to decay?

It was in her other name that Magdalene's safety was found—Mary, which in Hebrew means *bitterness*.

Mary, or Miriam, a name first given to the daughter of Jochebed. The mother's name signified '*whose glory is Jehovah*,' but her child was born in the *bitterness* of Egyptian bondage, and she thence derived her sorrowful name—bitterness as of the sea, waters of affliction, of which they drank from a full cup.

But the bondage of Mary Magdalene was the bondage of sin, and when once its *bitterness* was felt the hour of her freedom was at hand: 'loving much,' to her 'much was forgiven.' Strangely still sounds the name of Magdalene, the *Magnificent*, applied to the sorrowing daughters of shame.

How gloriously from her other name has its sorrowful meaning been rolled away! In every Christian land Mary is the name that most women love best to bear. Much sorrow had the mother of our Lord, and the sweet Marys of Gospel history, like Miriam of old, were born while their

---

* Migdol, *a tower*.

countrymen were in bondage, but they lived to see a far more glorious ransom accomplished. Of the waters of Marah they indeed also drank, but He of whom the tree was typical was Himself with them, and by Him was the bitter made sweet.

CHAPTER VII.

Name-giving Adam's first work in Paradise — Name-giving a natural instinct — Names of Stars — Saxon names of Months — Names of Animals, Flowers, Plants — Legend of St. Veronica.

'LE besoin de nommer'* is coeval with the use of words. We have seen that in Paradise it was the first act that Adam was called upon to perform. It is a natural instinct—from the hoary-headed Chaldean sages of old, who gave to each shining constellation, each twinkling star, separate and significative names, to the lisping little one in our nursery to-day, who, with her finger on her rosy lip, sits knitting her pretty brows, trying to think of some *nice* name for her kitten or her doll.

In the spangled heavens, as in some indestructible book, we read in lustrous characters these significant names of the highest antiquity. Some contain in themselves revelations of the past. Red Aldebaran, signifying '*he that goeth before*,' is said to point to that far period in the history of astronomy when this brilliant star, called by modern Arabians Ain-al-Thaur, '*the*

* Salverte.

bull's eye,' marched foremost of the celestial host, Taurus being then the first of the signs.* The names of others were as wise counsellors: the sweet Pleiades (in Hebrew, Cimah), whose Greek name signifies '*to sail,*' gave Grecian sailors notice that spring, the time most favourable for voyages, had arrived; while stormy Orion, signifying '*to agitate,*' warned them to stay at home. Even through the rugged disguises imposed on some of our week-days' names by our Saxon forefathers, we may still catch the shining of celestial orbs. With God's people, as from the beginning of time, we keep the week of seven days—the six days of creation, the seventh of rest. With the wise men of the East, Chaldea, Egypt, and ancient Hindustan, with the sages of Greece and Rome, we retain the recollection of the old 'planetary theory, itself founded, it is said, on the 'doctrine of musical intervals'—the 'music of the spheres,' a favourite thought in science as in poetry.

And through all the various systems to which men have successively subscribed, unchanging still to the glad ear of Faith is the matchless harmony to which unnumbered worlds of light move vocal to their great Creator's praise. Far off it is indeed, and human ears are dull. What wonder, then, that we can only catch broken echoes of the God-taught strain—here a swelling chord, and there a dying fall, as new planets are

* Encyclopædia of Natural Phenomena, by J. Forster, F.L.S. &c.

discovered, or familiar stars fade away? But are not these suggestive enough of the melody of all-perfect work that, mingling with angelic songs, encircles without end the throne of the Most High?

France and Italy unite in their week-days Christian and Pagan names. The first and the last day have, in Italian, sacred significations—Domenica, the *Lord's day*; and Sabbato, the *Sabbath* or *Rest*, as with the Jews. The French Dimanche is very expressive—the word dîme answering to our *tithes*, that portion of the land's produce which was appointed as the Lord's due. The moon and the stars shine through the other days—red Mars, pale Mercury, bright Jupiter, Venus radiant-eyed, and cold and distant Saturn moving slow.

The people of the North consecrated these days to divinities of their own, but they for the most part corresponded in their attributes to those of gods which the Grecian mythology had borrowed from the East. The first day was dedicated to the sun, the second to the moon. In the North the sun was regarded as feminine—she was said to be the wife of Tuisco; the moon was masculine. These genders are still so preserved to them in the German, Dutch, Danish, and Swedish languages, all originating from the Teutonic root. Tuisco, 'the most ancient and peculiar god of all the Germans,'* points to the far-away legends of

* Verstegan.

the Teutonic race, and their Indian god Deut, by whom the tribes were led from the countries of the rising sun to regions where a sterner atmosphere should reinvigorate the race.* Next come Wodin or Odin, god of battles, and father and chief of the gods; Thor, the thunderer, the first-born of Odin; Frigga or Freyga, the *beautiful*, the Venus and Juno of the North; and Seater, a Saxon idol resembling Saturn.

It is singular to remark that, while our week-days still bear Saxon names, the months of the year have reverted to those given to them by our Roman conquerors.

Excepting only January, from Janus, a keeper of doors—the two faced god looking to the past and to the future—the Saxon names were far more significative than the Latin.

The first month was called Wolf-monath, or Wolf-month, because at that rigorous season of the year men lived in dread of the attacks of these ravenous beasts.

February, the second month, was called Sprout-kale, from the sprouting of kale which was used as a winter broth; this name was afterwards changed to Sol-monath, from the returning sun.

March was Lenet-monath, because of the

* In High Dutch the third day of the week is called Erechstag, also in remembrance of the deified hero of old. The name Erech, originally from the word Heric or Haric, a *chief warrior*, became *significative* of a mighty lord, and has passed into countless forms—Eoric, Euric, Eric, Heinrich; and from it our name of Henry is derived.

lengthening days; hence we still call the fast preceding Easter, Lent, because the greater part of that season fell to Lenet-monath.

April, Oster-monath, took its name from the east winds which prevailed at that time.

May was called Tre-milke, because, on account of the fresh juices of the young grass, cows then afforded milk three times a day.

June was Sere-monath, or dry month.

July, Hay-monath, from the making of hay; or, Mæd-monath, from the meadows being then in bloom.

August was Barn-monath, from the harvest-time filling their barns with corn.

September was Gerst-monath, from *barley* being then reaped. The old Saxon name for barley was gerst; but this grain being looked upon with especial favour, 'from the drinke therewith made called beere,' it became first beerlegh, then berlegh, and finally barley.*

October was called Wyn-monath, or Wine-month.

November was Wind-monath, or Wind-month.

December was originally Winter-monath, or Winter-month; but after Christianity was established in the land it became Heligh-monath, or Holy-month, from its being the birth-time of our Lord.†

The Parsees assign each day of the month, and

* Clavis Calendaria. † Ibid.

each hour of the day and night, to superintending genii, and give to them the names of presiding deities.

Significant names, chosen either from those of their gods or from lofty mountains, were given by the people of Armenia to each separate day of the week and to each of the twenty-four hours of the day and night.

The wandering tribes of the Kalmuck Tartars, whose worldly possessions consist in vast herds of camels, horses, sheep, and a comparatively small number of cattle, give to months, days, and hours, names taken from those of animals.

Greece and Rome did honour, too, in a different manner, to the names of some animals. The winners of chariot races at the Olympic games consecrated in the temple of Jupiter the names of the horses to whom their triumph was owing, and ancient Latin inscriptions still exist which record the names of the winning horses in the circus at Rome. Of these names some recall that of their first master, others refer to their native land, while others are characteristic names, such as The Gentle, The Proud, &c.

In Thibet, not the men who ride, or those who own the winning horses, receive prizes, but the animals themselves; various privileges are conferred upon them—amongst others they receive new and honourable names.

But to the priceless steeds of Sahara, cherished as they are beyond all other possessions by the sons of the Desert—petted, caressed, and cared for as tenderly in their youth as the children of the family—to them human names are never given. Forbidden by their Prophet to make representations of the human form, it was also forbidden to the followers of Mohammed to call animals by the names of men and women.* And so amongst Arab steeds none answer to such names as correspond with our 'Miss Fannies' and 'Lord Johns;' but beautiful names are found for them, generally significative of jewels — Marjanah, *Coral*; Lu-lu-ah, the *Pearl*, &c.†

Thought travels back to sacred promises of old, and to the 'Good Shepherd' who 'calleth His own sheep by name,' when we read of flocks, sometimes exceeding a thousand in number, being all known by *name* to their keepers. Not only is this the case in Palestine, even as it was in our dear Lord's day, but it is so also in Terceira, one of the lovely Western Isles or Azores, so called by the Portuguese from Açor, a *hawk*, those birds abounding in the islands when they were first discovered.

We read also how in Italy vast flocks of sheep and herds of cattle are all known by name to

---

* Miss Beaufort, a late traveller in the East, mentions, as amongst the many causes of ill-will existing between the Moslems and the Maronites, the intentional insult implied by the Zuh'leh people calling their dogs 'Mohammed,' while we at home consider it as a compliment to have our names given to pet animals.

† Miss Beaufort mentions as names of dromedaries, Simri, *Black*; and Helweh, *Sweet*.

their vigilant keepers. Not only are the names of distinguished families in the land bestowed upon these beasts, but also their titles.

Travellers describe the movements of these immense flocks of sheep as full of interest and picturesque beauty. As cattle are in Switzerland yearly led to mountain pastures, so in Italy the sheep are pastured in the mountains of the Abruzzi and the highlands of the kingdom of Naples. When the summer heats begin, long processions ascend the breezy hills, sheep guarded by dogs, who, like their fleecy charges, all answer to individual names, which in their case are generally significant of fidelity and courage. The shepherds follow with their families, all laden with their domestic properties. When fruitful autumn's harvests have been gathered in, and the gleaning of the grapes and olives is over, the roads again become white with the snowy fleeces of the far-extending flocks, descending for the winter months to low-lying lands. The vast plains surrounding Rome for a circuit of six miles quickly assume the appearance of an immense sheep-fold, temporary huts being erected for the shepherds and their families.

Independently of names given to individual animals, it is curious to notice how certain proper names of men and women have become identified with particular animals as a class, and this most frequently apart from their signification, and seemingly unaccounted for.

In some cases such names, however, are most happily appropriate. The Englishman, in his wanderings over the globe, wherever he finds a red-breasted bird, calls it by the familiar name of 'Robin,' in remembrance of his trustful little favourite at home. We all know how this cheery little bird stays with us throughout the winter: the nightingales and the goldfinches do not tempt him to fly away with them to summer climes. We all know how, when snow is on the ground, his bright eyes peep through our window panes, while he taps on them with his tiny bill; and wherever heard, his gentle appeal is always responded to. But who knows why this name of Robin was given to him? Whatever the reason, certain it is no name could suit him better: bright-eyed Robin *answers to his name.* As in winter he thankfully picks up each scattered crumb—as in spring-time he cheerily sings to his mate—is not his happy trustfulness a sweet repetition of the holy lesson intrusted to the 'fowls of the air?' Oh, listen to the little bird, anxious and careworn human beings! Will your Father in heaven not 'much more care' for you?

Robin is a *bright counsellor.* Robin is from Robert, originally Rod brecht, from the Teutonic, signifying one who *speaks* or *counsels brightly, excellently.*

But why should the crafty fox be known as Reynard? Rein-hard, an old Teutonic name also, which has so lovely a signification, a *pure heart.*

And Marten, which, like Martin, must be originally derived from Roman Mars, the God of War—whence our *martial* or warlike—what has such a name in common with a member of the weasel family? the name of Martin itself being given to different kinds of swallows. A brilliantly coloured little mullet, found in the bay of Suédiyeh, is called by the natives 'Sultan Ibrahim.' In France, a still greater number of such instances may be found. Both the English and French have assigned the pretty name of Margaret, signifying a *pearl*, to a mischievous chattering bird—Magpie and Margot.

Glowworms, or St. John's worms—in German, Johannis Wurmchen—have their name explained by their beginning to appear about St. John the Baptist's day (24th of June), when St. John's Wort begins to blow. The same reason—its coming into bloom about the 22nd of February, St. Margaret's day—gives to the pretty daisy its old English name, Herb Margaret. In France it is always called 'Marguerite.'

Herb-Bennet, or Gold-star, the common clove-scented Aven of our hedge banks, was originally named Herb Benedicta, from its blossoming about Corpus Christi day (May 28th). In France it is feminised as 'Benoite;' and also in Italy, 'Erba Benedetta'—all having the same signification, *blessed*.

Herb-Gerard, or Gout-weed, flowering on St. Gerard's day (April 23rd), is supposed to share, with its namesake, the power of healing the gout. The plant may be healing, or, like the saint, powerless to heal. The issues of life and death, sickness and health, are in the Almighty's hand alone; but yet St. Gerard has an apt cure for much suffering—a noble lesson for all. A precious truth lies in the significance of his name: derived from the language of the warlike Teutons, Gerhard sig. *Brave heart.*

Sweet Williams take their name from St. William de Monte Vergine, whose festival is the 25th of June, when they are in full bloom. A narrow-leaved variety, now seldom seen, used to be called Sweet-Johns.

Wild Spinach is called by the French Bon-Henri.

To Chervil, one of our old medicinal plants, was given the name of Sweet Cicely; to one of the Milfoils, that of Sweet Maudlin, from Magdalene; but why was a native of North Africa called Sweet Marjoram? Marjorie or Margery, a pretty old English diminutive—gone out of fashion now—for Margaret, but surely prettier than Maggie or Meg. And the aromatic herb of the East, the Rayhan of Persia (in Arabic, Reyhan, a proper name, sig. *the favour of God*), which, because of its name, perhaps, as well as its fragrance, is planted in burial-places, and scattered by Egyptian women on the grave of those they loved. How comes Sweet Basil by its kingly name? Basileus, in Greek, sig. a *king.* The wild aromatic plant which is eaten by us when candied with sugar, the dried roots of which the Laplanders chew as tobacco, is called Angelica (from the Greek), sig. *a messenger from heaven.*

Is it because of its heavenly blue—unmatched in colour but by children's eyes—that the lovely Speedwell is called by the sainted name of Veronica, for on her day (the 13th of January) the wild flowers are all hidden away under their snowy coverlet?

Protestants do not accept the wild legend of St. Veronica, Vera Icon, a compound name, Latin and Greek—Vera, *true*; eikon, *figure*, likeness.

The impression of the Saviour's face was said to have remained on a cloth with which a compassionate woman wiped from His brow the drops of agony, as, bearing His cross, He passed her door on the way to Calvary.

We do well to reject miracles based only on tradition; we do well to shrink from all undue reverence to saints; but we do not do well to lose *one* lesson contained in the life of a holy man or woman.

We see, as it were, St. Paul and St. Barnabas rending their clothes in horror when unseemly worship is offered to them; we hear them exclaiming, 'Sirs, why do ye such things? we also are [were] men of like passions with you.' But we also hear our dear Lord's voice applying His parable of the good Samaritan to all hearers with the words, 'Go and *do* thou likewise.'

It may or it may not be that the blessed woman since called Veronica (from the supposed miracle) was Berenice, daughter of Salome, niece of Herod. Would that it were! for then she would have shown much courage as well as much compassion. But is it not more than probable that the legend had some foundation in fact?

What wonder would it be if, from amongst the daughters of Jerusalem who *did* weep for Him who 'went about doing good,' one pitying hand stretched forth, as the patient Sufferer passed by, and passed her woman's veil tenderly over the 'marred' face, wet with the dews of unutterable agony?

Sacred dews, that shall henceforth descend in showers of unspeakable mercy upon mankind!

The Saviour's image—not graven on the senseless cloth—would most surely be impressed on the woman's feeling heart, sanctifying her after-life, and making her for ever His own.

He who attached a reward to a cup of cold water given in His name—would He have passed on His way regardless of this act of womanly sympathy, nor left His blessing behind?

And not to Veronica alone! Sisters, are our veils ever wet with tears? Let them recall to us Veronica's veil of other days—*not pictured*, but simply wetted by our dear Redeemer's drops of agony. Hallowed by the thought, thrice blessed will our tear-wetted veils become, if they serve to imprint the Saviour, the Comforter, upon our hearts. The scene is reversed. It is we who must now bear the cross—it is He who will wipe our griefs away.

Do any bear the pretty name of Veronica? Oh, what a continual reminder they have of the holiness which their lives should reflect! *

---

* The Robin, called in Brittany *Jean le Gorge-rouge*, has his red throat and breast accounted for there by a pretty legend. His feathers are said to have been first crimsoned by his own blood, as he wounded himself in striving to pluck the thorns from the Saviour's crown.

Some flowers have been called after saints from growing abundantly in the neighbourhood of their shrines. The plant *Angelica* may have derived its name from its healing powers, and fanciful eyes have discovered in the markings of the leaves of the *Veronica* some resemblance to a human face. The flower was believed to be a charm against evil spells; hence its common name of *Speedwell*.

CHAPTER VIII.

Curiosities in histories of names — Superstitions in ancient Rome — Lucky and unlucky names — Diocletian — Hippolytus — Superstitions in various nations — Lucky and unlucky letters — Talismans and charms — Moses' Rod — Solomon's Seal — Abracadabra — Hebrew and Druidical alphabet of trees and plants — Anagrams and acrostics — The Imperial riddle of the vowels — Sad story of an anagram — Variations in a name.

IN days of old, ere Faith born of the Spirit was seen with radiant finger pointing ever upwards to a God of love, the human race, anxious-eyed and irresolute, followed blind superstition into many a darkling and crooked path.

Accomplished Greece and warlike Rome were alike bewildered by the conflicting claims of their many divinities, to whom in their ignorance and irreverent folly they attributed such idle jealousies and bitter animosities as would have disgraced humanity. They walked in fear and doubt all the day long. The minds of some of the wisest of their philosophers, the bravest of their commanders, were alike strangely and unhealthily affected by the commonest incidents of their daily life—they were unnerved or elated by the most immaterial circumstances.

Amongst these many causeless sources of undue

hopes and fears, none were looked upon as more pregnant with meaning, none considered of more moment, than lucky or unlucky names.

Oracles were consulted and sacrifices offered up, so that by their gods fortunate names might be revealed. In religious ceremonies, and in all public undertakings, the greatest precautions were observed, so that those who assisted in them, or at least all those to whom prominent positions were assigned, should have names of good augury. The children by whom the victims were led, the priests by whom they were to be sacrificed, or by whom the new temple was to be dedicated, were carefully selected according to the signification of their names.

When citizens were chosen for the formation of new colonies, or soldiers enrolled for military expeditions, or even when electors registered their votes, such names only as were supposed to presage good fortune were allowed to head the lists.

In Rome, Valerius, sig. of *strength*, and Salvius, sig. of *safety*, were amongst the lucky names; but Vespellian, derived from vespa, a *wasp* (a disagreeable companion indeed), Nævus, a *blemish*, and Egerius, expressive of *want*, were avoided as sure prognostics of evil.

Certain tribes were considered in consequence of their names to bring misfortune whenever they presented themselves first to vote, or to take part in any public ceremony. When criminals were assembled for judgment, the trials commenced with those whose names were reckoned as least fortunate.

Good or evil auguries were drawn even from the names of animals.

Lepidus Æmilius Paullus Macedonicus, a Roman consul, appointed for the second time to conduct the war in Macedon against Perseus, on returning to his house from the election found his little daughter Æmilia (No. 3) in tears. On his asking the cause, the child replied that her favourite dog Perseus was dead. The Roman general gladly accepted the omen for good. Assured of success, he set off on the expedition which terminated in Perseus, last of the Macedonian kings, being brought in triumph a prisoner to Rome, there to die of a broken heart.

Before the battle of Actium, Augustus was rejoiced by a favourable augury—a donkey and its driver were the humble instruments of his joy. Meeting an ass, he hastened to enquire its name. It proved to be Nikân, sig. in Greek to *conquer*. Thus encouraged to ask the name of the man by whom it was led, his triumph was complete, for it was Eutyches, *the fortunate*! After his victory over Anthony, Augustus built a temple in which were placed figures of the luck-bringing (?) ass and its master.

In later days an Italian physician found in his name a powerful letter of introduction to the court of the Imaum of Muscat. On being asked his name, he replied Vincenzo, which, translated into the Arabic, Mansour, announced him as the *victorious*, and secured for him the immediate favour of the prince.

In another name good fortune sprang from the addition of a letter.

Friendless and poor, a young Persian named Nuari bore about him a continually depressing reminder of his low estate, for Nuari sig. *destitute*. One day the master with whom he studied, struck by his promise of excellence, exclaimed that his name should no longer be Nuari, but that he should be known as Anuari, sig. *brilliant*. The changed name acted as a charm: the spirit of the lad was aroused, and the whole power of his mind was put forth. The clouds of neglect and contumely rolled away—as a newly found star the young poet shone forth, and to this day his admiring countrymen delight to sing the songs of Anuari, the *brilliant*.

Some names, alas! have lost all their prestige through the change of a letter. An R changed into an H has ruined one reputation irremediably! What cruel destiny presided over the transformation of Robin Goodfellow—the beneficent fairy of olden times, well known to all country lads and lasses—into HOBGOBLIN, now become the nightly terror of all waking inmates in dark nurseries?

But some names have in very truth brought misery on their possessors. To one of the early martyrs of the Christian Church a death of peculiar horror was assigned in consequence of his ill-omened name.

Hippolytus, a Roman soldier placed as a guard over St. Laurence—whose martyr's crown exceeded in glory the *laurel-wreath* sig. by his name—moved by the dying saint's exhortations, and inspired by his sublime courage, not only became, but boldly avowed himself to be, a Christian.

After the cruel martyrdom of St. Laurence, who was roasted alive on a gridiron, the brave Hippolytus, eager to prove his gratitude for the inestimable boon which the saint had bestowed on him, joined with some other fearless Christians in the daring act of carrying away the mangled body and affording it Christian burial.

Soon arrested by the lictors of the Emperor Decius, Hippolytus resisted all attempts to shake his faith, and, after having seen nineteen of his family beheaded, he was himself reserved for a more agonising death. His name, signifying in Greek *torn by horses*, suggested to his cruel persecutors the hideous mockery of fulfilling its meaning by tying the gallant soldier to the tails of wild horses.

In the following century a strange story was attached to one of these unlucky names, as it proved to the bearer of it.

A youth of obscure parentage received from his mother a name. Her name Doclea, from the village where she was born, was altered for her son into Diocles, sig. in Greek the *glory of Jupiter*. Enlisted in the Roman army, Diocles disputed one day with a woman the price of a meal which she had supplied to him. Reproached by her for his meanness, the young soldier mockingly replied, that when he became emperor he would become generous. 'You speak in jest, but your words will come true,' exclaimed the Druidess; 'after you have killed a *wild boar* you will become emperor.'

Haunted by this prediction, the ambitious soldier, as he pushed his way through each successive grade of his profession, eagerly sought every opportunity of slaughtering a wild boar. But it was not for many years that, far distant from his native land, on the banks of the Tigris, the hidden sense of the prophecy flashed on the mind of the then captain of the Palace Guards. The news of the death of the Emperor Numerianus had reached the camp—Diocles was chosen by acclamation of the troops as his successor. One obstacle alone remained—one only rival stood between him and the throne—the præfect of the prætorians, Aper, sig. *wild boar*. Seizing on the pretext of his being suspected of the murder of his son-in-law, Numerianus, Diocles killed Aper with his own hand, and as emperor assumed the sonorous name of Diocletian.

As I write the name Diocletian, does there not pass before the mind of my readers, even as it does before my own, an exquisite vision of such mingled beauty and mournfulness that none could look and few can think upon it without tears? A fair pale body—a woman's long hair floating around, dimly revealed through green translucent waves—a still and shadowy horror over all—the only light in the picture the fair pale body just sinking to rise again, and the circle of light which, hovering overhead, tells of the 'Martyr in Diocletian's Reign.'*

Was that murdered woman's drowning form amongst the crowd of avenging visions that scared from the throne of the Cæsars the man whose life-long ambition it had been to attain to that proud preeminence? The lowly-born Dalmatian achieved his wildest dreams, but when his sceptre reeked with the blood of Christian martyrs its weight became intolerable. With his own hand, in the presence of the army and the people, in the very spot where he had so triumphantly assumed them, he divested himself of the insignia of sovereignty to which he had attached unusual splendour.

His imperial robe was of cloth of gold; his silken slippers, dyed in purple, were incrusted with gems; his diadem blazed with jewels of inestimable value; and he caused himself to be addressed as Master, Lord, and God! But the prosperity of the wicked is no enviable thing. The Dalmatian slave did indeed ascend the

* The beautiful picture of that name, by De la Roche, in the French gallery of pictures in the International Exhibition of 1862.

Cæsars' throne, but of his own will he descended from it as from a seat of thorns. Worn out in body, distracted in mind, the murderer of so many men, women, and children, in a state of insanity, finally starved himself to death, to escape an imaginary death at the hands of Constantine.

Prophecies like those which fired the ambition of Diocles frequently, as we see in his career, lead to their own fulfilment; but it only needs to compare the superstitious fancies of different nations, which are often in direct opposition to each other, to show how far they are from resting on any sure foundation.

It was at one time considered unlucky in Ireland to give a son his father's name, supposing that it shortened the parent's life. So, too, amongst the Hurons, a warlike tribe of North American Indians, it is (or we should, perhaps, with a people continually wasting away, say *was*) the custom that only after the father's death a child is allowed to bear his name.

The Australian savages, on the contrary, dread no danger from the living, but shrink in terror from the name of one lately dead: survivors who bear the name hasten to take another, and even all utterance of it is avoided.

Far more intelligible is the mistaken but tender superstition of the natives of Tonquin, the northern part of Cochin China. Does the news arrive there of some dear one dying in a far-off land, his relations, jealous lest the strangers amongst whom he died should have neglected some needful observance in the last rites paid to the dead, are eager to fulfil these duties themselves. In the old home to which he will never return, they determine that his name at least shall be heard and honoured once more. The dead man's *name* is inscribed on a plank of wood — their love investing the rude symbol with reverence — and a mimic funeral takes place.

We have seen that with names, as with human beings, 'some have been born to greatness, some have achieved greatness, and some have had greatness thrust upon them.' The lustre which encircles many names has been cast on them by the deeds of those that bore them; while other names, fair in themselves, have been sullied and disgraced by their possessors.

Names so dishonoured were indignantly proscribed by noble families in ancient Rome. The beautiful name of Lucius, sig. *Light*—which has in all languages its synonymes — was once a favourite prænomen in the patrician family of Claudius; but rendered infamous by the crimes of two Luciuses, one convicted of murder and one of theft, the name was abandoned by the family.

Favour and disfavour have attached themselves not only to names, but even to the letters of which names are composed.

By sages of old each letter was connected with a particular star, so that astrological influence, as well as numerical value, contributed to exalt some letters above their fellows.

A, E, H, and I were considered fortunate; B, C, D, and F were looked upon as unlucky. T was also among the fortunate letters. The Greek Tau, τ, or St. Anthony's Cross, was in olden times the hieroglyphic of *security*. It was said: 'Kill not them upon whom ye shall see the letter Tau.'* For it was the initial of Theos.

But, disproving these idle fancies, the letter A proved most unfortunate to Alexis, married to the niece of Manuel Comnena. The Greek Emperor, anxious to fasten a quarrel on his niece's husband, affected to discover an indication of Alexis' aspiring to the supreme authority, in that his name began with the first letter of the alphabet.

Pythagoras is said to have originated the belief that an uneven number of vowels in a name was a sure presage of misfortune to the unhappy proprietor—loss of sight, a broken limb, or some other mischance.

In later days a French versifier accounted for the misfortunes of Margaret of Austria† in the

---

* Gwillim's Display of Heraldry.

† It was the morning of her life which with this princess was so overclouded. Margaret was the only daughter of Maxmilian I. and the beautiful Mary of Burgundy. She lost her mother, who was good as she was beautiful, while still in her cradle. Affianced to the Dauphin of France, son of Louis XI., the young

circumstance that the initial letter of her name was also that of the words malheur, misère, mal, martyre, malédiction, maléfice, mort. But, dear English Marys, Margarets, and Maudes, remember, I pray, that some of these terrible omens are destroyed by translation into other languages.

The four letters which compose the name of the first man, A D A M, being the initial letters of words which in Greek indicate the four cardinal points, Anatolia, Dysis, Arctos, and Mesembria, were supposed to signify that God made Adam from earth taken from the east, the west, the north, and the south.*

princess was sent to that country to be educated; but on Charles VIII. marrying Anne of Brittany, she was dismissed, with all honour, but dismissed—an insult which her father never forgave. Another husband was found for Margaret in Don John, only son of Ferdinand and Isabella. On her voyage to Spain she was nearly lost, off the English coast, in a tremendous storm. With great composure the young lady composed her own epitaph, which, with her jewels, she bound about her arms:—

'Ci gît Margot, la gente demoiselle,
Qu'eut deux maris, et si mourut pucelle.'

She did, however, live to reach Spain, and was married to John, who soon died. Again she married Philibert, Duke of Savoy. In three years she was again a widow, having then only reached her twenty-fourth year.

Her after life was peaceful and honourable. By her father first, and afterwards by her nephew, Charles V., she was intrusted with the government of the Low Countries. Invested by Charles with full powers, Margaret concluded with Louise of France, mother of Francis I., the Peace of Cambray, thence called 'La Paix des Dames.' Dying in her fiftieth year, she left behind an unblemished name, and was mourned alike by the Netherlands which she had governed, and by Charles whose vicegerent she was.

* Noël's Dictionnaire Historique.

It was once customary to write the name of Adam on the four corners of pigeon-houses, as a means of preserving them from the attacks of venomous reptiles.

A pleasant by-path here opens out from the broad track of the history of names. We dare not take time to enter far, but we cannot pass on without a glance. How curious it is to notice how, in all times and amongst all nations, strong men and wise men have looked upon bits of stones or small scraps of writing as actual preservatives from harm!

The learned Egyptian clung to the representations of his graceful Ibis or brilliant Scarabeus. In our day men irreverently take from the necks of mummies sacred gems which tens of centuries ago loving hands had tenderly hung about their dead, supposing them to be sure safeguards from all evil.

Greeks and Romans, too, had their amulets of precious stones, carved in the shape or engraved with the figures of sacred animals, or mystic symbols.

For our Anglo-Saxon forefathers a lump of amber sufficed, with a hole drilled through to hang round the neck of the living, or to place in the grave at the head of the corpse.

The African has his 'fetish,' some native charm, or a printed page from a white man's book, or some scribbled line from a white man's hand.

The North American Indian has his 'medicine,' feathers of a bird, bones or teeth of animals, or a rude representation of beast, bird, or fish.

And Christian men and women, too, have shown strange and undue reverence for the relics of saints—looking upon dead bones, or hair, or rags of garments, as holy things endued with power to preserve them from danger.

But with the seed of Abraham, the Faithful, the sons of Isaac and Ishmael, this superstition has been carried farther perhaps than with any other people. The Turks have adopted it from their co-religionists, the Arabs.

The word talisman has been sometimes derived from the Greek telesma, '*incantation*;' but it would seem rather to belong to the Arabic talsam, sig. '*mystical characters*,' and applied also to the seals, rings, and papers on which such characters are inscribed. The Latin amuletum also claims an Arabian origin, from hamalet, something '*suspended*,' as amulets generally are from the neck. Both names point to the East as the place whence Europe adopted this superstition, and where it is still most fondly and universally retained.

In the Hebrew Cabala is to be found, it is said, the origin of many of the tales of marvel connected with amulets and talismans.

Of those which strictly belong to our subject, the influence of *names*, we will but glance at two of the greatest importance.

Jewish *fables* tell of the Zaphir rod, the instrument by which they say Moses performed his miracles. On it the most holy name of God, the Tetragrammaton, or name of four letters, was inscribed. This rod, said to have been created in Paradise on the sixth day, was brought away by Adam, and passed successively through the hands of Noah, Abraham, Isaac, Jacob, and Joseph: on his death it was seized by Pharaoh. Jethro, one of the Egyptian monarch's counsellors, being friendly to the Israelites, conveyed it secretly away and planted it in his garden. When Moses took refuge with Jethro, beloved by Zipporah, she prevailed on her father to consent to their marriage, one condition being affixed—that Moses should pluck out of the ground the Zaphir rod, on which was written the incommunicable name. Other men were allowed at the same time to try their strength, but none could raise it except Moses, who did it by virtue of the sacred name which he alone could rightly pronounce.

How infinitely more sublime and impressive is the grand simplicity of Scripture! Moses, once the pride of the Egyptian court, kept his father-in-law's flock in the desert when God spake with him. 'What is that in thine hand? And he said, A rod.' . . . 'Thou shalt take this rod in thine hand, wherewith thou shalt do signs.' No glittering sword, or jewelled sceptre, or shining wand was bestowed on him; but his simple rod of almond wood, his shepherd's staff, which he was then using in his appointed work, became mighty through the word of God. Uplifted in Jehovah's name, water became blood, fire from heaven ran along the ground, armies of devouring locusts appeared, the Red Sea divided, and, behold, a pathway to the Land of Promise.

Ah! how often do we look abroad and covet instruments of power, when, lo! they are in our very hands, companioning with us through our daily work! God-blessed, the humblest instruments may do good service to God and man; but they must be 'proved' in prayer.

So in later days the sling and the pebble in the shepherd-boy's hand slew the giant; and, yet more gloriously significant, the transverse wooden beams—the despised Cross—when hallowed by a Saviour's blood, have become a symbol mighty to save, an instrument of world-wide power, high above all, unmatched in its infinite significance.

The Arabs, also, tell of Moses' rod, but they most delight to dwell on the wonders performed by the seal-ring of Suléyman Ibn Daood—Solomon the son of David. Partly composed of brass and partly of iron, its especial power consisted also in the 'most great name' of God, 'El Im al Aazam'—a name known only to the especial favourites of Heaven—being engraved thereon. By virtue of this magical ring, Suléyman was said to have commanded the mighty race of the genii inhabiting earth, and water, and air, both the good and the evil. His written commands for the good were stamped with the brazen part; those for the wicked with the iron—Hadeed, or *iron*, being considered unlucky. The Arabs say that thus were the whole race of the genii compelled to assist in the building of the Temple of Jerusalem. Beasts and birds, and even the lawless winds, obeyed this mighty talisman.*

The simple utterance of the name which it bore sufficed to transport the throne of the Queen of Sheba into the presence of King Suléyman in his palace at Jerusalem, and by it they affirm to this day that the dead can be raised.

Amongst talismanic names Abracadabra must not be forgotten. Said to be a Persian name, and one of the many synonymes of Mithra, the Sun-god, the word is still to be seen in English and French dictionaries, described as a superstitious charm which, written on paper in a triangular form and worn about the neck, was once a popular remedy for the tertian ague.

Serenus Sammonicus, a Latin physician of the third century, recommended this charm against intermittent fever in some Latin lines, which still exist.

* Lane's Notes to Arabian Nights.

```
A B R A C A D A B R A
 A B R A C A D A B R
  A B R A C A D A B
   A B R A C A D A
    A B R A C A D
     A B R A C A
      A B R A C
       A B R A
        A B R
         A B
          A
```

The connection between names and numbers is spoken of in Scripture: the number of 'the Beast' is said to be 666. Ill-directed ingenuity has at various periods of history discovered this fatal number in the names of several obnoxious individuals.

The Talmud is full of allusions to names and letters and numbers. It is there said that the letters which compose the name of Satan make the number 364, marking thereby that the power of the Evil One extends through all the days of the year excepting one, 'the Day of Expiation.'

Letters have also been connected with plants. An alphabet of trees existed amongst the Chaldeans, Hebrews, Arabians, and Celts. Nations in their infancy were taught even as we teach our little ones now—letters and words were connected with pictured devices of various kinds. Some of these ancient symbols were full of poetic beauty, and in them we may often find a key unlocking strange mysteries and making hidden allusions clear. Although they may sometimes give us a clue to the meaning of a name, the subject scarcely comes strictly enough within the range of our enquiry to be more than glanced at here.

We find that the Hebrew letter Beth (B) was symbolled by a thorn, Daleth (D) by a vine, He (H) by a pomegranate, Vau (V) by the kingly palm, Yod (I) by the ivy, Pe (P) by the cedar, Resh (R) by the pine.

These letters were differently represented by the Celts. With them the symbol for B was the birch, for D the oak, for T the yew, for P the pine, for R the elder and the privet.*

The Celts are said to have attached also to each letter and its symbolical plant the significance of some particular power. B was considered as expressive of *life*, D of expansive or *overspreading* power. This letter—symbolled in the East by the vine, which before her captivity was the cognisance of Judæa, the Holy Land; and in the North represented by the Druids' sacred tree, the oak, called in the Celtic Duir—has been in almost every land the initial letter of Deity.

In the Chaldaic and Celtic alike, Di, the omnipotent, the disposer; in the Greek, Διός; in the Latin, Deus; Italian, Dio; Spanish, Dios; French, Dieu.

It was forbidden by the Greek laws that any persons should be ridiculed on the stage by their real names; but the fictitious and significant

* Davies's Celtic Researches.

names which were adopted in their plays afforded a fertile source of puns.

The reproach which French writers have cast on English dramatists, including Shakspeare and Sheridan, for such play upon words, must be shared with the classic authors of both Greece and Rome. Even their orators, including Cicero, disdained not so to feather their darts of sarcasm; but in unskilful hands, or with a quick-witted adversary, it was dangerous play. The eloquent Q. Lutatius Catulus (which literally signifies *little dog*), denouncing with much vehemence the malpractices of an extortioner, was rudely challenged by one who sought to defend the criminal—'And why do you bark, little dog?' 'Because I see a thief,' Catulus instantly replied.

In a drama translated from the Sanscrit by Sir W. Jones we may see how far in the East also the practice of punning allusions on names has travelled. Sacontala hails a companion, Pryamvada, as one '*rightly named.*' Pryamvada signifies '*one who speaks kindly*' and graciously.

In our own day some happy hits have been made by expressive names, intelligible to all, and yet not clumsily apparent. Amongst a host of imitators few have been so successful as the inventors of the names Lord Verisopht and Lord Dundreary.

Long names were, as we have seen, amongst the Greeks and Romans confined to men of rank. Their great ladies, we may suppose, appreciated them also, for at the luxurious banquets of Greece and Rome men drank to the health of their lady-loves as many cups of wine as there were letters in their names. The fair Greek Charitoblepharos, sig. one who has *beautiful eyebrows*, was no doubt a popular toast.

Anagrams have already been alluded to as amongst the many curious subjects opening out from the history of names. The 'anagramma' of the Greeks was at one time in high favour amongst ourselves. By the transposition of the letters composing the names of individuals and countries, appropriate epithets were sometimes discovered. The name of the attorney-general to Charles I., William Noy, a laborious man, was read, '*I moyl in law*;' better still, old England was '*golden land.*'

The simpler these anagrams are, the better. The transposition of a letter would connect two German words—leid, *sorrow*; lied, *song*—and illustrate the line all poets have felt to be true:—

He learned in suffering what he taught in song.

In the fifteenth and sixteenth centuries many books were written, composed entirely of these 'Pleasant Fancies' and 'Fair Conceits,' as they were called. One published in France, 1662, contains French and Latin verses, principally panegyrics on princes and great men. Two of the best of these anagrams, untranslatable of course, were:—

> Anne d'Autriche,
> Reine de haut ran*g*.*
>
> Paulus Apostolus,
> Tu salvas populos.†

Though carried at one time to a ridiculous extent, the subject cannot be regarded as wholly without interest, remembering that Galileo, when persecuted by ignorant bigots, disdained not to make use of anagrams. In them he embodied some of his scientific discoveries, as the only means by which they could be preserved secret and inviolate.

Prophecies were also occasionally put forth in anagrams. Many such issued from a Provençal of the name of Billon, to whom Louis XIII. gave an annual pension of 1,200 livres, thereby securing, no doubt, the line which his prophecies should take.

Amongst the most remarkable anagrams are some connected with religious subjects.

The anxious enquiry which burst from the lips of the time-serving Roman governor, and which has again and again rung through the universe, uttered by the quivering lips of unhappy men who, like Pilate, are striving to serve two masters—that solemn enquiry, 'What is truth?'—has been made in Latin to answer itself in the person of Him to whom it was addressed: 'Quid est veritas?' by transposing the letters be-

---

* *g* to be accepted for *c*, we suppose.
† Noël's Dictionnaire Historique.

comes 'Est vir qui adest'—'It is the man who is here.'

Acrostics, or verses in which the initial letters of each line form a name or word, are amongst the instances of wasted ingenuity which may be found in connection with names.

To Eusebius *Pamphili* (so called in memory of his martyred friend Pamphilus), Bishop of Cæsarea, who lived in the fourth century, has been attributed the supposed discovery of a copy of verses, professedly by the Erythrean Sibyl. The poem put forth as delivered by her—who predicted, it was said, the Trojan war and its issue—described the coming of the Judgment-Day. The initial letters of the lines composed the Greek words, Iêsoûs Christos, Theou Uios, Sôtêr, sig. '*Jesus Christ, Son of God, Saviour.*' The initial letters of these words being then put together, the Greek word Ichthus, *fish*, is discovered, a fish having been early adopted by the Christian Church as a sacred symbol.

Acrostics, as many old books remain to prove, long continued in favour. In the fifteenth century, Frederic III. of Austria delighted in such exercises of ingenuity. A species of acrostic composed by him was printed on his books, engraved on his plate, carved upon his buildings: it consisted of the five vowels, and as a riddle excited much curiosity even amongst learned men of the time. After his death the secret was revealed by an interpretation written in his own hand:—

A̲lles ustria E̲rdreich st I̲st mperare O̲esterreich rbi U̲nterthan. niverso*

The Latin and German, freely translated, so as to preserve the conceit, may be read:—

Austria's Empire Is Overall Universal.

In the sixteenth century Sir John Davis, a poetical judge, compounded a dainty dish to set before a queen in a volume containing twenty-six poems, all acrostics on Elizabeth Regina. They took the form of addresses to 'The Rose,' 'The Lark,' &c.

Addison tells us that in his day there were compound acrostics — verses being composed much in the same way as a weaver manufactures his ribands, edged by a name at each extremity, with the same name running down like a seam through the middle of the poem. There were also pentacrostics, where the name was repeated five times.

To match with these English follies may be mentioned the labours of a Greek of ancient times, misnamed Tryphiodorus, sig. *Giver of delight.* His self-inflicted penance consisted in the composition of an epic poem on the adventures of Ulysses, each division of the poem leaving out in succession one letter of the alphabet—the first part being called Alpha, because *no* 'a' was found therein; the second Béta, for a similar reason; and so on till all the letters of the alphabet

* Fugger. Coxe's Austria.

were in turn rudely called up, to show that their services could be dispensed with.

'Moses & Son,' 'Rowlands' Kalydor,' and other advertising houses seem now to enjoy a monopoly of acrostics. It would seem to have been felt at last an unwise thing to prefer jolting along on Pegasus with hobbled feet, his wings (the especial glory of the celestial steed) the meanwhile trailing uselessly on the ground.

But lest there should still be some whose tastes incline them to the laborious amusement of anagram or acrostic writing, I would, as a warning of the fearful risks attendant on such pursuits. recall a lamentable story told by Addison as having happened in his day!

A gentleman, suddenly enamoured of a fair lady, whose name he was told was the Lady Mary Boon, determined to win her affections by the desperate achievement of an anagram on her name. For this purpose he shut himself up in the strictest confinement for six months. The enterprise was at last accomplished, but not without some liberties taken with his subject. Mary he found unmanageable: he ventured therefore on its diminutive Moll. His task completed—we are not told what he did make out— the hopeful lover hastened to present the fruit of his labours to the lady of his love. But the fair one frowns. She is, in the first instance, vexed to see her Christian name Mary degraded to Moll, and she then coldly informs the gentleman that her surname he has mistaken altogether—it was the lordly name of Bohun, not the plebeian Boon.

Horror-struck at the irretrievable mistake, the wretched lover—his mind previously weakened by long and continuous application to the anagram—being totally overthrown by the sudden downfall of his hopes, in a few days became a raving lunatic.

And yet one plea may be advanced for anagrams and acrostics, if they are composed with greater accuracy than that of the unfortunate lover of Mary Bohun. The laboured lines may be as the setting to encase some precious stone, as the fossil gum which has preserved uninjured some rare insect or unique leaf of far-off times. Amber is often quadrupled in value from the specimen which it contains. Anagrams and acrostics, sufficiently good to have outlived their day, might be esteemed as a means of discovering the original spelling of some sought-for name.

How numberless and perplexing are the various forms which names assume as they pass from mouth to mouth of successive generations, none but a name-hunter can tell.

We meet with these wonderfully varying names everywhere; but let us now turn to one of the pretty Cornish holy wells. It is on the Trelawney property. Its arched roof is overgrown with silvery willows. It is overspread by a huge oak-tree garlanded with ivy. It is known as St. Nun's Well. Her legend is still preserved. She is said to have been the daughter of an Earl of Cornwall, and mother of St. David, the famous Archbishop of Menevia (now called St. David's), the patron saint of Wales. The waters of this holy well were supposed to cure insanity. Her chapel has passed away, and her name, too, is passing away from her pretty well, which is often now called the 'Piskies'' (or the Fairies') Well; and yet there was an ample choice amongst the many forms which her name has assumed in various chronicles:—

St. Nun, Nunne, Nonnet, Nunnites, Nunice, Nynnina, Neomena, and Niemyne.

And after all these variations of her name, other chroniclers speak of the mother of St. David as *a* nun, called by the name of Malearia.*

* Brady's Clavis Calendaria.

CHAPTER IX.

Antiquity of our baptismal names — Bible names the favourites in England — Art of name-making died out — Names connected with French and English revolutions characteristic — English diminutives of names: their love for them of ancient date — Christian converts clinging to old names — Origin of the popularity of some names — Peter, Catharine, Paul, and Margaret — Successive causes influencing the adoption of names — Our patron saints — Heroes and saints, honoured men and women, romances, &c. — Names beginning with Z — Suggestions for new names from the Spanish, &c. — Nameless creditors — Names amongst Africans, North American Indians, Hindus — Jews and Arabians.

WITH but very few exceptions, all our baptismal names are older than—as a people—we are ourselves. Modern nations have done comparatively nothing to increase the treasury of individual names. Christianity—with its sublime inspirations, its deep and far-spreading influence over thoughts and words and deeds—has made but a very slender addition to the store.

It is by names borrowed from the Assyrian, the Persian, the Hebrew, the Greek, the Roman, the Celt, and the Goth, that Christian Europe enrols her children in the vast army of Christ.

To this rule the small exception will be found in a few names of Spanish, Italian, and French invention, of which the greater number have been derived from the Latin.

The religious element, which is more strongly developed in Spain than in any other Roman Catholic country, there assumes with regard to names a different form from its simple manifestation in England.

Our open Bibles have given to us our favourite names—of women's names especially, those most universally in use are all of Hebrew origin. Our poorer classes seldom care to go beyond 'Bible names,'* as they are most expressively called, for in that their charm enduring for many centuries consists, wholly irrespective of signification.

The great body of our people look upon names as typical of those that have borne them, and therefore it is that while Protestant England shrinks from undue homage to the Virgin Mary, her name, as that of the 'blessed among women,' the mother of our Lord, is heard in every house throughout the land; and almost as common among them is the name of the 'beloved' disciple John.

The sweet name of Mary, as '*Marie*' or '*Maria*,' is also the universal favourite in Roman Catholic countries; it is constantly prefixed to

* 'Bible names.' Amongst soldiers, sailors, agriculturists, and mechanics, even such names as Josiah, Jeremiah, Jesse, Noah, Obadiah, &c., may be commonly found; and Keziah, Rachel, and Ruth amongst the women of the same class. What joy to think that *possibly* a knowledge of the signification of such names may be blessed to some at least as an occasional *reminder*! Jeremiah, '*one who gives glory to Jehovah*,' or God; Obad-iah, '*the servant of God.*'

other names, and not unfrequently even to those of men.

We read that in part of Bavaria Maria is affixed to every woman's name, and Johann to that of every man.*

The musical Spanish name, Dolores, signifying *sorrow*, almost a synonyme with Mary, was adopted as commemorative of the sorrows of the Virgin mother: in spite of its sad meaning it is an especial favourite. In Italy and Spain—also introduced in honour of the Madonna—we find commonly used the names of Immaculata, Concepcion, and Annunziata, signifying the Annunciation. In connection with this last is the still prettier, simpler name, Ave, a favourite name amongst them.

Derived from the Hebrew 'haveh,' so beautiful an idea attaches itself to this word, that it may well have become a popular name.

In this *first* word of the angel Gabriel's salutation to the Virgin are reversed, both in Hebrew and Latin, the letters which compose our first mother's name, Hevah, Eva; and thus it becomes significant of the rolling back of the curse entailed by her upon mankind, by the blessing which at that moment Mary, as the mother of the Redeemer, was appointed to convey.

Some of these foreign Roman Catholic names jar painfully upon English ears. Unfitted surely

---

* Rev. J. Robertson's Narrative of Mission to Danish Islands.

for familiar use are the names, common amongst Spanish women, of Jesusa, and its diminutive Jesusita, and the yet more solemn appellation of Trinidada.

But others of these continental names unused by us refer to religious festivals in our church. The French Domenique, Italian Domenico, Spanish Domingo, signifies '*the Lord's day*,' or '*belonging to the Lord.*' Pascal, almost a saintly name, is from the Hebrew Pascha, *passage*, the Jews' Passover and our Easter. Epiphanie, Epiphany, from the Greek, to *appear*, to *shine*, as a woman's name had its French diminutive Tiphaine,* rendered in English by Tiffany, as in the old lines referring to one of the Breton knights who came to England in William the Conqueror's time:—

> William de Coningsby
> Came out of Brittany,
> With his wife Tiffany,
> And his maid Manfas,
> And his dog Hardigras.

In the name of Evangeline, Evangelista (from the Gr., sig. *bringer of good news*), there is a sound of joy-bells ringing; and sweeter still, from moonlit Bethlehem softly echoes the angel's song in the lovely name of Nathalie, sig. the Nativity.

* From Theophania, the ancient name of the festival of Epiphany. Out of this word, when it became a name—a name ever a fertile source for a legend—sprang an imaginary personage, Theophania, the supposed mother of the three kings of the East. Salverte.

Its corresponding man's name, Noël, was once—as it well might be—a cry of joy.

But it would seem that with rare exceptions the art of inventing names is one of those arts which have died out amongst civilised nations. On two occasions when revolutionised countries sought to inaugurate a new order of things by new names, the attempt in both cases proved a failure. But even in these unsuccessful attempts the guiding principles apparent in both were, in their direct opposition to each other, strikingly characteristic of the respective nations and the spirit of the revolutions.

Goaded, alas! by years of misrule—and, still worse, the mind of the nation having been corrupted by the sight of vice triumphant in high places—France, in her desperate and cruel madness, denied her God, and flooded her land with her children's blood.

Amongst other pagan names which, in that they were pagan, found especial favour, was one peculiarly appropriate—Brutus, sig. '*irrational*,' '*brutish*.'*

In another instance they were equally unconsciously but singularly correct in their choice of a watchword. In that frenzied cry, 'Les *aristo-*

---

* Vide Ainsworth's Latin Dictionary; our word *brute*, explained as 'senseless,' 'savage,' 'ferocious,' being derived from Lat. brutus. Vide Todd's Johnson.

> 'The *brute* philosopher, who ne'er has proved
> The joy of loving or of being loved.'—*Pope*.

crats à la lanterne!' (Death to the aristocrats!), the monsters who used the word to condemn others little dreamt that they were ever their own accusers. Aristocrates, the name of a king of Sparta, literally signifies the *rule* or *power* of the *best*.*

Did not the leaders of the French revolution seek to destroy 'the *rule of the best*—nay, all that was holy and good—when they forbade teachers to pronounce the name of God in their tuition of the children of the people;'† when the president and members of the commune outraged decency by paying homage to an infamous woman under the name of the Goddess of Reason; when, not content with inventing horrible deaths for the living—saintly men, virtuous women, innocent boys and girls, and sinless babes — they violated the grave itself to insult and mock at the silent dead?

None were spared, living or dead—no reputation, no age, no sex, no rank. Amongst the coffins of the royal dead one was missing: it was that which contained the body of a young daughter of Louis XV., who had fled from a gay

---

* ἄριστος (aristos), '*best*, and so in all sorts of relations, like ἀγαθός (agathos), to which it serves as superlative, in Homer usually *best, bravest, noblest* . . . . first transferred in Att. to moral goodness.'—*Liddell and Scott*, p. 182.

κράτος, ' might, power, rule.'—*Ibid.* p. 770.

Aristocracy is literally the 'rule of the best,' opposed to oligarchy, ' government in the hands of a few.'—*Ibid.* p. 959.

Aristarchy, sig. 'best men in power,' was a word once used in the English language. Todd's Johnson's Dict.

† Lamartine's Histoire des Girondistes, vol. iii. pp. 301, 303, &c.

but sinful court to lead a life of self-denial in a nunnery. The body of the blameless maid was sought for in its cloistered tomb, that it might be exposed to contumely with the rest. For about thirteen centuries the memory of St. Geneviève had been venerated by her countrymen, the holy and heroic peasant-girl, whose influence, extending to the fiercest of barbarian conquerors, had saved Paris from being crushed by the iron heel of Attila,* and by whose saintly life Clovis, King of France, and Clotilde, his wife, were subsequently converted to Christianity. These hallowed remains of the patroness of their city the madmen dragged from their resting-place, carried to the Place de Grève infamous as a place of criminal punishment, where they were burnt, and their ashes scattered to the winds.

The poverty of invention in the French revolutionists was apparent in the names given to their decade of days. In the dry bones of numerals there is no power of laying hold on the affections of man. Be it what it may, a name to *live* must spring from something which has *life*; colour or form, at the least, it must have, or the love of man will not cling to it; so the primedi, duodi, tridi of revolutionary days were soon abandoned. In the names of their months they attempted a more attractive style of nomenclature, but it had no claims to originality. Centuries before, our

* Anquetil's Histoire de France.

Anglo-Saxon forefathers had given significant names to the months, and for their ideas of the 'slippy, droppy, showery, flowery' names, the French were indebted to an almanack which had long been in use in Holland.

But, significant as were the revolutionary names of months, the horrors with which such names were associated sufficed to make them odious. The scent of blood was over them all; and when the Reign of Terror was fully overthrown, men, shuddering, turned from all possible reminiscences of a time when, as it has been well said by an historian of the period, 'the horror of living removed the horror of death.'*

Except in the one foul blot of regicide, the English revolution has no resemblance to the French. Violence, injustice, self-righteousness, and culpable ambition were the crimes of the Puritans; but they were not bloodthirsty—they never denied their God!

Compare for a moment the pictures we have of the leaders of the two revolutions. See that of Marat, Collot d'Herbois, Couthon, Carrier, and, above all, Robespierre, in his silken gala-coat, with cruel eye and cruel smile—alas for the innocent flowers he wore shivering on his hyæna breast! Now look through any gallery of old portraits—a child will tell you which are the pictures of the English regicides. Iron-

---

* Lamartine's Hist. des Girondistes.

clad, cropped-haired—how stern and joyless are their faces! Have they the look of men whose *pastime* was murder?

For them this much may at least be said. They must have often turned aside from, but they did not quench, the light of conscience. Are not their brows knitted like men oppressed by too strong a light? And in such painful consciousness may there not be hope in the end?

Such names as the Ironsides and Puritans generally assumed, do they not show—to such as sweep them not all away in a reckless charge of hypocrisy—a feeling after God?

We are shocked by the seeming irreverence of such names as '*Praise God* Barebones,' '*More fruit* Fowler,' '*Fight the good fight of faith* White,' '*Kill sin* Pimple;' while the ludicrous unfitness of the accompanying surnames cannot but provoke a smile. But if you give the subject a moment's thought, we shall find that in such a name as '*Praise God*,' strange and unseemly as it sounds to us, there is no more real irreverence than in three-fourths of the Hebrew names—such as Judah, '*Praise the Lord*;' Joel and Elijah, synonymes, transpositions of the words '*Jehovah is God*.'

Many Hebrew names, when translated, make sentences as long as 'Fight the good fight of faith.' Some of them, indeed, are absolute prayers; but in Hebrew a letter may express a whole word. In Eastern languages generally, the power of cutting off letters and syllables, and words being understood though not expressed, make sentences like these practicable for names, which in our language they never could be.

With regard to the fashioning of these strangely sounding Puritan names, in remembering how unmanageable were their materials, we must remember, also, how untaught and clumsy were the workmen's hands, for the work was attempted by uneducated men. The unfitness of these names, so apparent to all, made them short-lived. Those of their women, being simpler, were of longer continuance; but Prudence, Faith, Temperance, and Truth were, from their prosaic and positive form, not sufficiently attractive to gain lasting favour.

Had not the recollection of the significance of names been already allowed to pass away, men would have found, fashioned in beauty to their hand, sweet names expressive of the glorious qualities they prized. Long since had *Truth* been symbolised as a jewel by the Egyptians, a sapphire ornament worn by the high-priest, called by the Greeks 'aletheia,'* or 'alethe;' and idealised by the bards of the North as Gertrude, *the maiden trusted and true*; and simply named by the Latins ' Vera,' *true*. Faith might be read in Elizabeth, one who *worships* or *trusts*

* Liddell and Scott, p. 57.

in God; while Mildred, *gentle of speech*, might well represent one who was of a temperate and equable mind.

As may be seen, therefore, England does not possess the art of name-making. It is not that poetic feeling is wanting in our land. We are rich in poets—our misty atmosphere seems redolent of inspiration. From castle and hall, from the dark lanes of our cities, from the breezy uplands of our villages, they come forth—highborn and lowborn, sons of the shuttle, sons of the plough—true thinkers, sweet singers all. English poets have made themselves known and loved in all lands. But as a nation we are wanting in that, it would seem, indefinable thing that all nations have agreed to call *taste*—the wanting of an especial and right word to define it showing how rare a gift it is.

Women are laughed at for applying the word *nice* alike to people and puddings; but how is it that wise men do not think it equally unsuitable for one word, *taste*, to be in like manner applied to the definition of the flavour of these same puddings, and to the perception of what is befitting?

The word 'æsthetic' may be called affected; but what other word can we use to express a sense or perception of the beautiful and befitting in all things? In this sense, it would seem, we are deficient. It is not only that we cannot compose lovely and suggestive names, but we sadly spoil many that we have adopted from other languages.

How is sweet Mary degraded to Poll, without an excuse—not one letter of the original retained in the diminutive? The 'New Zealander' of future days, should he have a taste for name-hunting, will find it hard to prove to his satisfaction that Mary and Poll were the same name. Peggy and Meg, too, for Margaret, Patty for Martha, might puzzle him too; and many like instances may be found.

Susannah has Susan, Sukey, Susie, Sue. Elizabeth has a still wider choice—the name boasts more diminutives than it has letters; and some of them are really pretty. Eliza, Ellie, Lizzie, Lisa, Libby, Bessie, Betsy, Betty, Bettina, Betha, with the Scotch Elspeth and Elsie. Elisa reversed makes a pretty name, Asile, and has a pretty meaning in French—a *refuge*.

Our national fancy for diminutives is of long standing. We read that, A.D. 608, the sons of Sigebert, King of the East Saxons, demanded* from Laurentius, successor to St. Augustine, that he should give them, though unbaptised, the 'white bread' of the Holy Communion, which they had seen their 'father *Sæb*' (a professed Christian) receive.

Almost as bad as our Jue for Julia, and Matty for Matilda, is the German Trud*chen* for

* Thierry's Norman Conquest.

Gertrude; another of their diminutives is prettier —Sophi*ele*.

The pretty feminine termination, 'ine,' so common in French names, Evel*ine*, Adel*ine*, may have had its origin in, or is at least a pretty reminder of, the Teutonic 'wyn,' *beloved*.

The Italian and Spanish ella, illa, and ita, are all musical. Compare the Spaniard's Mariquita and Juanita with our Polly and Jenny. As we have seen in Dolores, and also in Mercedes (sig. *grace, favour*), the Spaniards have shown a more graceful and musical talent in the invention of names than any other modern nation. Their pretty Nina, signifying a *young girl*, has become in other lands a proper name, as its synonymes, Greek Cora, and Teutonic Hilda, might also be. In Spain, Inez grew out of Agnes, and Isabel out of Elizabeth; with French peasants, Isabella became Zabillet, the name of the mother of noble-hearted Joan of Arc. The Spaniards were also happy in their adaptation of Gothic names—many improved in their hands. Is not Gomez an improvement on Gomesind, sig. a *good youth*? It is curious to mark how, travelling from the far North, Gunstaff, *war-staff*, significant of courage, grew softer in sound as it drew near the South, assuming first a Latin form, Gustavus, and then in Spain becoming Gonsalez and Gonsalvo—a name dear to all lovers of heroes as that of 'the Great Captain' of the fifteenth century.*

The difficulty we have found so insuperable has never existed in the East. At this moment new names are happily conceived to express new states of feeling. Missionary records tell us of two Sikh soldiers, lately converted to Christianity, who were baptised by the respective names of Ummur Mesech, sig. '*Life from Christ*, or the *Messiah*,' and Mesech Cheran, sig. '*Footstool of Christ*,' figuratively *subject* to Him. In Abyssinia a name invented for a Christian convert was Zera Haimanot, '*Seed of Faith.*'

It would seem, therefore, that, so far as the classes of names in greatest favour amongst different nations may help us to judge of their characteristics, the test can only be strictly applied to nations of old, by whom they were invented, and with whom their signification was

---

* The language and the land of Spain were alike enriched by her Moorish masters. Never have conquerors left behind them so shining a track as the Arabs have left in Spain. Her palms and pomegranates and many a fair tree and lovely flower were gifts from the Saracens, children of the *rising sun*; her most beautiful buildings in their form, and many of her most musical and expressive words by their sound, betray their Eastern origin.

Ruy or Rodrigo Diaz de Bivar, a mighty conqueror of the Moors (A.D. 1040), is only known by the name bestowed by them on him—the Cid, from El Seid, or Seydna, the *Lord*, a title borne by Hassan, the mountain chief of the Ismaïlite Fedavec (the *devoted*), or Assassins. No fewer than 102 ballads of the thirteenth and fourteenth centuries are said at this moment to exist in Spain, of which the Cid—the King Arthur of Spain—is the hero.

never lost sight of. With the peoples of modern times, we may at least mark how the tide of public favour has set now in one direction and now in another, with more or less permanent effect, according as the impelling force was more or less powerful. There have been fashions in names as in all things else—sometimes a mere caprice, of which the effect was but for a day; sometimes the result of deeper feeling, of which the impression has been abiding. Such, we have seen in England, has been the case with Bible names.

One of the stumbling-blocks in the way of the standard-bearers of the Cross in our islands was our forefathers' attachment to the old names. To them the names of their dead were almost as sacred as their sepulchres. Men's hearts were bound about the old familiar names of that 'long ago.' In war they were the battle-cry of brave men; in peace they became the burden of the bard's and the maiden's songs. Even as with us now, loved names were living and abiding memories.

In those far days, when the faint dawning of Christianity had but gilded the hill-tops, not flooded with light the plains and valleys of the whole land, to the hermit preachers and the monks certain names sounded ominously of the darkness of paganism not yet passed away. The shepherd's flocks were but too apt to stray away, and mischief seemed to lurk in certain names.

To anxious ears, in Ulf, and Saewulf, and Ethelwulf, the howl of the *wolf* sounded dismally of superstitions still lying in wait: in the grand old name of Hugues (or Hugh), which was sacred alike in Celtic and Teutonic mythology, the flap of the raven's wing was heard—Huginn being one of the sacred birds of Odin, whose name sig. *spirit* and *power*.

This clinging to old names was a feeling also in other lands, and converts to Christianity everywhere amongst the Gaels and the Goths battled long for the right of bringing their fathers' names to the font. In vain St. Chrysostom preached and Gregory the Great (Gregory sig. in Greek *vigilant*) denounced the practice; a decree issuing from the Papal chair, which limited the choice of Christian converts to certain names, was sullenly and but partially obeyed.

The temporal arm was not more indulgent than the spiritual. In the fourteenth century, a king of Poland, on being converted to Christianity, added to his national name, Jagellon, that of Vladislaüs (Greek form of Wladyslaw), sig. the *glory of power*, the V being a contraction of Vasileus, *royal*; his brother Witwold took the name of Conrad (Kuhnrath), sig. *wise counsellor*. The king was graciously pleased to allow his nobles and warriors to receive separate baptism, and to have an individual choice of names; but the people were baptised *en masse*. To the first division of men and women were given respectively the names of Peter and Catharine, to the second those of Paul and Margaret: Catharine from the sainted princess of Egypt, Margaret from the martyred maid of Antioch, and Peter and Paul were perhaps from the two celebrated hermits rather than from the apostles of that name. Amongst those dirty darlings of mediæval times were Peter, the preacher of the Crusades, and the still more celebrated Paul of Thebes, founder of the Anchorites. He is said to have lived for ninety-eight years alone in a desert to the east of the Nile—his dwelling a cavern near a date-palm, his only food the fruit of the tree, his only garment a rude mat woven from its leaves.

But before such stringent rules were made as to what names Christians should bear, Gregory should have looked back at the list of his own predecessors as bishops of Rome. Amongst many others of similar import he would have found Eleutherius, a Greek name sig. *liberty*, and formerly used as a designation both of Jupiter and Bacchus; Zephyrinus, the west wind deified, sig. a *bringer of life*; and, stranger still, Hormisdas, the *sun-god* of Persia.

The names of heathen gods and goddesses are heard amongst Christians to this day; but so late as A.D. 1198 a king of Servia bore the not common name of Vulcan; and in a church at Venice a monument of about three centuries later records as the baptismal name of a wife of one of the Doges, Dea, *goddess*—Dea Morosini. In parts of Greece, bordering on Turkey, Christians frequently join Moslem names with their own—Fatmé-Katharine, Ayesha-Maria, Ali-John, and Mustafa-Constantine.*

The early Christian martyrs who bore such names as Jovian (descended from Jove), and Dionysius (or Denys), *consecrated to Bacchus*, did none the less bravely die for the faith. We do not find that St. Paul saw mischief in Christians bearing names which had been endeared to them by family associations; he speaks of his 'brother Apollos;' and his 'sister' Phœbe, as a servant of the Church, he affectionately commends to the disciples at Corinth. As a 'Bible name,' Phœbe is often heard in the cottages of our English poor, separated long since from all connection of ideas with the great goddess Diana of the Ephesians; its lovely meaning of *the light of life*, radiant and pure, may well be remembered by Christians, and laid to heart.

It has been observed as singular, by Roman Catholics themselves, that in Italy, the seat of the Papal power, little attachment has ever been shown to those names which the pure lives and glorious deaths of the martyrs of the early Christian Church have endeared to other lands. Rome's catacombs are illumined with saintly names; and pilgrims come from afar off to read them with kindling eyes and throbbing hearts; but she cares rather (her greater families at least)

* Salverte.

to recall such names as are linked with the triumphs of pagan Rome and the wild mythology of ancient Greece. France has largely shared this classical mania: England and the nations of the North have been less affected by it.

But the touching legends that Italy cared not so much to call to mind in her children's names found an undying echo in our distant isles. The story of the martyred Egyptian princess, Katharine the *pure*, gave to us one of our most favourite names; another came to us from the maid of Antioch, 'Mild Margarete that was God's maid.'

In the wild tale of St. Margaret, swallowed alive by a dragon, whose body bursting she issues from it unhurt, the same allegory appears which is common to most of the legends of the early Church, figurative of the power of faith in Christ to overcome the power of the Evil One. In the figure of the saint in Henry VII.'s chapel, Westminster, we see its representative upholding the Cross—she tramples on the dragon. In reference to the beautiful signification of her Greek name, St. Margaret generally wears a fillet of *pearls*, and, from the flower which has been devoted to her and called by her name, *daisies* are often placed in her lap.

Amongst the names of Englishwomen Katharine and Margaret rank next in favour to Mary, Anne, Mary-Anne, Elizabeth, Sarah, and Jane, all these last being of Hebrew origin.

In the warlike St. George of Cappadocia, patron of chivalry, we also see a conqueror of the dragon as figurative of sin. 'St. George for merry England!' was the battle-cry chosen for Englishmen by Richard the Lion-heart, while warring with the infidel to set the Holy City free, and place the Holy Sepulchre in the guardianship of Christian swords. Centuries have rolled by, and not yet has the Church's darling dream been fulfilled; but the day will come.

'Cœur de Lion' was almost a synonyme of our brave Richard's Teutonic name, which signifies *great heart*, of which a lion would be figurative. 'Ric' sig. *a chief*, one that was *great, powerful, valiant*, and like 'hard,' signifying *nature, heart*, entered into the composition of many names. Germans still express by the word 'art,' *race, nature, disposition*. St. George sig. in Greek *a cultivator*. Though long our patron saint, George has never been one of our most popular names: for a long succession of years Englishmen in all parts of the world have answered to the name of *John* Bull.

From Ireland's patron saint, St. Patrick, came 'Paddy,' the Irishman's sobriquet. As such it is now applied to a whole nation, but 'patricius,' *noble*, was in its original sense confined to three hundred ruling families of ancient Rome. May not patricians, as rulers, still find a suggestive lesson in the close connection in the original of the words *noble* and *fatherly*?

Taffy the Welshman takes the diminutive of

the name of his patron, St. David, which in Heb. sig. the *beloved.* The Archbishop of Menevia (now St. David's, called after him) was a son of the British Prince of Cereticu (now Cardiganshire) and uncle to King Arthur. He died A.D. 642, having, it is said, lived 146 years. The victory of Cadwallader over the Saxons, in memory of which the Welsh wear leeks on St. David's day (the 1st of March), was owing, under God, they believe, to the 'beloved' Archbishop, who wisely suggested that the Britons should wear some distinguishing mark; and leeks were hastily gathered from a garden adjoining the battle-field.* The harp, which for love of her ancient bards Wales chose as her cognisance, suits well with the name of her patron saint—the name of the Royal Harpist of Israel.

A Scotchman's nickname of Saunders is from Alexander: his patron saint is St. Andrew. Unthought of by many, the names are closely connected, both from the Greek, and in part derived from the same word—an epithet which Scotia's hardy sons have never belied. Andrew, from 'Andros,' sig. a *man of courage*; Alexander, connecting with this 'Alexein,' to protect, sig. a *brave protector* or *defender.*

Scotland's choice of her patron is said to have arisen in the fourth century, when some of his supposed relics were taken to that country. St. Andrew is also the patron saint of Russia, and of the

* Brady's Clavis Calendaria.

Burgundian order of knighthood of the Golden Fleece. And well might princes be proud to wear a badge with St. Andrew's name, and Englishmen cherish St. Andrew's Cross (united to that of St. George, as the Union *Jack*), for nobly did the lowly-born fisherman of the Sea of Galilee live up to his name, matchlessly brave, a true soldier of Christ. How terrible was his martyrdom! But, hallowed to him by the sufferings of his Lord, he hailed his cross as 'precious'—his faith, his courage never failed, as, tied with ropes to the transverse beams, he lingered for two whole days in his death of agony.

It is singular to remark how not one of these national sobriquets is derived from national names; yet England had her Arthur—

> The first of all the kings who drew
> The knighthood errant of this realm, and all
> The realms together, under him their Head.
> *Idylls of the King.*

Arth, the Bear, the dazzling constellation of our winter skies — Arcturus, the glory of the north — was, it is believed, the noble origin of this nobly illustrated name — the *Bear* having always been significant of courage. And after centuries had gone by, the grand old name again blazed forth, and Arthur, the name of England's invincible duke, became, as we shall see, a 'household word.'

Scotland has never forgotten her Fergus, Gaelic for the *strong arm*; nor Ireland her Dermot, from

Diarmid, derived (I would *suggest*) from the sacred tree of the Druids, Duir, sig. the *Oak* (preserved in Cornish dialect as Dar), and Meod, *Father*, a grandly significant name for a chief, the Oak-father (*S*). Wales, too, keeps her two old names, which so strongly contrast with each other—Llewellyn, the *Lion*, and Owen, the *Lamb*.

Many of our old names have never died away, and it is curious to notice amongst the poorer classes how almost distinctive of different counties are certain names. In Hampshire will be found very commonly the Saxon names of Ellen and Emma. In Cornwall, the last stronghold of the Celtic race in England, we meet with striking analogies with the kindred race in Ireland. The broad sea flows between—there is no intimate connection kept up by commerce or other means —yet again and again are we there reminded of the innate sympathies of race. It may be in little things; but little things have voices as well as great things.

In Cornish cottages you will often hear two Christian names rarely heard amongst the poor in any other part of England, but (though not of Celtic origin) they are amongst the commonest names in Ireland, both in the upper and lower classes. They are two of the loveliest of Latin names, with the additional charm of requiring no translation—Grace and Honor, from which last has come the sweet name of Norah.

Dear, unspoiled, warm-hearted, kindly Cornwall has rather a peculiar taste in Christian names. The superb Greek name of Zenobia,* sig. *Life from Zeno,* Lord of Life, or Jupiter, and Philippa (Gr.), *Lover of Horses,* will there be found amongst farmers' wives; and amongst ladies the simpler but singular name of Sage. But Cornwall has stranger names than these. In a village not far from Falmouth, two farmers, brothers, are called Cherubim and Seraphim Johns! But strange names are heard out of Cornwall also. In Portsmouth, but a short time back, lived a girl called Azimuth! Her name, derived from an ancient Arabic word, sig. a *path,* a *track,* was no doubt bestowed by a sailor-father on his child in grateful recollection of the true old friend who had accompanied him in his voyages to and fro—the azimuth compass.

To 'Bible names,' and those first suggested by legends of saints and heroes of old, must be added such as have been adopted from time to time in honour of living characters. The preponderance of certain names almost make chronological tables in England.

Amongst our gallant soldiers, who, amidst the snows of the Crimea and on the burning plains of India, have shown that our race are still what they have ever been—unconquerable—there was

---

* In the neighbourhood of the ruins of Palmyra, amongst the women of the Anazeh, a Bedouin tribe, Zenobia is a common name to this day. 'They pronounce it Zenobēeah, which is said to be the original pronunciation.'—Beaufort's *Travels.*

many an Arthur; for, when those brave men were infants in their mothers' arms, from battle-plains and besieged cities in Spain and Portugal, blast after blast of the war-trumpet rang 'Victory!' 'Victory!' and the women of England, as they clasped their darlings to their breasts, in triumph called them by the name of England's conquering Duke.

A still greater darling of the nation was our naval hero, Nelson; but his Christian name, Horatio (said to be of Etruscan origin, and sig. *worthy to be beheld*), had a strangely foreign sound, so, for their children born in his day, John Bull and Mary his wife made a Christian name out of Nelson itself.*

As a general rule, there is a shyness amongst English poor people of giving to their children any name at all out of the common.

I was once anxiously asked by a poor woman if I thought the name of Rhoda 'too fine for a girl who would have to work for her living.' Reminding her that it was a Bible name, I told her its pretty meaning—a *rose*; but I did not frighten her by saying that it was Greek! On another occasion I warmly supported a young mother's wish that her first little girl should be named Janet. It was simple enough, one would think; but some of the family objected to it as

---

* Thereby restoring part of the name to its original station. Neil son, or Nelson, the son of Neil: abbreviation of Nathaniel, Jamieson says; others say of Nigel.

'out of the way'—'Why could n't she just call it Jane?'

That the name of Adelaide (Teutonic Adelhilda, sig. *noble lady, noble maiden*) should have made its way into English homes of all classes, was therefore the higher compliment to the good Queen whom the nation desired to honour. And is not Albert a 'household word' with us? Well will it be for all, both rich and poor, if they—like the noble Prince England has so truly mourned—*answer to their names*, for only the *pure* in heart are truly *bright*. Albert is *bright, excellently bright,* derive it which way we please, from Al-brecht, *altogether* bright; or from Adal- or Ethel-bert, *noble and bright, illustrious*.

Romances which have left such determined tracks on the Christian names of other nations have not, at least in later days, left much impression on ours. The days of chivalry—the days of the chronicles of martyred saints—once past, it would seem that England, having once chosen her household names, cared little to add to them except at rare intervals when powerfully moved. Even Shakspeare's magic wand failed to conjure up Ophelias, Desdemonas, Imogenes, and Perditas.* For a short time it was in England, as elsewhere, the fashion for poets to

---

* To avoid repeated breaks in the sentence, when many names come together, their significations will be deferred to the classified list at the end.

sing of their mistresses as Delia, Chloe, Phyllis, &c.; but these names seldom or ever passed into real life. The Lady Bettys and Lady Kittys of Richardson's day wept over his 'Pamela' and 'Clarissa Harlowe,' but all the same did they give to their little daughters their own names of Elizabeth and Katharine, which their mothers and grandmothers had borne before them.

It may, therefore, be a just cause of pride to an American writer of our day to know how many little Evas England has in all classes. Not only Evas, but dark-eyed pretty little Topsies, too, answer to their names in English infant schools. Happy little English 'Topsy Steele,' unconscious are you of the wide contrast, as of light and darkness, which divides your life from that of the class of which the slave-child whose strange name you bear was a type.

The French take more easily to new names than we do. Dante's Beatrice, Petrarch's Laura, Tasso's Erminia, and Clelie, Isaure, Aurelie, &c., of other romances, once adopted by the upper classes, soon found their way to the lower ranks of the people. At an English hotel you will scarcely be wrong to call a chambermaid Mary Anne, Elizabeth, or Jane; in France you are far more likely to be right if you hazard Virginie, Zéphyrine, Adèle, or Cécile.

At one time a novel idea seized French romance and play-writers. The last letter of the alphabet, after a long life of comparative obscurity, was suddenly raised to preeminence. Every heroine was provided with a name beginning with a Z. It became, par excellence, *the* letter of the alphabet. Zulma, Zelie, Zenaïde, Zaïre, Zelidie, and a very long list besides. A writer of the day ridiculed the fashion by announcing the forthcoming History of Prince Zzzzzz!*

But may not a few of these names beginning with Z be acceptable in England? We sadly want a little more variety, and amongst Arabic names there are some as pleasing in significance as they are musical in sound.

Zulma or Zuleima (also spelt Suleyma) is from Selim or Salim, sig. *healthful*; Zarifa, sig. *graceful*; Zara, *splendour*, the *brightness of the East*; and Zaidee, *abundance* or *prosperity*.

From the Greeks we may have Zelie, *zealous*; Zoë, a synonyme with Eve, sig. *life*; and Zenaïde, one who *lives modestly*, almost a synonyme with *violet*, which is itself in English and in Greek, Ianthe, a lovely name. How seldom do we hear the sweet names of lily, rose, and violet! Giacinta is the pretty Italian feminine form of *hyacinth*, which as a man's name is common in Ireland and France. Besides our large stock of unused though beautiful names, may we not, as they do in the East, find many new names of pleasant sound and significance amongst trees and flowers? *Iva* (a name given to one of the milfoils) has a soft simple

* Noël's Dictionnaire Historique.

sound, and, though 'bad Latin,'* may recall the idea of ivy, ever the symbol of a loving constant nature. In the far-away forests of Brazil and Guayana a palm-tree grows which is found in no other part of the world. Its botanical name is Mauritia flexuosa; but the beloved and kindly tree from which their almost every want may be supplied is called by the natives of Brazil *Miriti*, and by those of Guayana *Itá* (pronounced *E*ta). English hearts cling closely to old familiar things, nor would we for an instant wish that one long-loved Christian name should ever drop away from the shining circlet of gem-like names which crowns so many English homes with happiness. Let us cherish our Marys and Elizabeths still; but we have room for many new names without losing any old ones. In families with large connections the constant repetition of the same Christian names (in some cases accompanying the same surnames) makes confusion, and somewhat of the individuality of the name is lost. It also leads to many of those very eccentric compositions, English diminutives, which of themselves would form a curious chapter.

These dear old names are frequently thus repeated over and over again, out of true love; but sometimes it is only because they come handiest. In poor people's families it is by no means uncommon for sisters to be called Elizabeth and Eliza, Mary and Maria, and Mary Anne.

* Ainsworth's Latin Dict.

Juana and Juanita,* the pretty Spanish forms of Jane and Jenny, might sound foreign and strange at first, but ere long they would be naturalised. Elizabeth is thought of and spoken of as a 'good old-fashioned English name;' but the land of its birth was far Palestine, and from the Hebrews did those merchant-sailors—our visitors of old, the Phœnicians—adopt it. Their Princess, the founder of Carthage, Queen Dido, in the home of her childhood, was called Elissa, and her mother's name was Anna. We have other names as familiar, and yet more ancient, and of more far-away extraction than Elizabeth. Have we not Persian lilies making glad our homes? Before the royal city of Shûshan, 'city of lilies,' took its name from the radiant flowers covering the plain upon which it was built, an Assyrian Princess had been called after them Sosana or Susana, daughter of Ninus before his marriage with Semiramis. From one of those bright 'lilies,' which in beauty excelled Solomon in all his glory (Iris Susiana, or Chalcedonia), the sweet name of Susan comes to us as a 'Bible name,' having been adopted by the Jews. As Souson, the Eastern lily's name was familiar to the Greeks, and to the Arabs as Soosan. Sophia has for its diminutive Sophy (in France and Germany the name is Sophie); but supposing the word (as I believe) to have been derived from the Sofi of the ancient Persians.

* The *j* in Spanish pronounced as a soft aspiration.

then is Sophy the original of the name, and of greater antiquity than the Greeks as a nation.*

With so many names of far-off origin naturalised amongst us so long, we need not shrink from admitting into our families a few more new and pretty names, particularly when they, in telling us where they come from and what they mean, bring, as it were, their credentials with them. The small number of Christian names made use of in England has long been a subject of remark; it leads to many inconveniences. The 104 'William M'Kays,' in the Sutherland regiment of 1793, is a well-known fact;† and in Army Lists of a few years back, 1, 2, and 3 were attached to 'John Gordons' as the names of officers. And with greater variety of choice, one would fain hope better taste (if not even higher views) may be brought to the pleasant task of choosing our children's names.

Without taking into account such names as the Registrar-General's documents afford— 'John Bottle of Beer,' 'Will Bill,' 'Faith Hope Charity Green,' which would seem rather to have been registered as idle jests than to be true designations—ridiculous names do meet us on all sides. To 'Anna Maria Julia Statira Johnson Thomson Kettleby Rundell,' and 'Joyful Moses

---

* Such suggestions as I venture to make are entirely and eagerly submitted to the kind correction of learned readers, if any such deign to look through my little volume.

† Stewart's Sketches of Highland Clans.

Lazarus Solomon,' *real* names as they are, every reader can supply many more from his or her recollection.

Beyond our subject, indeed, for they are not *names*, but within the scope of laughable designations, may we for an instant peep into the accounts of a small tradesman in a town in the West of England? The poor man, becoming bankrupt, reckoned amongst those to whom he had given credit, 'Fat Coal-woman,' ' Mrs. in the Cart,' 'Mrs. Feather Bonnet,' other ' Bonnets' of various kinds, and 'the Woman that told me of the Man!'

We have glanced at some of the causes which have influenced modern nations in their choice of names. The names themselves will tell us in what various directions lay the strongest sympathies of the nations of old.

Do any weary at the impending list of names? Think yet again! What are names? *Words* of especial meaning, instinct with life, lifted as they have been out of their fellows to be clothed with human individualities.

Names of the dead are as pictures or statues, but more imperishable are they than either canvas or marble. Each name, as the representative of an individual, has its true story to tell; and some of these stories are of noble and lovely lives.

Sometimes in a single name is a revelation of great joy or great sorrow, through which, at the moment of the child's birth, the people to whom it belonged might have been passing through.

Miriam, the *bitterness* of bondage, and the unhappy Hebrew mother's dying cry, Ichabod, *the glory has departed*, have their synonymes in other lands. We read of a traveller who, in far Kamschatcha, met amongst one of the tribes a girl, whose name, Ka-souktch, was explained to mean ' she who weeps,' for the mother, who at the moment beheld her country ravaged by strangers, had so baptised her infant with her tears.

In our own West India Islands, from which long since, thank God, the curse of slavery has been rolled away, a touching reminiscence of the dependent old days may be found in a name which is an especial favourite amongst the blacks —Mercy!

Grand-sounding names, such as Cleopatra and Anastasia, are also popular amongst negroes. An amusing peculiarity at one time existed in their assumption of not only the family names, but also the titles, of their former white masters. An old black man, of by no means a good character, was rather a scandal to a family in one of the islands—Sir Somebody Something's name appearing in the local papers as having been taken up—drunk.

It may perhaps be doubted by those who have no personal knowledge of Africans, but it is nevertheless true, that amongst them really handsome men and women may be found. The personal characteristics of various tribes are very distinct. A dear good old woman, and as pretty as she was good—for her features were too regular to be [injur]ed by age—was known to me as 'Princess.' Of the Ashantee tribe, it was said that she was descended from the royal race of her own country, and in remembrance she had been so named in the land of her exile.

Curious instincts of race meet one often in a search after names. Amongst the natives of Shangalla, names frequently express some trifling incident occurring at the moment of the infant's birth. One of these names is recorded by a traveller as sig. '*Born while the bouza* (a preparation of corn) was preparing.' A negro woman in the West Indies invented for her child the name of *See-fire*, she having been born while a fire was raging in the neighbourhood.

What a striking contrast do the Indian races of North and South America afford in all respects to the Africans domiciled on the continent and the neighbouring islands!

Put a few palm-leaves into the hands of an Indian on the banks of the Demerara: in a few moments you will see growing in beauty, beneath the dark slender fingers, a basket of graceful shape, or some domestic utensil neat and durable. To a red Indian girl of the North give a bit of cloth, some porcupine quills, and a few beads of bright colours: you will soon receive back a brilliantly-embroidered bag or a gay pair of moccasins. But offer the negro the most suggestive materials you can think of, and he or she will shake their woolly heads, show their white teeth, and with a peal of merry childlike laughter protest to their 'dear missy,' 'dose tings no good at all for poor blackie; dat white man's, white woman's work.'

From this entire absence of all innate sense of the beautiful, we cannot wonder at the difference which African names afford to those of other coloured races.

The brave Delaware, and the fierce Dacotah, whose war-cry is like the bark of an angry dog, are never at a loss for significant names, suggested to them on the instant by images of grandeur or beauty, either surrounding them or impressed on their memory—'*Bursts of thunder at a distance*,' or '*the pleasant sound of wind amongst the trees*,' will furnish poetical names for a son or a daughter.

In the Spanish parts of South America, the Indians have mostly adopted Spanish names, but such of their national names as do remain are significant of such images as 'Glittering Light,' 'Sunlight,' 'Fine Gold.'

But most of all do we find in our Indian Empire names and name-giving surrounded with all the elements of poetry.

Missionaries and travellers seldom, alas! care to repeat the actual names, but they tell us of many of their charming meanings.

Their ancient laws are remembered still, and Hindus choose, for their daughters especially, 'musical names of pleasing signification,' 'which sound like a blessing.' An inexhaustible treasury of names for men as well as women is furnished by the fairest of flowers, the brightest of jewels, beasts and birds if distinguished by beauty and grace, the dark-eyed gazelle, the majestic swan, radiant stars and shining rivers, lofty mountains and stately trees. To these are added the names of their gods and goddesses, and their peculiar attributes, 'Six-face,' 'Fiery face,' 'Three eyes'— exceptions certainly to their generally attractive list; but such names find great favour with them, inasmuch as the mere repetition of sacred names is in itself considered meritorious. Their 'praying cylinders' may be remembered as a strange example of such 'vain repetitions.'

There is much to interest in Arabic names. The reader may smile if, apropos to the sons of the desert, an old French proverb of aristocratic tendency is quoted, 'Bon sang ment jamais.' We should not forget that the sons of Ishmael are the sons of princely Abraham, Father of the Faithful. The seed of Ishmael, '*Heard of God*,' became, according to promise, a great nation; and, despite the deadening influences of a religion of fatalism, they long retained many of the elements of greatness. Let Europe say who caught the torch of Learning as it fell from the hands of exhausted Greece? From whom did Europe's physicians learn their first lessons in the healing art, if not from wise Arabians well skilled in all the circle of sciences? And who but our childhood's delight, Sindbad the sailor, and his brave countrymen, first dared the distant seas, to furnish the shivering North with the countless luxuries of tropical climates?

We find in Arab names, as in those of the Hebrew race, expressions of eager whole-hearted service to God. They delight in avowing dependence on Him, and love to recall His attributes. Abd-er-Rahman, *Servant of the Compassionate*; Abd-el-Melik, *Servant of the King* or the Most High; Abd-es-Selam, *Servant of* (the God of) *Peace*; for Allah, though not mentioned, is always understood in these compound names. Many of the Hebrew names are retained by them. Another of our nursery friends, Haroun-el-Rasheed, is *Aaron the Orthodox*; Mousa or Muza is Moses; Ayub, Job; Yusef, Joseph; Hanna, John; and amongst their women's names it is singular to find Hosn Maryam, sig. *The Beauty of Mary*, or Miriam. They are said, in some inexplicable manner, to confound in a model of female excellence Miriam the sister of Moses, and Mary the mother of our Lord.

We shall find that generally, throughout the East, the ideas of light, flowers, and jewels prevail in their names.

The Japanese, passionate lovers of flowers, cull from their gardens the *names* as well as the flowers themselves, to bestow on their women.

Arabs also add to their lists of fragrant flowers

a catalogue of sparkling gems—'trees of pearls,' and 'seas of treasure;' but most of all do they delight in names of light—'Sun of the Forenoon,' and 'Smiling Full Moon.'

Light has ever been like life in the East. The blazing sun-god of ancient Assyria and Persia shed its far rays even to our island in the misty North. In their long and mysterious pilgrimage from the East by land and 'hazy' sea, the Celts led by Hy Cadarn, or Hu the *Strong* or Mighty, must have brought with them the name and worship of Belus. Our king of Britain, Cymbeline, was in truth Cuno-bel-in, *Lord of the Sun.* Even amongst the cannibal natives of the Figian or Vitian Islands, we find the name of Valu-gaiaki (or '*rising moon.*') *

Love, too, has its synonymes in all lands. Even the Chinese have some names more befitting women than hateful numerals—their '*Little Darling*' may match with the Greeks' '*Little Love*,' and our Anglo-Saxon '*Dearly loved*' and '*Beloved.*'

Courage is met everywhere; lions and eagles are its highest types: Cyaxares the lion-king of Persia, Leonidas the truly lion-hearted king of Sparta, and our own Welsh Llewellyn. In the North, too, as significant of bravery, men have loved to call themselves *Bears* and *Wolves*, those fierce animals once so dreaded in our land. Our Anglo-Saxon forefathers had '*Noble Wolves*,' '*Bright Wolves*,' and '*Wolves of the Sea.*' The

* Seemann's Mission to Viti.

beasts have long since been extirpated, but the name is still strangely dominant in our gentle liege Lady's family name of Guelph.

But amongst human beings' individual names are to be found names of all creatures, from the Syriac rendering of Pharaoh's name, ' *Crocodile*,' [*] to Greek Psyllus, a *Bug*, which we do not read was abandoned by its owner for a more aristocratic-sounding name.

An ample list is before us, therefore, from which to cull and classify some specimens of the names of various nations.

Sun, moon, and stars to begin with—many a noble quality of mind, and exquisite personal charm—down to the poor African's Bourma Kassar, sig. '*Broken Vessel.*'

[*] Cruden.

CHAPTER X.

The four nations from whom our Christian names are principally derived, Hebrew, Greek, Latin, and Teutonic — Dominant note in each — Characteristics of Hebrew and Arabic names, of Greek, of Latin, of Teutonic — Origin of some — Celtic and Gaelic names — Cherished names, their undying value—'Le premier Grenadier de France' a Breton.

INDIVIDUAL names may be broadly classed under four heads:

1st. Names of Religion.

2ndly. Abstract Qualities, and figures typical of them.

3rdly. Personal Characteristics, and figures typical of them.

4thly. Miscellaneous.

The nations from whom the Christian names in general use amongst us are principally, almost entirely, derived are four:

Hebrew, Greek, Latin, and Teutonic.

Hebrew names we shall principally find in Class 1, Names of Religion. There, too, would be found almost all the names of highest antiquity—Assyrian, Persian, Egyptian, and Phœnician.

Names from the Greek (some of them of great beauty) will for the most part be included in Class 2, Abstract Qualities.

The practical Romans, whose conquests and discoveries lay not so much in the realms of thought, were indebted to the Greeks for many of their finest names. Those of their own invention, and in their own tongue, are most numerous in Class 3, Personal Characteristics; and Class 4, Miscellaneous.

Names from the Teutonic, which, as the mother tongue (to simplify classing), may include those of the Germans, Anglo-Saxons, and Scandinavians, will be found to predominate in Class 3, Abstract Qualities and figures typical of them.

In a word, the dominant note in Hebrew and their kindred Arabic names is *Religion*; in those of the Greeks, *Mind*; in names from the Teutonic, *Power*; in those from the Latin, *Personal Appearance*.

But few, comparatively, of our names are derived from the Celtic. Separately classed (of course) from the Teutonic, they will be found to bear a resemblance to them in the character of their significations.

As a first step towards understanding the Babel of voices, as a list of names may appear to some, when it is acknowledged that each name has a voice, the recollection of a few of the words principally used in the composition of names may be useful. These words will of themselves be characteristics of the several nations.

Hebrew names have naturally been always a subject of interest to learned Christian men, from St. Jerome of the fifth century to the scholars of our own day. We learn from such authorities that more than a thousand Hebrew names are compounded of the titles of Jehovah; so that a knowledge of the prefixes and affixes which signify the sacred names will help us at once to understand a large number of Hebrew names.

' It has been observed that the great epochs of the history of the chosen people are marked by the several *names* by which in each the Divine nature is indicated.' ' In the Patriarchal age, the oldest Hebrew form by which the most general idea of Divinity is expressed is "El-Elohim," "the Strong One," "the Strong Ones." As El-Shaddai, " God Almighty," was He also known to them; but the New Name revealed to Moses was Jehovah, the great " I AM," expressive of self-existence, " the same yesterday, to-day, and for ever." In " Adonai " and " Kurios," "*the Lord*," was beheld the approaching dawn of " the Sun of Righteousness," even Christ, " our Lord." ' *

Jehovah is contracted to Jeho, Jo, Jah, and Iah. ' El ' sig. God; ' Shaddai,' the Almighty. Thus Ahaz-iah, Jeho-ahaz, and Jah-azi-el, all sig. ' *Sustained of God.*' The latter name, containing a repetition of the Holy Name, seems yet

* Stanley's Jewish Church, pp. 110, 111.

more significant, and may, one would think, be read as *Jehovah is God, He sustaineth me.*

Such emphatic repetitions are not unusual in Hebrew names. As a nation, stiff-necked, alas! and idolatrous, God's true servants in the land seemed all the more earnestly to desire to set forth their entire devotedness to Him. Their love for God was absolute *worship*—not a cold acknowledgment of a Superintending Power, a chilly act of reason alone, unaccompanied by love, which can never warm the heart or animate the life.

Ab, *father*; Abd, or Obed, *servant*; Ah, *brother*; Bar and Ben, *son*; Ur and Ner, *light* and *fire*; and Hanan, *grace*, are a few of the ideas most commonly expressed by Hebrew names.*

Ab and Abi, *father*, was sometimes used metaphorically, as it is in the present day. Abi-noam may have *signified* father of Noam (*handsome*), or, as 'Father of beauty,' may have been *significant* of an exceedingly handsome man.

So, also, the Arabs say Abu-Saadat, 'Father of Prosperities;' figuratively, 'a fortunate person.' A traveller is spoken of by the Arabs as Ibn-es-Sebil, 'son of the road.' The name is also used figuratively of one who is journeying to Paradise by the way of good works.†

In some of the Hebrew feminine names, there are also metaphors of great beauty: Keren-

---

* Sunday School Teacher's Treasury.
† See Knight's monthly vols., 'Middle Ages.'

happuch, '*my box of eye-ointment*;' expressive of one the sight of whom 'was good for sair een'—a healing presence!

Zillah, a name of sweeter sound, and more fit for general use, *signifies* '*Shadow*,' a word which, in an Eastern land, is doubly *significant*.*

In a hot climate, shadow is expressive of refreshing coolness; and in a land where oppression is rife, shadow is figurative of protection. For a man's name, Ab-ner, '*the father's lamp*,' exquisitely suggests a darling son, as the light of his parents' home.

In following out the meaning of Hebrew names, the Bible itself derives additional interest. In the name which unhappy Cain gives to his firstborn, Enoch, '*dedicated*,' is there not a welcome whisper of repentance—an offering which was made in faith? In the next generation, Mehu-ja-el, '*Smitten of God*,' tells of the awful curse still darkly brooding over the unhappy race; but then, with a dawning of hope in the end, comes Methusa-el, ' Man of God.'

The waters of the Deluge have rolled between the crumbling bones of those men and ourselves; but in their names we hear living voices still!

For many successive years the conquering sons

---

* Whenever the abbreviation *sig.* is used, *signification*, or some tense of the verb to *signify*, is to be understood; but when, as now, the separate meanings of signification and *significance* come together, to prevent mistake both words are written in full.

of Rome wrote with their sharp swords everywhere—north, south, east, and west—those proud words, 'Rome, Mistress of the World.' But universal dominion once attained, its limits gradually began to narrow day by day, like the iron chamber of the Italian torturer. Province after province was wrested away, and distant colonies were abandoned one by one, till in her very capital Rome's haughty neck finally bowed beneath the foot of the conquering Goth.

But the empire of Greece was of the mind, and it has been the more lasting of the two. Still through her eyes we read the histories of the nations of old; still through her voice are their names repeated to us; and the exquisite beauty and endless variety of actual Grecian names secured them a welcome everywhere.

On the throne of Palmyra sat, in the purple robe which Rome had accorded to her, Zenobia, sig. *Life from Zeno*, 'Lord of life;' and casting his nets into the Sea of Galilee, a Jewish fisherman, toiling for his daily bread, was Andrew the *man of courage*.

Significant indeed of noble qualities is the rich treasury of names which ancient Greece left as a legacy to the whole world; but, read by Gospel light, we are struck by one great want.

Names of religion are numerous. Greece did not forget her many gods; nay, Athens had her altar even 'to the Unknown God.' Like the inarticulate cry of a child who, in the dark, cannot *see* the Father who it *feels must* be near, is the yearning after ideal good which echoes through the names of Greece.

They are attuned to the lofty pitch of Glory, Wisdom, and Virtue. The prefix *Eu* sig. what was eminently *good* and excellent may be found in no less than 125 names of men and women. The pages of Grecian history sparkle with glorious names, many of which are illustrated by the lives of those that bore them.

How admirably did the life of *Socrates* correspond to his name—a *healthy power* (of mind) temperate and self-controlled!

And Pericles, *surrounded with glory*—he, who (hardest of all places to fill), ruler of a republic, was intrusted with almost absolute power, could, when dying at seventy years of age, declare his chiefest glory to be, that he had never caused one fellow-citizen to mourn.

In these names of Greece, by itself, and with innumerable compounds, the word Areta, *virtue*, meets us everywhere; so, too, does Charis, *love*;[*] Elpis, *hope*, is more rare; but where is Pistis, *faith*?

In two, three, nay, perhaps four names, we read of Pistis, Faith. Pistus occurs as a slave's name.

Ah! the natural man may nobly strive after Virtue; Love and Hope are instincts in some natures; but Faith, with its unutterable gladness,

[*] '*Goodwill*,' '*kind feeling*;' also *grace, beauty*. Charieis, *graceful, beautiful.—Liddell and Scott.*

its immeasurable, all-pervading power, cometh only from above. It is the gift of the Holy Spirit through Christ; and through it alone can finite man behold the Infinite.

Latin names are far less interesting than those of the Greeks; they are like the cartes de visite of to-day as compared with portraits by Van Dyck. Has your friend a big nose, a large mouth, or small eyes? They are plainly to be seen; some striking beauty, too, may be recognised —a tall figure, or abundant hair; but where are all the more exquisite charms of an expressive face illumined by the soul within—the kindly beaming eyes, the enchanting smile?

This is no fanciful sketch; the names are here. Naso, *large nose*; Chilo, *thick lips*; Ocella, *small-eyed*; Longinus, *tall*, and Cæsar, *having much hair*.

Compare, too, the Latin Junia, *young*, with the Greek Petala, which expresses in one word a *tender leaf just unclosed*. With the Romans a fair beauty was Albinia, *white*; for a brunette we find no name at all. With the Greeks a dark beauty was Ioessa, *the hue of a violet*, and a fair one Cymopolios, *white as the sea-foam*.

But we hasten to do justice to Latin names in recording some that all would be proud to bear. Beatrice, the joy-giver; Vincent, the invincible; Constantine, Constance, Victoria, Honor, and Grace.

In names derived from the Teutonic race we

joyfully meet again, as in the Greek, a preponderance of the nobler class of names, signifying, or significant of, abstract qualities. Courage, power, and nobleness are the dominant ideas in German, Scandinavian, and Anglo-Saxon names. One other striking characteristic we find: The manly tenderness and respect which 'Goths and Barbarians' felt for the weaker sex have been recorded by an enemy—Tacitus, the *silent*, whose voice has gone out into all lands.

The Teutons believed the sex to be inspired. Truly they were—inspired as women will always be when, in the answering eyes of those most dear, they read that their whole-hearted devotedness is believed in and responded to. Woman's nature is as some noble instrument of music—the soul of harmony is within, but there, too, discord dwells; as the hand that plays on it is true or false, so too will be the answering sound. *Trusted* and *true* is woman's motto, whoever, wherever she may be.

The Teuton women's names are as revelations of the past; they are records to all time of women's trustworthiness. Listen to them.

Ethelreda, *a noble counsellor*. Do we not see it all, that scene of centuries gone by? Aged chiefs in solemn council—the old men look irresolute; wise and experienced as they are, where is their wonted decision gone? Some undiscovered hitch makes the wheels of power drag heavily—time passes, and mischief lurks behind!

Behold, suddenly, in the midst, a stately woman stands! a mother in Israel, like Deborah of old, the Hebrew prophetess dwelt beneath the palm; but the northern Vala has a yew-branch in her hand. Inspiration has come to her—come from where all good gifts come, even to those who do not know their Father in Heaven; the right word is said, and the coming evil is averted.

Look again! It is now a battle-field: not there surely is woman's place; ah, no! yet see, brave men are faltering; some inexplicable panic has seized those heroes of a hundred fights—they fly! But not for long. In the confines of that bloody field they are met—by whom? Fresh soldiers with whole weapons and untired frames, who will sweep back together with them in a desperate charge? No! Pale women are there with dishevelled hair, and uncovered breasts, and shining eyes that speak what lips cannot. Dare those that love them be defeated now? As men who are cased in iron, those half-naked warriors surge back; as stormy waves in their wrath, they fling themselves against the breasts of their foes Their foes! where are they? Melted away. And the golden-haired girl, whose whisper summoned the mothers and wives from their homes, she is named Macht hilda, the *Damsel of Might*, from Hildr, the War-goddess of the North!

Once again listen and look! Listen for the name of Elgiva; look, for the battle is won; but that crimson field must be flooded with tears ere the green grass grows over it again. Mothers, and wives, and sisters are there—pillowed on their loved ones' arms, conquering heroes die joyfully. But one curly-haired boy lays alone—he has come from afar, and none know him there; but a chief's daughter knows that where sorrow or suffering is, there is her place!

Was the cup of cold water given in the name of the 'High Father' unblessed? Was the prayer to the only god she knew unheard by the God of Love? The brave boy blesses her as he dies, and the soft-eyed maiden has won the sweet name of Ethel-gifa, the *Noble help-giver.*

Would that our store of Celtic names was as large as that preserved from our Saxon and Norsemen forefathers! But we know that the Gaelic race honoured women: their priestesses are historic characters, and names like the Teuton *Counsellor, Help-giver,* and *Lady of Might,* have their Celtic synonymes, telling that in our own England at no time was woman despised. The Ancient Britons had Cwen-burh, a *woman who assists,* or who is a *tower* (of defence); and Boadicea, is it not derived from Bu add, *Victory?* (s.) a synonyme with Victoria, the happier Queen who rules over English hearts to-day.

We read that the most ancient names in Britain related to colour; but in those that remain, we find only *White* and *Black*—the two extremes, fairness often accompanied with red hair, and dark complexions and black hair, which are still the distinguishing characteristics of 'Old Gaul.' The Highland race still boast their Du galds— Dhu-gallu-edd, the *black-haired powerful man.*(s.)

For the epithet of the 'fair sex,' it would seem that women are indebted to the Celts. Cwen, Gwen, Gwyn, originally *White*, having been accepted as signifying *Fair*, was then applied to the sex in general, either as *woman* or *lady of rank*. One of these British beauties of ancient days rejoiced in the name of Gwen wyn wyn, *Thrice Fair*.

The form of the final syllables of this name assimilating it to the Teutonic Wyn, *Beloved*, we may read, if we will, in the one little word Gwyn, a *fair woman beloved*.

Both the names and the mythological traditions of Celts and Teutons, as they have been handed down to us, do sometimes seem to assimilate strangely—distinct races as they were, but both claiming an Eastern origin, and becoming united in our isle. The Celtic Hu Cadarn, the Mighty, and Morvran, Raven of the Sea, connect themselves, though mistily, with one of the sacred birds of Odin, Huginn the Raven. Revealing faint and far traditions of the Deluge, I believe that in Muginn, the Bird of *Memory*, we behold the Dove, who did *remember* her old home, bringing back across the trackless waste the olive-leaf.

Morvran, as preserved in Mervyn, the enchanter of later days, is a name of to-day, and Cordelia, the loving daughter of King Lear, may be recognised in Creirwy or Creird dylad, sig. '*the token of the flowing*,' her father's name Lyr, sig. '*the sea-shore.*'

Of names compounded of Celtic and Teutonic words, that of the wife of Dagobert, King of France, affords an example, Nant Hilda; Nant, a Celtic word sig. *torrent*, and Hilda, Teut., sig. *lady* or *young girl*, the compound name taken to mean '*Child of the Torrent.*' *

Such compound names meet us on all sides. From Sanscrit, the sacred language of ancient Hindustan, came (it is said) * the name Amala, sig. *faultless*. This name, borne by the founder of the kingdom of the Visigoths, joined itself in succeeding generations with the Teutonic terminations, Ric, *ruler*, and Berga, *tower*, so often used as a feminine designation, Amalaric, Amalaberga.

Amongst compound names, Maximilian of Austria, first of the name, is said by a learned writer † to have owed his hitherto unheard-of appellation to his eccentric father, Frederick III., who, after consultation with the stars, composed this name of royal sound from those of Fabius *Maximus* and Paulus *Æmilius*.

In Anna-bel, Hebrew and Latin are combined; so are they also in Luci-anne, once a favourite name in England, and in Lu-anna, a different form of the same names.

The names both of Gael and Celt are in

---

* Salverte, Noms d'Hommes.
† Fugger, Coxe's *Hist. House of Austria,* vol. i. 278.

themselves nobly significant—the one derived from Galluedd, *strong, powerful*; the other from Caled, *hard, intrepid*. The Celt *intrepid*, to dare; the Teuton resolute, *to do*—noble roots, from which upsprang the nation whose empire girdles the globe. The 'Gallant Six Hundred,' the ' thin red line,' and Havelock's hero-band, did they not show, with countless examples besides, that the vigour of those precious roots is undecayed ?

A Bréton proverb retains the meaning of Celt as ' hard, intrepid;' ' got callet densan Armorig,'* sig. it is a hard (or intrepid) man of Armorica. The proverb applied to Theophilus Corret Latour d'Auvergne, ' prémier grenadier de France.'

The thrilling story is well known how the brave men whom the gallant Bréton had so often led to victory would never part with their dead hero's name. Still day by day at the head of the regimental roll it is called aloud; the generation that loved him have passed away, but their sons and their sons' sons still ever and always hear the idolised name—Corret Latour d'Auvergne; still first of the brave band is summoned, and ever and always a soldier steps forth from the ranks to reply, ' Dead on the battle-field! '

Ah! who can speak lightly of names when our heart-beats tell us how vast and undying is their influence?

* Salverte.

CHAPTER XI.

Classified List—Class I. Names of religion. II. Divisions and notices—including names from the Assyrian, Persian, Egyptian, Hebrew, Greek, Latin, Teutonic, Celtic, Arabic, &c.

CLASSIFIED LIST OF NAMES.

CLASSED ACCORDING TO THEIR SIGNIFICATIONS AND SIGNIFICANCE, AND ACCORDING TO THE LANGUAGES FROM WHICH THEY WERE DERIVED.

> 'For every word men may not chide or pleine,
> For in this world certain ne wight ther is,
> That he be doth or sayth sometimes amis.' *

CLASS I.

NAMES OF RELIGION.

Division 1. Names of Deities assumed by Men and Women.
  „   2.   „   relating to Deity.

---

* May these old lines (quoted in the preface to Bohn's edition of Mallet's Northern Antiquities) go before the writer as she now ventures into the more immediate domains of the learned—not to deprecate criticism, but to plead for *kindly* correction wherever it may be needed?

In attempting so *new* and venturesome a task as the classification of upwards of 1,500 names, according to their signification and significance, and according to the languages from which they are supposed to be derived, the writer feels that, of course, she must be liable to errors and oversights, although, in giving her whole heart to her work, she has tried her best to avoid both. Far and wide she has sought for the trustiest guides; but with all her most diligent search she has failed to discover any notice of some names, about which history, poetry, or living worth has (at least in her eyes) cast a charm. Their meaning she has striven to discover for herself. Where a signification rests entirely on her supposition, an (s) is attached, sig. *suggested*.

CLASS II.

ABSTRACT QUALITIES.

Division 1. Names signifying or significant of Life.
,, 2. ,, signifying or significant of Virtue.
,, 3. ,, of Love, including Jewels as significant of Preciousness.
,, 4. ,, of Light, Brightness, and Purity.
,, 5. ,, of Truth, Sincerity, and Fidelity.
,, 6. ,, of Help-givers.
,, 7. ,, of Courage and Strength.
,, 8. ,, of Wisdom and Intellect.
,, 9. ,, of Noble Birth and Station, Glory and Power.
,, 10. ,, of Peace and Gentleness.
,, 11. ,, of Charm, Winsomeness, and Melody, and Perfume as figurative of them.
,, 12. ,, of Joy, Joy-givers, and Good Fortune.

CLASS III.

PERSONAL CHARACTERISTICS.

Division 1. Names signifying Beauty and Youth, and Flowers as typical of them.
,, 2. ,, descriptive of Complexion, Hair, Height, &c.
,, 3. ,, descriptive of Personal Defects.

CLASS IV.

MISCELLANEOUS.

Including Names signifying Animals, Plants, Places, Letters, Numbers, &c.*

---

* Occasionally a name will be found to which different significations are attached. When both interpretations rest on apparently good authorities, both are given. For instance, Owen, or Owain, has been said to signify a *lamb*—while others see in it the Celtic form of that universally popular Christian name, John. So, too, Nant has been translated as *torrent*—while at this moment in Wales it signifies a *dingle*.

CLASS I.

NAMES OF RELIGION.

Division 1.
Names of Deities assumed by Men and Women.

MEN.

Assyrian. Shalmaneser, or Sallum Anu—Noah deified.
" Belus—The sun.
" Jerah (Jericho, city of moon worship)—The moon.
Sanscrit. Vaji-Zatha (a son of Hamon's)—Moon-god.
Persian. Hormuz, Hormisdas, Orosmodes, &c.; Khosrow; Mithra—Sun.
Egyptian. Osiris, Pharaoh (Ph *the* Re or Ra)—Sun.
Hindu. Krishnur, Rama, Nana,[1] &c.
Phœnician. Thammuz, Thomas?[2] (*s.*)—Sun-god.
Celtic. Cuno-bel-in, Cymbeline—Lord of the sun.
Greek. Artemas, from Artemis (*perfect*)—The moon.
" Epaphros, from Aphrodite (foam of the sea)—Goddess of love and beauty.
" Dimitri, from Demeter (liberal mother)—Ceres, or the earth-goddess, &c. &c.
Roman. Diocles, Diocletian, from the Greek—Glory of Jupiter.
Latin. Vedius—Evil-god, Pluto, &c. &c.

Amongst early Christian martyrs, St. Jovian, St. Mercurius, &c. &c.; amongst Italians, Bacco, Nettuno, Zefirino, Ercole, Saturnino,[3] &c. &c.

Otho, from Odin, Wodin—Father of the Gods.

WOMEN.

Greek. Phœbe; Selene, Selina; Artemis, Artemisia (*perfect*)—The moon.*
Latin. Diana (bright as day)—The moon, &c. &c.

---

* Very few names have been given in this list. It was thought little interest would be afforded by multiplied synonymes of the sun and moon, and a repetition of the names of false gods.

Division 2.
Names relating to Deity.—Jehovah the true God.

Hebrew.

MEN.

Elijah, Joel—Jehovah is God.
Abi-el, Eliab, Joab—God is my Father.
Abdi el, Obad iah—Servant of God.
Matthias, Matthew—God's gift.
El Nathan, Nathan el, Jonathan, &c., John; *Arabic,* You hanna, Hanna; *Armenian,* Ohannes; *Sclavonic,* Ivan; *Gaelic,* Ian; *Welsh,* Owen, Evan; *Breton & Cornish,* Ives; *Italian,* Giovanni; *Spanish,* Juan—God's grace, or God's gift.
Judah—Praise the Lord (or Jehovah).
Hananiah—Grace of the Lord.
El dad, Jedidiah—Beloved of the Lord.
Michael, Michaela (*w.*)—Who is like God?
Gabriel, Gabriella (*w.*), Joachim [4]—God is my strength.
Raphael, Raffaela (*w.*)—Healing of God.
Daniel—God is my judge.
Ishmael—Heard of God.
Israel, Ezekiel—Who sees God.
Joseph; *Arabic,* Yusef; *Italian,* Giuseppe, dim. Beppo—'He will add,' sig. of Trust in God.
Emmanuel, dim. Manuel, Manuela (*w.*), Manuelita (*w.*)—God with us.
Enoch—Dedicated.

Ari el—Lion of God.
Shelemiah—Peace of God.
Zephaniah—The secret of God.
Esrael, Lazarus,[5] Azariah, Joshua, Eliezer—God is my help.
Uriel, Uriah, Neriah—Light, or Fire of God.
Jeremiah—Exaltation of God.
Eli—My God.
Elimelech—My God is king.
Ib har—The chosen.
Pascal—Passage, significant of deliverance through God.

WOMEN.

Jochebed—Whose glory is Jehovah.
Judith—Who praises God.
Joanna, Jane, Janet, Jeanie; *Spanish,* Juana, Juanita; *Italian,* Giovanna; *French,* Jeannette; *Bréton,* Yvonne—God's grace, or God's gift.
Mehetabel—How good is God.
Seraphino—Full of love to God.
Bethiah—Daughter of Jehovah.
Elisheba—In God is her rest.
Elisabeth, Eliza, &c.; *Spanish,* Isabel; *Russian,* Lescinska—God is her oath, or a worshipper of God.
Bathsheba—Daughter of an oath or seventh daughter.
Josepha, Josephine; *Italian,* Giuseppina; *Spanish,* Pepita.

Greek.

MEN.

Christian, Christina (*w.*), Christabel—Follower of Christ.
Christopher—Christ-bearer.
Jerome, from Hieronymus; *Italian*, Geronimo—Sacred name, sig. of consecration to God.
Eligius, Eloy, Lo—Chosen.
Epiphanius, Epiphania (*w.*)—Manifestation, glory.
Baptist, Baptista (*w.*)—Washed.
Theodore, Theodora (*w.*), Dorothy (*w.*), Dora—God's gift.
Theodosius, Theodosia (*w.*)—Given to God.
Theophilus, Theophila (*w.*)—Lover of God.

WOMEN.

Hebrew & Greek. Veronica—The true image of Christ.
Evangelista, Evangeline—Bringer of good news.
Angela, Angelina, Angelica—Messenger from God.

Latin.

MEN.

Donatus; *French*, Dieu-donné—God-given.
Amadeus, Amadis—Lover of God.
Spanish, Domingo; *Italian*, Domenico, Dominichina (*w.*)—Belonging to the Lord.
Noël, Nathalie (*w.*)—Nativity of our Lord.
Redento, Redenta (*w.*)—Redeemed.
Renatus, Réné—Born again.
Benedict, Benedicta (*w.*), Beata (*w.*)—Blessed.

WOMEN.

Electa—Chosen.
Immaculata—Immaculate.
Annunziata—Annunciation.
Spanish, Dolores; *Italian*, Dolora—Sorrow of the mother of our Lord.
Spanish, Mercedes—Grace, favour (also title of honour).
Verena—One who venerates God.
French, Dévote—Devoted to God.

Teutonic.

MEN.

God frey—God's peace.
God win—Beloved of God.

WOMEN.

Gudule—God's help.

FALSE GODS.

MEN.

Chaldaic, Abd u Shems—Servant of the sun.
Assyrian, Belshazzar—Bel has formed a king.
Belteshazzar, Balthasar—Bel has formed a prophet.
Abed Nego—Servant of Nebo.
Egyptian, Rameses—Begotten of the sun.
Amosis—Begotten of the moon.
Potiphera, Hophra—Consecrated to the sun.

Persian, Korshid—Splendour of the sun.
Mithrabarzanes — Resplendent as the sun.
Khurdad, Mithridad—Gift of the sun.
Asp-a-tha—Gift of the horse.
Phœnician, Hamilcar—Favour of Baal.
„ Asdrubal—Help of Baal.
Caucasian, Bajazet—Abode of the gods.

Greek.

MEN.

Diogenes—Son of Jupiter.
Diodotus—Gift of Jupiter.
Diomedo—Dear to Jupiter.
Diogiton—Neighbour of Jupiter.
Dionysius, Denys, Denise (*w.*)—Descended from Bacchus.
Zenobius, Zenobia (*w.*)—Life from Zeno, lord of life.

Heraclius, Hercules—Glory of Hera (Juno).
Isidore—Gift of Isis.
Heliodorus—Gift of the sun.
Spiridion, Spiro[6]—Breath of the gods.
Demetrius, Dimitri (*w.*)—Consecrated to Demeter (Ceres), &c. &c.

Teutonic.

MEN.

Thor-wald[7]—Thor's chief.
Thor-mod—Courage of Thor.
Thor-geir—Vulture of Thor.
Thor-kell—Thor's club.
Esmond, Osmond—Protected by the gods.
Oswald—Chief appointed by the gods.
Osbert—Divinely bright.

Oswin—Beloved by the gods.
Anselmo[8]—Helmet of the gods, significant of a powerful protector.

WOMEN.

Thor-disa, Thora, Thyra—Consecrated to, or given by Thor.
Thor-gerda — Girdle of Thor, signifying protected by him.

NAMES OF RELIGION.

Arabic.

MEN.

Abd Allah—Servant of God.
Abd el Ahad—Servant of the One (God understood).
Abd el Melik—Servant of the King (of kings).
Abd el Kader—Servant of the powerful.
Abd el Wadood—Servant of the loving.
Abd er Rahman—Servant of the compassionate.
Abd el Kudoor—Servant of the most holy.
Abd el Meshid—Servant of the lofty-one.
Neamet Allah—Gift of God.
Reyhan—Favour of God.
El Mustafa—The elect, chosen.
Mohammed—Greatly praised.
Haroun el Rasheed—Aaron the Orthodox.
Amin[9]—Faithful.

Amine Deen—Faithful to the religion.
Sofi ed Deen—Pure of faith.
Sofian (*s.*)—Devoted to God.
Shems ed Deen—Sun of the religion.
Bedr er Deen—Full moon of religion.
Ala ed Deen—Glory of religion.
Nour ed Deen—Light, or lamp, of religion.
Salah ed Deen (Saladin)—Goodness of religion.
Fadl ed Deen—Excellence of religion.
Seif ed Deen—Sword of religion.

WOMEN.

Khadija (*s.*)—Holy.
Amina, Amineh—Faithful.
Safiyeh; *Turkish,* Sofiyeh—Chosen (of God, if from Sofi).*

NOTICES TO CLASS I. DIVISION 1.

[1] *Nana.*—This name, rendered lately of such infamous notoriety, is of great antiquity, as the name of a goddess worshipped by the Babylonians.

---

* Class I. Division 2.—This division also may have been enlarged to almost any extent. Hebrews and Arabians loved to profess themselves *Servants* of God; the Greeks especially loved to call themselves (as noticed by St. Paul) the *offspring* of God; they also delighted in naming their children a *gift* from one of their many divinities. *God's gift* has its synonymes in all languages. But to each division a few characteristic names—in due proportion to the numbers out of which they are selected—will, it is thought, be sufficient.

² *Thomas.*—The signification of a *twin* is generally attached to the name of Thomas; but is it really so? If synonymous with the Greek Didymus, why should the two names be repeated together? 'Thomas which is called Didymus;' Simon is spoken of 'as called Cephas,' and as 'surnamed Peter,' the two Greek names being synonymes, but different to his Hebrew name, which signifies *obedient.* The writer ventures to suggest: may not the origin of our familiar name of Thomas be found far away amongst the countless synonymes of the sun-god, Phœnician Thammuz, from whom the Greeks borrowed their Adonis? In his vision of Jerusalem Ezekiel mourned to see Jewish women 'weeping for Tammuz,' the beloved idol in which was personified the summer sunshine, yearly blotted from the sky by the rude hand of winter. This festival was in June, part of the month was called Tamuz, and we may well believe that to sons born to them at that time the daughters of Judah, who worshipped him, would love to give his name. Once established as a favorite name, it would continue to be used long after its idolatrous significance had passed away, even as many heathen names are used by us.

³ *Saturnino.*—This name, in the days of St. Cyprian, the martyred bishop of Carthage, in the eighth century, was at the same time so common and so distasteful to him, that in epistles written by him in the name of the principal members of his church, it is mentioned as 'Saturnino, another, and again another.' It would seem still to find strange favour amongst the Italians. A short time back, at a London police-office, *Saturnino Terribile* was brought up on a charge of murder—this name of terrible import, unfortunately, seeming in his case to have been too suggestive.

NOTICES TO CLASS I. DIVISION 2.

⁴ *Joachim* is said to be the Hebrew name given to Moses by his parents before he was carried as an infant from his home.

⁵ *Lazarus.*—How much significance there is in the names of Lazarus and Bethany in connection with Christ's first victory over the *grave*! Bethany sig. *house of dates,* a village of palms; palm-branches in all lands and in all times being symbolical of victory. The village venerated by the Arabs is called by them El Azariah, in Arabic and Hebrew a synonyme for Lazarus. *Azrael** is their

---

* In Arabic, Azr signifies *strength.*

angel of death; was not that name also derived from the Hebrew Esrael, the meaning of which is identical with the former names, all four signifying the *help of God*? If so, then in the words 'Lazarus, come forth!' we have the angel of Death himself summoned, and in his name all the dead ransomed from the power of the grave. By *God's help* with Lazarus will be our victory over death, by *God's help* with Joshua our entrance into the promised land.

⁶ *Spiridion, Spiro.*—This name and its diminutive, belonging to a bishop of Cyprus in the fourth century, patron saint of Corfu, is a favourite name amongst modern Greeks. The grand old classical names have a strange sound to us, used, as they are there, so commonly: Leonidas, Lycurgus, &c.; and, amongst women, Calypso, Calliope, Cleopatra, Aspasia. Besides these, some of their most favourite names are: (*Hebrew*) Michaelis, (*Latin*) Constantis, their own Petros, Kyrios (was it not originally from the Persian Kouresh, *the sun*?), and Kyrillos, our Cyrus and Cyril; for women's names, Helena, Aglaia, Agathonia, Polyxene; and for men and women both, Dimitri.

⁷ *Thor.*—In the Land nama-bok of Iceland, one-third of the names given have reference to Thor (the Daring), the favourite divinity of the Scandinavians, as his father Wodin, or Odin, was of the Anglo-Saxons.

⁸ *Anselm.*—Anses, As, Os, inferior gods worshipped by the Teutonic race, corresponding to the deified heroes of Greece and Rome.

⁹ *Amin*, the name of Mohammed when young, his mother's name having been Amina. The strange combination of Jewish traditions and Christian reminiscences is supposed to have been owing to his mother having been a Jewess converted to Christianity by the Syrian monk Sergius.[*] Deen, or Dîn (*religion*), signified the practical part, and Imân (*faith*) the doctrinal part of Islamism, Islam, *salvation*, or, as some translate it, to mean originally *resignation*—are they not the same? and in Christianity also? Man must renounce his own will in all things; he must look up to, depend upon God as a child upon his *father*, ere he can accept and rejoice in His will, and His revealed will become his guide in life, his hope in death. Is not Heaven's song 'Amen! Alleluia?' *So be it! Praise the Lord!*

---

[*] Von Hammer.

CHAPTER XII.

Classified List—Class II. Abstract qualities—Twelve divisions and notices— including names principally from the Hebrew, Greek, Latin, Teutonic, Celtic, Arabic, North American Indian, &c. &c.

CLASS II.

ABSTRACT QUALITIES.

Division 1.
Names signifying or significant of Life.

Hebrew.

WOMEN.
Hevah, Eve, Eva, Evelina, Eveleen, Evelyn; *Arabic*, Howwa—Life.

Greek.

MEN.
Ambrose, Athanasius, Athenaïs (*w.*)—Immortal.
Anastasius, Anastasia (*w.*)—Rising again.
Zeno—Life.
Zenobia (*w.*)—Gift of life, or gift of Zeno.
Zephirino, Zephyrine (*w.*)—Carrying life (the west wind).

WOMEN.
Zoë—Life.
Zozimia—Living.
Zopyra—Fire of life.
Amaranth—Unfading flower.

CLASS II.—ABSTRACT QUALITIES.   243

Division 2.
Virtue.

Hebrew.

MEN.	WOMEN.
Abitub—Father of goodness.	Michal—Perfect.
Chilion, Shallum—Perfect.	Hannah, Anna, Anne, Annie; *Spanish*, Anina, Anita; *French*, Annette, Nanette—Grace.
Simon—Obedient.	
Simeon—Who hears.	
Zadoc—Just.	

Greek.

MEN.	WOMEN.
Asyncritus—Incomparable.	Hiera—Holy.
Evaristus—Most excellent.	Penagia[1]—All-holy.
Aristides—The best.	Agatha, Chrestilla—Good.
Epaminondas—Better than the best.	Lois—Better.
	Hypatia—Superior.
Aristotle—Having the best end in view.	Agarista—The best.
	Panarista—Altogether best.
Aristocles—Glory of goodness.	Perialla—Excelling.
Themistocles—Glory of justice.	Telesia—Perfect.
Eustace—Steadfast.	Sophrosyne—Temperate.
Agathon—Good.	Sophronia—Modest.
Agathenor—Good and brave.	Evodie—Who follows the right path.
Philarete—Lover of virtue.	
Polycarp—Bearing much fruit.	Zenaïde—Who lives modestly.
Eusebius, Eusebia (*w.*)—Honoured for goodness.	Areta—Virtue.
	Phœnarete, Clinarete—Of shining virtue.
Socrates, Sosthenes—Temperate, self-controlled.	Aretaphila—Who loves virtue.
Mnechus—Who rules his spirit.	Timarete—Who honours virtue.
Eurymenes—Large-minded.	Mnesarete—Memory of virtue.
Euthynoüs—Just-minded.	Eunice—Fair victory, one who wins by her goodness.
Chrysander—A man of gold.	

Latin.

MEN.	
Celestinus, Celestine (*w.*)—Heavenly-minded.	Innocent, Innocentia (*w.*)—Blameless.
	Pius, Pia (*w.*)—Pious.

Probus—Good; *Italian*—Omobuono—Good man.
Spanish, Sanchez, Sancha (*w.*)—A saint.
Justus, Justinian, Justine (*w.*)—Just.
Honorius, Honor (*w.*), Norah (*w.*)—Worthy of honour.
Tullius, Tullia (*w.*), Tulliola (*w.*)—Worthy of being brought up.

WOMEN.
Una—One, expression of matchless perfection.
Bona—Good.
Emerentia—Deserving.
Casta—Chaste.
Mathurine—Perfected.
Meliora—Better.

Teutonic.

MEN.
Vibert—Of eminent holiness.
Wimund—Holy peace.
Godard—Heavenly disposition.
Engelbert—Bright as an angel.
Amalaric; *Sanscrit*, Amala—Faultless ruler.
Gomesind; *Spanish*, Gomez—Good youth.
Guthman; *Spanish*, Guzman—Good man.
Betstan—The best.

WOMEN.
Amalia—Faultless.
Amalaberga—Faultless tower, fig. steadfastness.
Bathilde—Good girl.

Celtic.

MEN.
Saidi, Sâd—Firm, just. | Angus, from *ango*—Undeviating.

Arabic.

MEN.
Saleh—Virtuous and just.
Abu 'l Fazl—Father of excellence.
Aziz, Azeezah (*w.*)—Excellent.
Omar—Better.
Persian, Anushirwan—Of a generous mind.

Hindu.

WOMEN.
Mher ul Nica—First of women.

Division 3.
Love and Jewels as significant of preciousness.

Hebrew.

MEN.
David, Hobab—Beloved.
Jedidiah, Jedidah (*w.*)—Wellbeloved.
Benjamin — Son of my right hand.
Abner—The father's lamp.
Absalom—The father's peace.
Saul—Asked for.
Adlai—My ornament.

WOMEN.
Abigail—The father's joy.
Hephzibah—My delight is in her.
Keren Happuch—My box of eye ointment.
Peninnah — Precious stone or coral.
Ispah—Jasper-stone.
Pinon—Pearl.
Sapphira—Sapphire.

Greek.

MEN.
Erasmus—Loved.
Erasthenes—Greatly loved.
Agapetus—Beloved.
Polytimeus—Very precious.
Philetas, Philemon, Philander —Loving.
Philopater,[2] Philomater, Philodelphus—Loving father, mother, brother.
Patrocles, Metrocles—Glory of father and mother.
Pamphilius—Beloved by all.
Damian—Popular.

WOMEN.
Erato, Elma—Love.
Erotium—A little love.
Deiphile—Twice loved.
Pasiphila—Beloved by all.
Philumena—Of a loving mind.
Charis, Phintias, Phila, Phillina—Loving and loved.
Eudora—A good gift.
Medora (*s.*)—A mother's gift.
Imogene—A beloved child.
Delphine—A loving sister.
Margaret, Margarita, Marguerite —A pearl.
Menie (*s.*)—Cared for, cherished.

Latin.

MEN.
Amand, Amanda (*w.*), Amias, Aymon—Beloved.
Desiderius, Didier, Desiré—Desired.
Italian, Benvenuto—Welcome.

Publius, Publicola—Popular.

WOMEN.
Amata, Amabel, Amy—Beloved.
Volumnia—Longed for.

Spanish.

WOMEN.

Niña,[3] Ninita—Darling, little darling (Old Spanish Dict.)

Mercedes[3]—A gift, a favour, also 'thanks.' transl. as 'apple of the eye').

Teutonic.

MEN.	WOMEN.
Leofwyn—Love-winner.	Wyn, Holdlie—Beloved, lovely.
Leofstan—Best beloved.	Deorwyn—Dearly loved.
Leofric—Beloved ruler.	Deorswytha—Very dear.
Leopold—Beloved and brave.	Minna, Minnie—Borne in memory, beloved.
Alwyn, Alwy—Beloved by all.	Vala—Chosen.
Ethelwyn—Noble and beloved.	Valborge—Chosen tower.
Berthold—Beloved and bright.	Adeline—Noble wife.
Reynold[4]—Pure love.	Audovere—Happy wife.
Edwin, Edwy—Happy and beloved.	Ghiselle, Giselle—Companion.
Harold—Beloved leader.	Beage—Bracelet, fig. precious.
	Beage stan—Bracelet-stone.

Celtic.

MEN.

Madoc—Fatherly chief. | Mungo—Beloved.

Arabic.

MEN.

Mustafa—The chosen.
Aziz, Azeezah (w.)—Dear, excellent.
Sa'ed—Forearm (expression of nearness, dearness).

WOMEN.

Mahboobeh Shoh—Beloved.
Rahmah—Gift of God's mercy.
Tohfeh—A gift.
Safiyeh ; *Turkish*, Sofiyeh—Chosen.
Looloo Luluah ; *Persian*, Murwari—Pearl.
Johareh—A jewel.

Zumurrud—Emerald.
Persian, Statira (s.)—A gold coin.
Denaneer—Pieces of gold.
Bahr el Kunooz—Sea of treasures.
Shejeret el Durr—Tree of pearls.
Nuzhet el Fuad—Delight of the heart.
Nuzhet es Zeman—Delight of the age.
Lezzet el Dunya—Delight of the world.
Hazut en Unfoos—Life of souls.
Kurrat el Eyn—Delight of the eye.
Koot el Kuloob—Food of hearts.

CLASS II.—ABSTRACT QUALITIES.

Hindu.

MEN.
Door dowran—Pearl of the age.
Soem—Emerald.

WOMEN.
Mootie—Pearl.
Ani Mootie—Precious pearl.

Chinese.

WOMEN.
Ghiang Koo—Little darling.

North American Indian.

MEN.
Wingēmund—The beloved.
Netis—The trusted friend.

WOMEN.
Nenēmoosha—Sweet heart.
Eeh-nis-kin—The crystal stone.

Division 4.
Light and Purity.

Hebrew.

MEN.
Malachi—An angel.
Zaccheus—Pure.
Er, Neri, Jairus—Light.
Abner—The father's lamp.
Japhia, Nogah—Splendour.
Samson—Sunny.

Barak; *Carthag.* Barca—Lightning.

WOMEN.
Ruth—A vision (of brightness?).
Almah—A maiden.

Greek.

MEN.
Fosco—Light.
Phano, Lychnos—A lamp.
Phaon—Brilliant.
Periphas—Most brilliant.
Ælianus, Aland, Alan—Sunbright.
Anatole—Rising of the sun, the East.
Lampadius—A torch.
Ignatius—A kindled flame.

Lycurgus—Work of light.
Apelles—Without shade.

WOMEN.
Heloise, Helena (*s.*)—Bright as the sun.
Phœbe, Selina—Pure radiance, as the moon.
Asteria—Radiant as a star.
Marmarium—Radiant.
Aurora—Morning light.

Actis—Ray of light.
Aglae, Eudoxia—Splendour.
Inclyta—Illustrious.
Delia, Phædra, Lampisium—Brilliant.
Parthenia, Neottis, Cora, Corinne, Coralie—A maiden.
Lampeto—I shine.
Olympia—Shining afar off.
Psyche—The soul.
Zora—Pure.

Hyale—Crystal.
Margaret, Margarita, Marguerite, Margery—Pearl.
Katharine, Katinka, Katrine, Catalina, Kathleen, Katie, Kate—Spotless, pure.
Petala—A young leaf, fig. a young girl.
Phædora, Feodora—A shining gift.

Latin.

MEN.

Fulgens—Brilliant.
Flaminius, Flaminia (*w.*)—Flame.
Lucius, Lucullus, Luke, Lucia (*w.*), Lucy (*w.*), Lucille (*w.*), Lucinda (*w.*)—Light.
Clair, Clara (*w.*), Clare (*w.*), Clarinda (*w.*), Clarissa (*w.*)—Clear light.
Lilius, Lilian (*w.*), Lilias (*w.*), Lilla (*w.*)—Lily, fig. purity.
Virginius, Virginia (*w.*)—Pure.

WOMEN.

Diana—Bright as day.
Luna—The moon.
Stella, Estelle—A star.

Teutonic.

MEN.

Engelbert—Bright as an angel.
Bertrand—Bright, generous.
Albert, Adalbert, Ethelbert—All bright, noble and bright.
Hildebert—Illustrious lord.
Childebert—Illustrious prince.
Gilbert, Willibert—Light of many.
Dagobert—Bright as day.
Herbert—Illustrious ruler, or chief.
Hubert—Mighty and illustrious.
Egbert—Eminently bright.
Berthelm—Helmet of light.
Humbert—Light of home.
Philibert—Beloved and bright.

WOMEN.

Icelandic, Mona—The moon.
Bertha—The shining one.
Dagmar—The mother of day, the dawn.
Hilda—The maiden.

Celtic

MEN.

Taliessin—Radiant brow.

WOMEN.

Gwendaline—Lady of the white bow, the crescent moon.
Essylt, Isolt, Ysolt—A vision (of brightness).
Aëron—Queen of brightness, splendid one.
Gladys, Gladusa—Brilliant, splendid.
Bûn—The maid.

CLASS II.—ABSTRACT QUALITIES.

Spanish.

Niña—A young girl.

Arabic.

MEN.

Abu Noor—Father of light.
Doel Mekan—Light of the place.
Kamar es Zeman—Moon of the age.
Bedr Basim—The smiling full moon.
Es Semendal—The salamander.

WOMEN.

Shems en Nehar—Sun of day.
Shems ed Doha—Sun of the forenoon.
Budoor—Full moons, excess of splendour.
El Bedr el Kebeer—The great full moon.
Nejmet es Sabák—Morning star.
Noor el Huda—Light of day (also fig. guidance).
Noor Mahal—Light of the Harem.
Noor Jehan—Light of the world.
Nehar es Sena—Pharos of splendour.
Zara—The brightness of the East.

Persian.

MEN.

Kouresh, Khosrow, Mithra, &c.—The sun.
Korshid—The splendour of the sun.

WOMEN.

Lab—The sun.
Roxalana, from Roushen—Splendour.

Assyrian.

WOMEN.

Sitareh; *Hebrew*, Esther, Hester—Star.
Sosana, Susan, Suzette—A lily.

North American Indians.

WOMEN.

Seet-se-be-a—The midday-sun.
Hee-la'h-dee—The pure fountain.

Division 5.
Truth, Sincerity, and Fidelity.

Hebrew.

MEN.
Ammon, Amana (*w.*)—Faithful and true.

Caleb—A dog (as significant of fidelity).

Greek.

MEN.
Evages—Truthful.
Piston—Trusting, trustworthy.

Philalethe—Lover of truth.
Alethe (*w.*), Alethea (*w.*)—Truth.

Latin.

MEN.
Fides, Fidelis, Fidelia (*w.*)—Faithful, true.

Vero, Vera (*w.*), Verax, Veranius, Verania (*w.*)—True.

Teutonic.

MEN.
Roger—A man of his word.
Beornoth—A noble's oath.

WOMEN.
Gertrude—Maiden trusted and true.

Celtic.

MEN.
Gruron—A true man. | Gwair—A just man.

Arabic.

MEN.
Amin, Amineh (*w.*)—Faithful.
Kuleyb, Celb, Celba (*w.*)—Dog, fig. fidelity.

Abu 'l Wefa—Father of fidelity.
Sawab—Rectitude.

North American Indian.
MEN.
Shonka—The dog.

CLASS II.—ABSTRACT QUALITIES.

Division 6.
Help-givers.

Hebrew.

MEN.

Azur, Esdras, Hoshea—Helper.
Raphia—Healer (title of honour with Egyptian monarchs).
Manaen—Comforter.
Hanani, Ananias—Grace, mercy.

WOMEN.

Zillah — Shadow, fig. shelter, protection.
Hamutal—Shelter (from heat or rain).
Hannah, Anna, Anaïs, Annette, Annie, Nanette, Nanina, Nanon, Anina, Anita [5]—Grace, good-will.

Greek.

MEN.

Soter, Sosthenes, Sosia, Sosandra (*w.*)—Saviour, preserver.
Alexis, Alexia (*w.*), Amyntas (*m. w.*), Alcides, Boetius, Epicurus—Helper.
Jason—Healer.
Onesiphorus—Bringer of help.
Alexander, Alexandra (*w.*), Alexandrina (*w.*), Alaster, Allister — A brave protector or defender.
Lysias, Lysander—Liberator.
Egidius, Giles, Gillian (*w.*) — A shield.
Evergetes—Benevolent.
Megaliter—Large heart.

Aristobulus — Excellent counsellor.
Menelaus — Who strengthens the people.

WOMEN.

Panacea—A healer.
Euryone—Of vast usefulness.
Pyrgo—A tower, fig. protection, shelter.
Charixene, Polyxene—Lover of strangers, hospitable.
Charis, Charity—Good-will.
Ophelia—A help-giver.
Eucharis—Gracious, Good, and Fair.

Latin.

MEN.

Salvator—Saviour.
Sulpicius—A refuge.
Fulk—Support.
Scipio—A staff.
Gratian, Gratia (*w.*), Grace (*w.*), Gracienne (*w.*); *Italian*,

Graziosa; *Spanish*, Engracia—Courteous, kindly.
Auxilius—Helpful.
Benevolus—Well-wisher.
Publius, Publicola—Universally esteemed.
Expeditus—One who expedites.

Extricatus—One who extricates.
Ponce—A bridge, fig. of succour.

WOMEN.
Mercedes—Favour.

Carita—Charity.
Genereuse—Generous.
Portia—A harbour, fig. safety.

Teutonic.

MEN.
Adolphus, Adolphine (*w.*), Ildefonzo—Noble helper.
Alfonzo, Alphonsine (*w.*)—Always a helper.
Ludolf—The people's help.
Udolph—Happy helper.
Rodolph, Rolf, Raoul—Counsel and help.
Randolph and Ralph—Pure, disinterested help.
Chilperic—Kingly helper.
Botolph—Ship of help.
Gyffard—Liberal heart.
Gaston—Hospitable.
Roland—Saviour of his country (?).
Beornhelm—Helmet of the nobles.

William, Wilhelmina (*w.*)—Helmet, or helm, of many.

WOMEN.
Ethelgifa, Elgiva—Noble helpgiver.
Heldewig, Hawisa, Avico—Lady of defence.
Lutgarde—Protectress of the people.
Emma; *Icelandic*, Ammie—A nurse.
Hildegarde—A lady who is a protectress.
Bridget (brygge)—Bridge, fig. of succour.
Ingeborge—Tower, fig. of defence, shelter.
Lina (*s.*)—A support.

Celtic.

MEN.
Celtic & Teutonic, Ceol mund—Ship of protection.

WOMEN.
Cwen burgh—A woman who is a tower, fig. trustworthy.

Arabic.

MEN.
Azim—Defender.
Hhafiz; *Persian*, Hafiz—Preserver.

Maaroof—Kindness.
El Feizad—The overflowing, fig. generosity.

North American Indian.

Mecheet a neuch—The wounded bear's shoulder.

Division 7.
Courage and Strength.

Hebrew.

MEN.
Ari, Arieh, Laish—A lion.
Areli—Son of a lion.
Phœnic. Hiram—High-souled.
Lebbeus, Boaz—Manly.
Elon—An oak, fig. strength.
Gideon—Who breaks.

Herod, Herodias (w.) — Fiery dragon.
Zeeb—A wolf.

WOMEN.
Eshtaol—Strong woman.

Greek.

MEN.
Andrew, Adrian, Alcander, Antenor—Manly, brave.
Evander—Good and brave.
Leander—Gentle and brave.
Iphis—Courageous.
Iphicles—Glory of courage.
Iphicrates—Strength of courage.
Nicias, Nicanor, Nicander, Nico (w.), Nicium (w.)—Victorious.
Nicephorus—Bringer of victory.
Domitian—A conqueror.
Nicholas,[6] Nicola (w.), Colette, Nicodemus—Victorious over the people.
Andronicus—Conqueror of brave men.
Inachus, Alcestes, Alcestis (w.), Alcibiades—Full of strength.
Callimachus — One who fights gloriously.
Aper—Wild boar.
Eetion—Eagle.
Lycos, Lycostrates — Wolf, strength of a wolf.
Cephas, Petros, Petrea (w.), Peter, Petronilla (w.); *Italian*, Pietro, Pietra (w.); *Spanish*, Perez; *French*, Pierre, Pierrette (w.); Perrine (w.)—Rock.
Hector—An anchor, fig. champion, defender.
Machæra—Sword, fig. warlike.
Chæremachus — Rejoicing in war.
Panthoüs—Always brave.
Triptolemus—Thrice brave.
Pammenes—All-enduring.
Telemon, Mentor—Patient and brave.
Demosthenes—The strength of the people.
Adamastus—Indomitable.
Thrasymene—Brave speaker.
Thrasybulus—Brave counsellor.
Leo, Leonidas, Lionel, Leonce (m. w.), Leonora (w.), Leonie (w.), Leontine (w.), Læna[7] (w.)—Lion-like.

WOMEN.
Eunice—Good victory.
Zelie—Zealous.
Berenice—Bringer of victory.

Elpinice—Hope of victory.
Deidamia—Dauntless.
Dorymene—Courageous.
Archileonis—Chief lioness.

Iphigenia—Of a courageous race.
Callisthenie—Full of strength.
Timandra—One who honours brave men.

Latin.

MEN.

Victor, Victoria (*w.*), Victorine (*w.*), Vincent—Victorious, invincible.
Romulus, Romola (*w.*)—Strength, power.
Marcus, Mark, Martin, Marcellus, Marcia (*w.*), Marcella (*w.*), Marcellina (*w.*)—Martial.
Valentine, Valerius, Valerie (*w.*), Nero [8]—Strong.
Firmin, Firmilianus—Firm, unshaken.
Lupus, *French*, Loup; *Sabine*, Hirpus—Wolf.

Anthony, Antonia (*w.*), Antoninus, Antonina (*w.*), Antonio, Antoinette (*w.*)—Anton, race of Hercules, sig. of strength.
Aquila, Aquilinus—Eagle.

WOMEN.

Tanaquil [9]—Eagle chieftainess.
Romilda—Lady of power, *Latin & Teutonic*.
Ursula, Ursina—Little bear, sig. of courage.
Elvira—Of manly courage.

Teutonic.

MEN.

Archibald, Erkinbald, Baldric, Baudry—Chief of the brave.
Algernon, (*s.*) Algar, Holgar—Noble weapon, fig. noble and brave.
Hugh (*also Celtic*)—Mighty.
Frank, Francis, Francisco, Frances (*w.*), Fanny (*w.*), Francesca (*w.*), Fanchon (*w.*)—Indomitable.
Edgar—Happy weapon, fig. successful in war.
Germain, Germaine (*w.*)—Man of war, warlike.
Gerald, Geraldine (*w.*)—Warlike chief.
Gerard—Brave heart.
Richard—Great heart, valiant, powerful.

Sigurd, Sigeard—Ruling spirit.
Sigismund—Victorious peace (*mund* also sig. protector).
Sighelm—Helmet of victory.
Sigbert—Illustrious conqueror.
Berenger, Berengaria (*w.*)—Warlike chief.
Bertram—Eminent for strength.
Engelram—Of supernatural strength.
Gustavus, Gonsalvo, Gonçalez, Gunstaf—Staff of war.
Gunther—Warlike leader.
Gunthram—Strong in battle.
Meyrick—Renowned chief.
Hargrim, Grimoald—Fierce chief.
Hildebrand—Sword of war. (Hildr—War-goddess.)
Canute—Knot, fig. strength.

CLASS II.—ABSTRACT QUALITIES.

Sœbald—Fearless at sea.
Modred [10]—Brave counsellor.
Charles, Karl, Carlos, Charlotte (w.), Caroline (w.) — Valiant, strong.
Leonard—Lion-heart.
Leonric—Lion-chief.
Arnold—Eagle-chief.
Arnulph—Eagle and wolf, fig. matchless bravery.
Everard—Heart of wild boar.
Bernard, Bernardine (w.) — Bear's heart.
Ulf, Olf—Wolf.
Wulfric—Wolf-chief.
Ethelwolf—Noble wolf.
Ranwulph—Generous wolf.
Wulfheah—Tall wolf.
Sœwulph—Wolf of the sea, &c.
Ferdinand; (s.) *Spanish*, Hernando (fœrdig)—Daring.

WOMEN.

Matilda, Maude—Brave girl.
Thora, Thordisa, Thyra—Daring.
Velleda—Powerful.
Gonda—Brave.
Hildegonde,[11] Modgudor — Female warrior.

Celtic and Gaelic.

MEN.

Cadwallader—Supreme disposer of battle.
Fingal (s.) (fion-gael)—Strongest of the strong.
Colgar — Warrior with the proud looks.
Boiorigh, Brian—Terrible chief.
Cedric (s.) (cead righ) — War chief.
Cadmar—Strong in battle.
Fergus — Strong arm, strong man.
Ard gal—Exalted valour.
Dugald (s.)—Black-haired and strong.
Caradoc (Caradawg) — Captain of fighting chariots.
Dermot (s.), Diarmid (duir meod) —Oak-father, fig. a chief.
Morhold—Ruler of the sea.
Morvran, Mervyn—Raven of the sea.
Tuileach—Overwhelming flood.
Merideth—Roaring of the sea.
Gniphon—Battle-spear.
Flamddwy—Firebrand.
Llewellyn—Lion-like.
Gryffyn, Griffith, Gruffyd — Dragon.
Arthur—A bear.
Bathanal — Son of the wild boar.
Budignat—Son of victory.
Boadicea—Victory.

Persian.

MEN.

Baharam—The planet Mars, a king, a sword.
Behadar; *Hindu*, Behadur; *Arabic & Turkish*, Behadir — A hero.
Kahraman—A warrior.
Carcas—Eagle.
Fareksavar — Intrepid horseman.
Turkish, Ildherim — Thunderbolt.

Arslân Sher; *Arabic*, Assad Dirbas, &c.—Lion.
Sherkok—Mountain lion.
Alp Arslân—Strong lion.
Cyaxares—Lion-king.
Arisai—Lionlike.
Kelig Arslân—Sword of a lion.
Kesel Arslân—Red lion, &c.

Arabic.

MEN.
Er Raad el Khasif—The loud pealing thunder.
Alp—Strong.
Ghanim—Taker of spoil.
Hallouf—Wild boar.
Marfain—Hyæna.
Melek el Mansour—Victorious king.

Chinese.

MEN.
Hwang Lûng—Yellow dragon.
Tsing Lûng—Azure dragon.
Chaon-Kin-Lûng—Golden dragon.
Lûng So—Dragon renewed.

North American Indian.

MEN.
Soangetaha—The strong-hearted.
Kwasind—Strong man.
Pahtoocara—He who strikes.
Munnepuska—He who is not afraid.
Goto kow pah a—He who stands by himself.
Eeshakkonee—The bow and quiver.
Kenen, Pehta, Nixwarroo, &c.—War-eagle.*
Eeahsapa—The black rock.
Nekimé—Thunder.
Tunt aht oh ye—The thunderer.
Ea chin che a—The red thunder.
Wa saw me saw—Roaring thunder.
Mahtothpa—The *four* bears, fig. of fourfold courage.'
Shome cosse—The wolf.
Chaheechopes—The four wolves.
Kah gah gee—The raven.
Ladooke a—The buffalo bull.
Pez he kee—The bison.

WOMEN.
Oo jeen aheha—The woman who lives in the bear's den.
Me cheet a neuh—The wounded bear's shoulder.
Katequa—The female eagle.
Ah kay ee pixen—The woman who strikes many.

---

* A few only of these almost unpronounceable names are given as being characteristic, but every tribe has its various names signifying more particularly Thunder, Eagles, Eagle's ribs, &c., and Bears, red, white, grizzly, old, &c., Bear's child, Buffalo's child, &c. *The wounded bear's shoulder*, as the name of a wife, suggests a pretty idea of tender and soothing support, to which a terrible contrast is afforded by *the woman who strikes many*! (Names quoted from *Catlin's N. A. Indians*.)

CLASS II.—ABSTRACT QUALITIES. 257

Tahitian.

MEN.	WOMEN.
Pauma—A kite.	Pomare—Perhaps the feminine.

Division 8.
Wisdom and Intellect.

Hebrew.

MEN.	WOMEN.
Zephaniah—The secret or counsel of God.	Dinah—One who judges.
Darda—Pearl of wisdom.	Deborah—A bee, fig. industry and art of governing.
Chilmah—Learned.	
Barnabas—Son of exhortation, or prophecy.	

Greek.

MEN.

Cleomenes, Climene (*w.*) — A glorious mind.
Sophocles, Clisophus—Glory of wisdom.
Callinoüs—Fine mind.
Nicomedes—Powerful mind.
Euphron, Euphronia (*w.*) — Right-minded.
Sophronius, Sophronia (*w.*), Sophroniscus—Temperate, wise.
Cleobulus—Glorious counsellor.
Aristobulus—Best counsellor.
Chrysostom—Golden-mouthed, fig. of eloquence.
Pythagoras—Who speaks as an oracle.
Numa—Law.
Cosmo—Order.
Bulis—Well-advised.
Nestor—One who remembers, or is experienced.
Archimedes—A master-mind.
Melesias—Thinker.

Pythias—Enquiring.
Dædalus—Ingenious.
Cadmus—Who adorns.
Metiochus—Prudent.
Gregory—Vigilant.

WOMEN.

Sybil—Counsel of God.
Theano—Divine intelligence.
Sophia, Sophy, Sophiele, Sophonie—Wisdom.
Sophronia, Sophrosyne, Sophronium—Temperate, modest.
Ida (*s.*), Idaline—Far-seeing.
Arsinoë—Lofty-minded.
Ismena, Athenaïs, Minervina—Learned.
Eurymene—Large-minded.
Eurydice—Liberal judgment.
Urania (from *Sanscrit*), Varouna—Who studies the skies.
Eudocia—Who thinks well.
Phantasia—Imagination.
Icasia—Who conjectures.

Latin.

MEN.
Cato—Well advised, prudent.
Facundus—Eloquent.

WOMEN.
Sapientia—Wise; *French form,* Sage.
Prudence.

Teutonic.

MEN.
Ernest, Ernestine (*w.*) — Earnest-minded.
Egbert, Cuthbert—Eminent for wisdom.
Robert, Rupert, Robin, Robinetta (*w.*)—Bright counsellor.
Cuthwin—Winner of wisdom.
Wistan—Wisest.
Conrad—Wise counsellor.
Alured (*s.*) — Universal counsellor.

Ethelred, Ethelreda [12] (*w.*), Audrey—Noble counsellor.
Roderick; *Spanish,* Rodriguez, Diaz—Chief counsellor.

WOMEN.
Edma—Mind.
Radegunde — A woman who counsels.

Arabic.

MEN.
El Abtan—The most profound. | Meh di—A guide.

North American Indian.

MEN.
Chesh oo hong ha—Man of good sense.
Not oway—The thinker.
Mash kee wet—The thought.
Wa hon gaskee—No fool.
Hahnee—The beaver.
Pah me cowetah—The man who tracks.

Division 9.
Glory, Power, Noble Birth, and Station.

Hebrew.

MEN.
Abraham — Father of a great multitude.
Malchus—King.
Adrammeleck — Power of the king.

Sharai—Prince. Jared—Ruler.
Jesse, Jessica (*w.*), Jessie (*w.*)— Wealthy.
Adonizedek—Lord of justice.
Adonibezek—Lord of lightning.
Aaron—Lofty mountain.

CLASS II.—ABSTRACT QUALITIES.

Ephraim—Increasing.
Bartimeus—Of honourable birth, or the son of Timeus.

WOMEN.

Milcah—Queen.
Sarah—Princess.

Deborah—Bee, fig. female ruler.
Aholibamah—'My tent is exalted.'
Magdalene, Madge, Madeleine, Madeline — Tower, magnificent.

Greek.

MEN.

Basil, Basilis (*w.*); *modern Greek*, Vassilis, Vassilissi (*w.*), Vasileia (*w.*)—King and Queen.
Anaxis, Anaxo (*w.*)—King and Queen.
Kyrios, Kyria (*w.*), Kyrillos, Cyrus, Cyril, Cyrilla (*w.*), Cyra (*w.*)—Lord, lady.
Archelaus—Chief of the people.
Porphyry—Purple, fig. royal.
Stephen, Stephanie (*w.*); *Spanish*, Esteban; *French*, Etienne—Crowned.
Epiphanius—Most illustrious.
Sebastian—Reverenced.
Creon—'I command.'
Crœsus—Who commands.
Pericles — Surrounded with glory.
Entimeus—Honoured.
Cleitus—Illustrious.
Cleogenes—Son of glory.
Cleon, Cleander — A glorious man.
Cleodemus—Glory of the people.
Cleostrates—Glory of the army.
Cydias—Glory.
Euclid—True glory.
Eugene, Eugenie (*w.*), Eupator—Well-born, of noble descent.
Hegemon—Leader.

Pancrates—All-powerful.
Trismegistus — Thrice great (counsellor to Osiris).
Patrocles—Father's glory.
Metrocles—Mother's glory.
Archebulus — Chief counsellor, chief of the senate.
Archestrates—Chief of the army.
Archippus—Chief of the cavalry.
Aristocrates — The power, or rule, of the best.
Demosthenes, Democrates — Power of the people.

WOMEN.

Iphianassa—Brave queen.
Panthea—Divine.
Pantaclea—All-glorious.
Celia, Medea—One who commands.
Phenice—Palm-tree, fig. victory.
Monimia—Self-sustained.
Eleutheria—Liberty.
Clio, Clelie, Cleine, Clorinda—Glorious, renowned.
Cleonimia—Glorious name.
Cleodora—Glorious gift.
Cleopatra—A father's or a country's glory.
Clearista—Best glory.
Clytemnestra—Glorious wife.
Cleophila—Lover of glory.

Latin.

MEN.

Regulus, Regillianus — Kingly.
Regina (*w.*), Reine (*w.*)—Queen.
Augustus, Augusta (*w.*), Augustine (*m. w.*), Crescentius, Crescens (*w.*)—Increasing.
Maximus, Maximin, Magnus—Great.
Celsus—Elevated.
Titus, Tita (*w.*), Titian (*Etrusc.*)—Honoured.
Patrick—Noble.
Liberius, Camillus, Camilla (*w.*) Freeborn.
Tancred (*s.*)—Aged chief.
Tanagra (*w.*)—Aged chieftainness.
Lorenzo, Laurence, Laurentia (*w.*), Laura(*w.*)—fig. Crowned with laurel.
Palma, Palmatius, Palmyre (*w.*) —Palm-tree, fig. of victory.
Respectus — One whom people turn back to see.
Caius, Caia (*w*) — (used to sig.) Master and mistress.

WOMEN.

Couronne [13]—Crown.
Digna—Worthy of honour.

Teutonic.

MEN.

Otho, Odo, Odette (*w.*) (from Odin)—Significant of supreme power.
Sanscrit & Teutonic, Amalaric—Faultless ruler.
Alaric, Athalric; *Spanish*, Alvarez—Noble ruler.
Reginald; *French*, Regnier—Godlike or chief ruler (regni, gods).
Theoderic — Fatherly chief or ruler of the people.
Louis (*s.*),[14] Ludwig, Ludovic, Clovis, Cloud, Louisa (*w.*), Louise (*w.*), Louison (*w.*) (*Old French*), Aloys; *Russian*, Lodoiska (*w.*) — Hero of the people.
Attala, Ella (*m. w.*)—Noble.
Athelstan—The most noble.
Landric—Lord of the country.
Sigeric—Victorious lord.
Dudda—Head of the family.
Dunstan—The highest.
Marmaduke, Waldemar—Most mighty.
Ethelward, Aylward, Ethelwold—Noble governor.
Meyrick, Almeric, Ethelmer, Aylmer—Great and noble.
Aldred, Eldred, Wildred—Revered by many.
Henry, Harry, Eric, Erica (*w.*), Eoric (eorl, *earl*), Henrietta (*w.*), Harriet (*w.*), Hetta (*w.*) —A mighty lord or a hero.
Herman, Hermanric, Armand—Commander in chief of an army.
Walter, Waltheof—Chief of an army.
Sœfreth—Freedom of the sea.
Evremond, Ebermund [15]—Wild boar, protector.

WOMEN.

Cunegonde—Royal lady.

CLASS II.—ABSTRACT QUALITIES.

Aldegonde, Olga—Noble lady.
Ethel—Noble.
Ethelswytha—Most noble.
Adelaide, Adeline, Adelicia, Adèle, Adela, Adeliza, Adeliz, Alix, Alice, Ethelinda—Noble maiden.
Hermenegilde, Hermione, Erminia, Ermengarde, Irmentrude,[16] Irma—Maiden of high degree.
Clotilde (s.), Othilde, Ottilie, composed of Clovis and Hilda—Sig. of a chief's daughter.
Alodie, Elodie—An heiress.
Ethelwyne—Noble and beloved.

Celtic and Gaelic.

MEN.
Rhys, Ruiz, Ruy, Conan[17]—A prince.
Gallawyg—War-god, fig. mighty chief.
Fineack—Noble.
Fingal (s.)—Noble and strong.
Hugh, Hugues (Hu-cadarn)—The mighty, indomitable.
Gwanar—The ruler.
Murdock, Murtagh—Great chief.
Verken-kedo-righ—Great chief of a hundred heads.
Or-kedo-righ—Chief of a hundred valleys.
Trystan—The proclaimer.

WOMEN.
Gwen-hywar—Lady of the summit of the water, fig. queen of the sea.

Sclavonian.

MEN.
Vladimir[18]—Glory of princes.
Droghimir—Good prince.
Casimir—Prince of the chief house.
Ladislas, Wladyslaw, Lancelot—Glory of power.
Stanislaus—Glory of the state.

Persian.

MEN.
Melchior—Kingly.

WOMEN.
Ariana—Honoured.

Arabic.

MEN.
Malek Shah—King. Mellaky—Princess.
Almir—A prince.
Shems al Mulook—Sun of kings.
Tajah Mulook—Diadem of kings.
Seyf el Mulook—Sword of kings.
Seyf ud Dowlah—Sword of the state.
Hamed—Praised.
Mohammed, El Amjad—Greatly praised.

Shamikh—High, lofty.
Turkish, Togred bey—The falcon lord.

WOMEN.

Zita—Mistress.
Sharaf al Benat—The glory of damsels.

Hindu.

WOMEN.

Perrya Amma—Great lady. | Pun Amma—Golden lady.

Mexican.

MEN.

Montezuma—Severe master.

North American Indian.

MEN.

Stee cha co me co—The great king.
Hongs kay be (synonymes in every tribe, not titles, *names* given to children)—The great chief.
Ha na tah me mauk—The wolf-chief.
Chee me na na quet—The great cloud.
Koman nikin—The great wave.

Division 10.
Peace and Gentleness.

Hebrew.

MEN.

Solomon, Salome (*w.*)—Peace.
Noah, Manoah—Rest.
Jonah—A dove.
Barjonah—Son of a dove.

WOMEN.

Jemima; *Syrian,* Hamami—A dove.
Rachel—A ewe lamb.

Greek.

MEN.

Irenæus, Irene (*w.*), Iris (rainbow)—Messenger of peace.
Leander—A *gentleman,* gentle and brave.
Melisander (a poet)—Significant of a man with honied lips.
Meteo—Gentle.
Parmenio—Patience.
Eudius—Serene.

WOMEN.

Ianessa—Who governs gentle.
Ianira—Who softens men.
Melissa—Bee, fig. honey.
Millicent, Milly, Melicerta, Melita—Honey, sweet.
Melina—Balm, gentle.
Drosée—Dew, fig. both of soothing and refreshing.
Glycera—Sweet.

CLASS II.—ABSTRACT QUALITIES.

Amaryllis—A refreshing stream.
Ethrosyne—A serene sky.
Elais—Olive-tree.
Azelie—Not emulous.

Orca—Oil-vessel, fig. healing and peacemaker.
Paula (s.), Pauline—Rest.
Rhene—A lamb.

Latin.

MEN.

Celestinus, Celestine (w.)—Heavenly-minded.
Clement, Clementina (w.), Clementia (w.), Clemence (w.)—Courteous, affable.
Oliver, Olivia (w.), Olive (w.), Olivarez — Olive-tree, fig. peace.
Placidius, Placidia (w.), Placilla (w.), Tranquillus, Tranquilla (w.), Quietus, Mansuetus, Lenius, Lena (w.), Latona — Quiet, gentle.

Pudens, Pudentia (w.)—Modest.
Tacitus—Silent.
Tace (w.)—*Be* silent!
Old French, Aignan, Agnes (w), Nancy; *Welsh*, Nest; *Spanish*, Inez—A lamb.

WOMEN.

Dulcibella, Douce—Sweet and fair.
Serena, Terentia—Soft, gentle, patience.

Teutonic.

MEN.

Frederic, Fritz, Frederica (w.), Alfric, Afra (w.) — Peaceful ruler.
Alfred—All peace, or the genius of peace (ælf—genius).
Humphrey—Home-peace.
Wilfred—Peace of many.

Raymond, Reinfred—Pure peace.
Manfred—Man of peace.
Offa—Mild, gentle.
Winfred, Winifred (w.)—Peace-winner, or Lover of peace.

WOMEN.

Mildred—Gentle of speech.

Celtic.

MEN.

Columba, Colombe (w.), Malcolm (coulm)—Dove.

Tegid—Serenity; also Beauty.
Owen—Lamb, or form of John.

Arabic.

MEN.

Salam, Salameh (w.)—Peace.
Es Samit—The Silent.

WOMEN.

Ten 'om—Soft, gentle.

Syriac.

WOMEN.

Semiramis (hamami)—A dove.

Division 11.
Charm, Winsomeness, and Melody and Perfume figurative of them.

Hebrew.

MEN.

Naamah—Pleasant.
Phœnician, Sidonia—Enchantress.
Bithron—Daughter of Melody.
Mahala, Anah—Sweet singer.

WOMEN.

Rebekah — One who draws as with a noose.
Hadassah—Myrtle.
Keziah—Cassia.
Keturah—Incense.

Greek.

MEN.

Æmilianus, Maximilian — A winning speaker.
Emilius, Emilia [s.] (w.), Emily (w.)—Of winning manners.
Pisander, Peitho—One who persuades men.
Eulalos—Eloquent.
Erasiphron—Of a kindly voice.
Eumenes—Charming.

WOMEN.

Charis—Grace.
Epicharis—Full of grace, exquisitely charming.
Aspasia—Winning.
Hedia, Hedyla—Pleasing.
Euphemia, Effie, Phemie, Eulalie—One who speaks sweetly.
Emmeline, Amelia (s.)—Full of melody.

Lyra, Lyris—A lyre, fig. of harmony.
Evadne, Ariadne—Sweet singer.
Hymnis—A singer.
Euterpe—Charming.
Calliope—A beautiful voice.
Ligia—Silvery-voiced.
Philomela—Lover of song.
Œdomium — Nightingale's throat.
Erianthe — Sweet as many flowers.
Muriel, Thya—Perfume.
Ianthe, Ione, Ia—Violet, fig. Modesty.
Haidee (s.)—Modest.
Aura, Isaura—Soft air.
Rosaura—Breath of a rose.
Cassiopeia—Fragrance of cassia.
Myrrha, Myra, Myrtah, Myrrhena—Myrtle.

Latin.

WOMEN.

Gratius (m.), Gratia, Gratianus (m.), Gratiana, Grace, Gracieuse, Gracienne, Graziella, Graziosa; *Spanish*, Engracia—Graceful, winsome, charming.
Violet, Viola, Violetta, Violante—fig. Modest grace.

French, Réséda—Fragrant weed, mignionette, fig. Little darling.
Carmen (s.) (favorite *Spanish* name), Carmenta—Song, also sig. a charm.
Vinnulia—Winning.
Blandine—Caressing.

CLASS II.—ABSTRACT QUALITIES.

Arabic.

WOMEN.
Shereen, Hulweh—Sweet.

Enees el Jelees—Charming companion.

North American Indian.

WOMEN.
Shawon dazee—The south wind.
Pshanshaw — Sweet-scented grass.

Minne ha' ha—Laughing water.
Minne wa' wa—Pleasant sound of wind in the trees.

Vitian or Figian Islands.

WOMEN.
Naiogabui—One who smells sweetly.

Division 12.
Joy, Joy-givers, and Good Fortune.

Hebrew.

MEN.
Baruch—Blessed.
Sardis—Prince of joy.
Terah—Flourishing.
Ephratah—Fruitful.
Isaac—Laughter.

Joseph; *Spanish,* José; *Bréton,* Joscelyn; *Italian,* Giuseppe; Josepha (*w.*), Josephine (*w.*), Giuseppina (*w.*)—Increasing.
Ave—All hail! sig. of welcome.

Greek.

MEN.
Evelpis, Elpidius—Hopeful.
Elpis—Hope.
Eudemon—Fortunate.
Chæremon, Charmion (*w.*), Charmis—Glad.
Thales, Thalia (*w.*), Thallusa (*w.*)—Flourishing.
Euthalia—Flourishing richly.
Charops—Rejoicing the eyes.
Charimene (*w.*)—Rejoicing the spirit.
Tychichus, Eutyches, Syntyche—Fortunate.

Polydor, Pandora (*w.*) — Much gifted.
Plutarch — Who commands riches.
Procopius—Successful.
Charilaus—Rejoicing the people.
Chæriphiles—Lover of joy.

WOMEN.
Euphrasia, Euphrosyne — Joyous.
Gelasia—Laughing.
Amenaïde—Satisfied.

Latin.

MEN.

Benedict, Benoit, Benoite (*w.*), Beata (*w.*)—Blessed.
Beatrice—Making blessed.
Felix, Felicia (*w.*), Felicité (*w.*), Felise (*w.*), Fortunatus, Faustus, Fausta (*w.*), Faustina (*w.*)—Happy.
Salvius, Salvia (*w.*), Salvina (*w.*)—Sage, fig. safety.
Hilary, Gaudentius, Jocunda (*w.*)—Joyous.

Bonaventure—Good fortune.
Boniface—Pleasant face.
Prospero; *Italian*, Properzia—Prosperous.
Sallust—Healthy and happy.

WOMEN.

Letitia, Lettice—Gladness.
French, Espérance—Hope.
Spanish, Mercedes—Favour.
French, Opportune—Welcome.

Teutonic.

MEN.

Odo, Eudes—Happy, powerful.
Odalric, Ulric, Ulrica (*w.*)—Happy ruler.
Edwy, Hedwig (*w.*)—Happy chief.
Edwin—Happy and beloved.
Edward—Guardian of happiness.

Edmund—Happy peace.
Geoffrey, Jeffrey—Joyful peace.

WOMEN.

Edith—Blessed.
Ida (*m. w.*)—Happy.
Eleanor, Ellen, Lenora, Nellie—Fruitful.

Arabic.

MEN.

Abu Saadat, Umr' Sood (*w.*)—Father, mother of prosperities.
Sa'ad, Sa'a dek (*w.*), Zaïdee (*w.*)—Prosperous.
Ferook—Fortunate.
El Asad—Most prosperous.

Selim, Selimah (*w.*)—Healthful.
Mes'ood, Mes'oodeh (*w.*), Meymoon, Meymooneh (*w.*)—Happy.

WOMEN.

Noam—Felicity.

Persian.

MEN.

Feroz—Fortunate.
Ferozeshah—Fortunate king.
Ferdusi, Feridoon—Paradisiacal.[19]

WOMEN.

Ayesha (*s.*) (aische)—Happy.
Hindu, Narmada—Bestower of pleasure.

NOTICES TO CLASS II. ABSTRACT QUALITIES.

¹ *Penagia*, Pan-Hagia, *All-holy*, the name given to the Virgin Mary by the modern Greeks.

² *Philopater, Philomater.*—With all their boundless wealth of words, and their ingenuity in forming names by endless combinations of them, the Greeks had a strange, uncomfortable fancy for calling people by their opposites. A shepherd-guardian and defender of the sheep would be named Lycidas, from Lycos, *a wolf*, the enemy of the flock; to a cold, unimpassioned orator would be given a name signifying *warmth* and *fire*. Some of these mocking names were given on graver grounds. Two of the Ptolemies were surnamed as above: the first, *because* he poisoned his father; the second, because of his undutifulness to his mother, who, in consequence, endeavoured to exclude him from the succession to the throne. This curious fancy for misnomers seized also on the mind of an Eastern monarch. His wife, who was exquisitely beautiful, was named by him Cabihat, sig. *ugly*, so that the effect of her charms might be heightened from their striking contrast to her name.

³ *Niña.*—This word, or name, as it has become to us, is used by the Spaniards as a term of endearment, sig. *darling*; Ninita, *little darling*; or simply to express 'a young girl,' and also in addressing a young lady, answering (but rather more familiarly) to our modern 'Miss,' 'the English *Mees*,' as our French neighbours say. Every other European nation has a better-sounding title for unmarried ladies than we possess. In frock-and-pinafore days, Miss sounds not *a miss* (though even then it will not do to dwell upon the actual meaning of the word, *a loss, a want*); but surely as applied to elderly ladies in spectacles, it has a silly sound. In Pope's and Addison's days, young ladies after ten years of age assumed the title of Mistress, which was given to both married and unmarried women. Miss, applied to a grown-up girl, was a term of reproach. Could not some scholar in a chivalrous spirit take up the cause of the unmarried daughters of Great Britain and supply them with a more befitting title?

Mercedes, a favorite name for Spanish women, is also used by Spaniards as a term of respect, answering to 'your honour' in English. 'Muchas mercedes' signifies 'many thanks,' as in modern Greece the surname of one of the Ptolemies, Eucharisto, sig. *very gracious*, is the common word for expressing thanks, being the exact rendering of the French 'mille grâces.' Mercedes, as a name, with its pretty double signification of 'a gift' and 'thanks,' may be to the parents as an acknowledgement for the blessed gift of a child, and to the child as a reminder that her life should be indeed a cause of thankfulness.

[4] *Reynold.*—The clear waters of the *Rhine* may illustrate this name; in the German word 'rein' is still preserved the signification *pure, clear.*

[5] *Anna,* or *Hannah.*—That word of melody, *grace,* as significant of 'good-will,' has echoed unceasingly through this fair world of ours since 'the morning stars sang together' of God's favour to man, and the crystal streams and pleasant trees of Paradise gave back the sound. High above all the discords of earth, it has rung, it will ever ring on the ear of faith, but sweeter far has it become since angels sang it over the cradle of Bethlehem. The word grace, so infinite in significance even to the heathen world, has its synonymes in all languages, and men have loved to make of it a name, and dower with it their children.

As a Hebrew name, Anna, *grace,* has a double significance, belonging to *Virtue,* God-given grace, as illustrated by Prov. xi. 16: 'a gracious woman retaineth honour;' and belonging to *Help-givers,* in that grace implies *kindliness, good-will.* In Hebrew, the prefix Jeho to Hanan makes it a *Name of Religion,* signifying *God's grace,* or *God's gift.* From Jehohanan come John, Jane, &c.

Grace, in the Greek Charis, and the Latin Gratia, also bears a double signification. Charis, as *good-will,* the original of our Charity, *inward grace,* belongs to *Help-givers;* and, in the sense of *outward grace,* charm of manner, greater than the charm of beauty, it belongs to what I have called *Winsomeness.* The Latin Gratia I have looked upon in like manner.

[6] *Nicholas.*—This name would suggest matter for a chapter, which must here be compressed into a little note. It has the singular distinction of making two diametrically opposite impressions. When we hear it, we think of a holy man, a lover of children, the protector of the defenceless and weak—we think also of the devil! The bravest English schoolboy, however lightly he may utter the name, would have a very wholesome dread of the appearance of 'Old Nick.' The most timid little Greek, Russian or German girl, as she lays her fair head on her pillow one night in the year, has no dearer wish (supposing always that she knows that she has been good) than that her (in German) Santa Claus should visit her bedside before morning; for then she will surely discover in the stocking laid ready to his hand, the toys that she longs for most.

For the evil repute of the name of 'Nick' we must go much farther back than to Niccolo Macchiavelli, the wily Florentine politician of infamous memory, upon whom some learned writers once fathered it. 'Old Nick' had his origin in the malignant water-sprites of Northern mythology. They were male and female, Nix and Nixe, Neckar derived from *necce*, to kill. In the semblance of a fair youth or girl, or an innocent-looking child, these dreaded beings were supposed to haunt the most beautiful streams; wiled onward by the enchanting melody of their songs, unwary travellers were lured to the water's edge, and then — their destruction was secure. Have the Nixies fled? Would to God they were! Evil spirits, both male and female, with enticing words accomplish still the ruin of immortal souls.

Not only by the river side, but far below the surface of the earth, in the gloomy depths of the Harz-mountain mines, we again catch the echo of the fatal name. Kupfer-Nickel, the fumes of which are poisonous, has for its deadly compounds arsenic and cobalt, so named from Cabalus, the once so-dreaded demon of the mines that the Church-service of Germany had a special form of prayer used for the expulsion of the fiend.

But the children's loved Santa Claus, or Claussen, as he is affectionately called, must not be forgotten. The Christian Saint's Greek name was prophetic, *Victorious over the people*, with that best victory winning their hearts. In all Roman Catholic countries this holy man is looked upon as the protector of the weak against the strong; he is emphatically the Saint of the people. Marvellous tales are told of his babyhood — standing up with joined hands to pray, when an infant of but a few hours old, and other incredible performances. Pity it is that foolish inventions should thus throw discredit on the realities of a good man's life.

The origin of St. Nicholas's stocking may well be true, for his vast wealth was spent in acts of charity. Three daughters of a distressed noble are said to have been relieved from a threatened life of misery by marriage portions contained in stockings, which were thrown in at their window on successive nights by the Saint. Therefore it is that in Greece, and Russia, and Germany stockings are laid out on the eve of St. Nicholas (December 6) for the Saint to fill.

Mixing the false with the true, a terrible tale hangs over the three children which usually accompany St. Nicholas in his pictures. At a time of famine, the Bishop of Myra, travelling in his diocese, lodged at the house of a man supposed to be of good reputation. The monster, however, since provisions had become scarce, had been accustomed to steal children, murder them, and serve them up as food to his guests. But the revolting dish placed before the holy man told its own tale, and the bishop, rising from the table, discovered a tub of dismembered limbs, over which he made the sign of the cross, and three children instantly arose alive and well, to be restored to their overjoyed mother.

The irreverent custom practised in England, in Roman Catholic times, of electing 'a boy bishop,' originated in the name given to St. Nicholas of the 'Child Bishop,' on account of his early piety.

The synonyme of Nicholas, Nicodemus, is applied in France as a term of reproach; *c'est un Nicodème*, means a silly man, who seeks for popularity. This application of the name doubtless refers to the Nicodemus of Scripture, who at first visited our Lord by night, 'for fear of the Jews;' but his after-fearlessness should have wiped away the reproach. It was the voice of Nicodemus that was raised before the assembled rulers to inquire: 'Doth our law judge any man before it hear him, and know what he doth?' And it was Nicodemus who brought an hundredweight of myrrh and aloes to embalm the body of the Crucified.

7 *Læna.*—A bronze statue in Athens of a lioness without a tongue commemorated the noble spirit of this woman of lion-heart. Concerned in the conspiracy of Harmodius and Aristogiton, to overthrow the tyrant Hippias, Læna was dragged to the torture; on her way she bit off her tongue, lest her coming agony should wring from her the name of an accomplice.

8 *Nero.*—This name, so constantly given to black dogs, may seem to the general reader wrongly translated. It is, however, on the best authorities said to be a Sabine word, sig. *valiant*; others have derived it from the Greek *neuron*, nerve. Not *valiant*, but of iron *nerve* the monster must have been whose hand kept true to time in the dance music he played while the cries of his victims in the burning city resounded on all sides. Nero, as black, comes to us from the Italian; from the Latin niger, *black*, we have Nigel, sig. *a dark, black-haired man.* Nero was wrongly painted in the great French picture in the International Exhibition: the tyrant's especial pride was his golden hair.

9 *Tanaquil.*—Tana, a word found on Etruscan inscriptions, signifying *master, lord*, and, as applied to women, corresponding with the Roman prænomen Caia, i.e., *mistress of the house.* * It is sin-

---

* Salverte.

gular to find also a Persian word, Tan, signifying strength, power, while amongst the ancient Scots a Thane was a chief.

[10] *Modred* and *Respectus.*—Lucifer, the *light-bearer*, accepted now as the 'proud,' and Abigail, the *father's joy*, only accepted as a 'maid-servant,' have shown us how names have been wrested from their original meanings—how many words also have been similarly wronged. In digging about the old roots of languages when name-hunting, we come upon some in whom are discovered the title-deeds, as it were, of words long since dispossessed of their birthright. Too late to hope to restore them to their high estate, it is at least curious to read their original grant.

See now Respectus, a Roman name. What would have been thought of the sanity of anyone who had spoken of the late Duke of Wellington as respectable? And yet we find Respectus a name of high repute, signifying, as it did, a man whom all *turned back to look at*; it would therefore have been no inappropriate word to use.

And Modig, too! Ask anyone the meaning of the word Moody, they will tell you: 'out of humour.' Not so did the hardy Norsemen, the Vikingr of old, look on the original word. Mod, Modig (still preserved in the German 'Muth') signifies *courage*, or *a brave spirit*, and as such the noblest of the land were proud to bear names of which it formed a part: Modred was one who counselled bravely, Thormod was one of supernatural courage. But the old spirit clings about some old names; it would seem, from the armorial bearings of the family, that Moodys were *modig* still, however their name might be read. An achievement of honour shows two hands grasping the Rose of England, for a King's life was saved at the risk of Edmond Moody's own; and the motto they bear is, 'Risk to save.'

Reversing the usual order of things, in another Northern name we find the probable origin of a word, which from such origin derives additional significance. The wife of Lok, the evil genius, or devil, of Scandinavian mythology, was named Signa, or Sinna—Sin,

. . . the snaky sorceress that sits
Fast by Hell-gate, and keeps the fatal key.

[11] *Hildegonde* and *Modgudor.*—In the warlike race of the Teutons we not only find amongst the names of men *wolves* and *bears*, the *spear*, the *staff*, and the *helmet of war*, but many of their women's names are strangely warlike too. For the progenitors of a race which should make little England first amongst the nations of the earth, it needed that every element of success should

combine; the Celtic blood was intrepid to *dare*, the Teuton nerve resolute to *do*, and valiant men were matched with women high-couraged beyond the wont of the sex. Significant of this, we find that the three terminations most common in Teutonic feminine names are all significant of courage. Hilda, from Hildr, the war-goddess of the North; Gunda, or Gonda, from gunnr, *war* (both of these were indeed names of themselves); and wiga, from the masculine wig, or vich, sig. a *hero*. Freyga, the beautiful, was represented with a drawn sword in her right hand, and in her left a bow, signifying thereby that in time of need women as well as men should be ready to fight.

[12] *Ethelreda, noble counsellor.*—How inappropriate to such a source seems the word of vulgar meaning, *tawdry*! At St. Ethelreda's or St. Awdrey's fair cheap laces were sold, and gay but worthless gewgaws, to attract the simple country wenches and their swains, who came prepared to buy, however limited may be their choice; and so, from Ethelreda's fair, showy things of little value came to be called tawdry.

[13] *Couronne.*—Names expressive of royalty are commonly borne by private individuals in all countries, except our own. In Italy, Regina is often heard, and still more frequently in France the name of Reine. Amongst the peasant women of Alsace, Couronne was at one time a very favourite name.

[14] *Louis.*—To this name has been attached the signification of 'an illustrious hero.' I have ventured to change it to 'hero of the people,' Lud or *Leod* wig. The C in Clovis makes it a royal designation.

[15] *Evremond, Ebermund.*—Mund signified both *peace* and *protection*. In connection with this last it had amongst the Scandinavians the additional meaning of a *hand*. The *wild-boar protector* would be the designation of a man high in power and of great courage. The wild boar was held in especial honour, as the means whereby mankind was supposed to have been taught the use of the plough. It was said by the Teutons that the first plough was made on the model of its snout, with tusks of iron on either side to tear up the ground.

[16] *Irmentrude.*—In this name of the mother of the Guelphs was combined two of the favourite ideas of the Teutons. Irminsula was a chief idol of the nation. Eormen, sig. *great, vast*, entered into the composition of many names, Hermanric, Hermione, &c. Trudr sig. *fortitude, firmness*—was considered a peculiarly feminine designation. Many names composed from it have passed

away, some of them, such as Mimidrud, would sound harshly in our ears; but Gertrude, once Gerdrud, remains, sig. one strong-hearted and true. Lina, as a termination or as a name by itself, has a lovely signification: a 'support on which to lean.' Hllina was a tutelary goddess of the North, to whom men looked for help in their hour of need. For true woman, could any name be more significant?

[17] *Conan.*—The Celtic word for a *prince* comes near to the Teutonic Cuning or Cyning, which illustrates the words 'knowledge is power,' kunnan being the Gothic word *to know*. Cuning is also said to signify valiant: well might the crown be worn by knowledge and valour combined. The initial C, as significative of royalty, is seen in Chilperic, Childebert, &c. Childe signified a youth of noble or knightly birth; we often meet with it in old ballads, and in that later noble poem, 'Childe Harold.'

Amongst the Sclavonians V (or W) as an initial was a royal letter, a contraction of Vasileus, from the Greek Basileus, a king.

Vassilis, Vassilissi, is the modern Greek for King and Queen.

[18] *Mir.*—This word is of Eastern origin, Emir, a *prince*. Under the title of Ameer al Omra, *prince of the princes*, a family of humble origin exercised in Persia a power nearly regal during a century and a half. One of them, Prince Azed ud Dowlah (sig. *the prosperity of the state*), having constructed a *dyke* across the river Keer, near the ruins of Persepolis, it was named Bund Ameer, the *prince's dyke*. Travellers ignorant of the meaning of the words have given this name to the river itself, and poets, misled, have sung of 'a bower of roses by Bendameer's stream.'

The word Mir, from its double meaning in Sclavonic, is suggestive, signifying a *prince* and a *wall*. A strong wall, for support and defence, should a prince ever be to his people.

[19] *Ferdusi.*—The Persian poet so named was originally called Isaac. His 'Shah-nameh,' *Book of Kings*, a history of Persia, is said to contain 60,000 rhymed couplets.

Feridoon is a name to this day significant to the Persians of their ideal of a perfect monarch. Four lines quoted by Sir J. Malcolm from the Gulistan of Saadi are thus literally rendered in words and measure:—

> The blest Feridoon an angel was not,
> Of musk or of amber he formed was not,
> By justice and mercy good ends gained he;
> Be just and merciful, thou'lt a Feridoon be.*

---

* Secret Societies of the Middle Ages: History of the Assassins.

CHAPTER XIII.

Classified List—Class III. Personal characteristics. Three divisions and notices—including names principally from the Hebrew, Greek, Latin, Teutonic, Arabic, Celtic, North American Indian, &c. &c.

CLASS III.

PERSONAL CHARACTERISTICS.

Division 1.
Names signifying Beauty and Youth, and Flowers as typical of them.

Hebrew.

MEN.

Abinoam—Father of beauty, or father of Noam (*the handsome*).
Japhet, Adoram, Naaman,[1] Naamah (*w.*)—Beautiful.
Adin, Ada (*w.*) — Ornament, adorned.
Dishon—Antelope.
Zibiah—Deer.

WOMEN.

Naomi, Sephora, Tirzah, Thyrza, Theresa (*s.*)—Beautiful.
Ruth—A vision (of beauty?)
Tamar—Palm-tree, fig. upright graceful figure.
Tabitha—Gazelle-eyed.
Jael, Jaaleh—Gazelle.
Orpah—A fawn.

Greek.

MEN.

Calixtus, Calista (*w.*), Narcissus, Hyperides—Of great beauty.

WOMEN.

Theophanie — Divine appearance.
Kalonice—Beauty's victory.

Callidora—Beauty's gift.
Calligenia—Daughter of Beauty.
Abra—Beautiful.
Charitoblepharos — Beautiful eyebrows.
Hebe—Youth.
Parthenope—Young face.
Thaïs—Lovely.

CLASS III.—PERSONAL CHARACTERISTICS.

Glaphyra—Elegant, graceful.
Dorcas—Gazelle-eyed.
Europa—Large-eyed.
Chloe—Blooming.
Cleanthe—A glorious flower.

Anthemia, Polyanthe—Blooming as many flowers.
Ampelis, Ampelisca—A vine.
Philyrea—A willow, fig. grace.
Pyrallis—A brilliant bird.

Latin.

MEN.
Etruscan, Horace, Horatio, Horatia (*w.*)—Worthy to be beheld.
Formosus, Formosa(*w.*); *French*, Bevis—Handsome.
Florus, Florian, Florence (*w.*), Flora (*w.*), Florinda (*w.*)— Flower, fig. beauty.

Junius, Junia (*w.*)—Young.

WOMEN.
Pulcherie—Most beautiful.
Arabella—Fair altar.
Hortense—A garden.
Poppea—A doll, fig. beauty without mind.
Italian, Gelsomina—Jasmine.

Teutonic.

WOMEN.
Vœnn, Vanessa (*s.*)—Beautiful.
Holdlie—Lovely.

Linda—Lovely maid.
Theodelinde (*s.*), Yolande — Fairest in the land.

Celtic.

MEN.
Pryd-ain—Father of beauty.
Prûdwen (*w.*)—Lady of beauty.

WOMEN.
Essylt, Yseult, Isolt—A spectacle, a vision (of beauty).
Gwen wyn wyn—Thrice fair.

Flur—Flower.
Gwend dydd—Fair lady of day.
Gwen frid—Fair face.
Gwenever; *Old English*, Ganore; *Italian*, Ginevra, Genoffeffa; *French*, Géneviève—Fair wife.
Dervoigil—Daughter pure and fair.

Arabic.

MEN.
Hassan—Handsome.
Persian, Behras—Beautiful as the day.

WOMEN.
Bustan—Garden.
Zahr el Bustan—The flower of the garden.

Zahr el Naring—Orange-blossom.
Yasimeen—Jasmine.
Zarifa, Zareefah, Ghazaleh — Graceful.
Shehrazad (Scherazade)—Open, ingenuous countenance.

Gullanar; *Persian*, Gulnare—Pomegranate-blossom.
Sasafeh—Willow.
Marjaneh—Coral, fig. coral lips.
Kadeeb el Ban—Willow-branch, fig. of exquisite grace.

Alif (letter *A* Arabic)—Tall and slender.
Persian, Geiran—Antelope.
Assyrian, Susan—A lily, or an iris, fig. radiantly bright.
Egyptian, Lalahzer—A garden of tulips.

North American Indian.

MEN.
Kokah—Antelope.
Shinga wossa—The handsome bird.

WOMEN.
Tahmiroo—Startled fawn, fig. soft dark eyes.

Olitipa—Prairie-bird.
Owaissa—Blue bird.
Mong shong shaw, Wee ne onka—Bending willow.
Mahnahbezee—The swan.

Division 2.
Complexion, Hair, Height, &c.

Hebrew.

MEN.

Edom—Red.

Greek.

MEN.
Seleucos—Brilliantly fair.
Leucosie (*w.*)—Fair.
Melander, Melanie (*w.*)—Dark.
Melanthus, Melanthusa (*w.*)—Dark flower.
Hyacinth (*m. w.*), Giacinta, Jacinthe—Dark flower and gem.
Glaucus, Glaucopis (*w.*)—Blue-eyed.
Miltiades, Milto (*w.*)—Vermilion, brilliant complexion.
Pyrrhus, Pyrrha (*w.*)—Red-haired.
Diochates—Splendid hair.
Plato—Broad-chested, or wide forehead.

WOMEN.
Liriope—Face of a lily.
Rhodope—Face of a rose.
Kalyca—Rosebud.
Rhoda, Rhodocella—Rose.
Galatea—Milk-white.
Chione—Like new-fallen snow.
Cymo—Waves, fig. white as sea-foam.
Cyanea—Fig. eyes blue as the sea.
Chloris—Pale.
Phryne [2]—Toad, fig. very pale.
Argyrea, Argentine—Of silvery whiteness.
Ione, Ianthe, Ioessa—Dark as a violet.

Aurora—Beauty of morning, fig. fair.
Lycoris—Beauty of twilight, fig. dark.
Chryseis, Chrysilla — Golden-haired.
Electra—Amber-haired.
Xanthe—Yellow-haired.
Leucophyra—White eyebrows.
Minutia — Small, delicately made.

Latin.

MEN.

Alban, Albinia (*w.*), Albyn, Aubyn—Fair.
Candidus—Brilliantly fair.
Eburnus—White as ivory.
Maurice, Maury—A Moor, fig. dark-complexioned. (Greek, *amauros.*)
Longinus—Tall.
Gracchus—Slender.
Paul, Paula [3] (*w.*), Pauline (*w.*)—Little.
Cæcilius, Cecilia (*w.*), Cecile — Grey-eyed.
Aurelius, Aurelia (*w.*)—Golden-haired.
Rosius, Rosianus, Rose (*w.*), Rosa (*w.*), Rosina (*w.*)—Rose, fig. rosy complexion.

Cæsar, Cæsonia (*w.*) — Having much hair.
Julius, Julian, Julia (*w.*), Giuletta (*w.*)—Soft-haired.
Cincinnatus [4]—Curly-haired.
Nigel—Black-haired.
Rufus,[5] Rufina (*w.*), Sulla — Red-haired.
Rutilius, Rutilia (*w.*) — Fiery red.
Flavius, Flavia (*w.*) — Yellow-haired.

WOMEN.

Rosalie—Rose and lily.
Rosalba—White rose.
Bianca, Blanche, Lily, Lilian, Lilias, Lilla — All significant of fairness.

Teutonic.

MEN.

Alberic, Aubrey — Fair-haired chief.
Sweyn—Young man.

WOMEN.

Teutonic & Latin, Rosamund — Rose of the world.

Rosalind—Maiden like a rose.
Golde—Golden-haired.
Brunehilde—Dark-eyed maiden.
Griselda—Grey-eyed maiden.
Heaburge — High tower, fig. tall.
Bugega—Nimble as a hind.

Celtic.

MEN.

Dugald (*s.*)—Black-haired.
Gael—A strong man.
Vhir dhu Mohr — The great black-haired man.

WOMEN.

Gwyneth—The fair one.
Rowena—The white-necked (?).
Foinnghuala—'Fair-shouldered woman.'

Brenna, Brenda (s.) — Dark-haired (bran, *raven*).

Faith fail ge —'Honeysuckle of ringlets.'

Arabic.

MEN.

Abu sh Shámat — Father of moles.

WOMEN.

El Ward fi'l Akmann—A rose-bud.

Soosan—A lily.
Zuleika, (s.) Zeleekah—Brilliantly fair.
Leyla, Leila [6] (s.)—Night, fig. a dark beauty.
Rahab—White cloud, fig. fairness, also of fickleness.

Division 3.
Personal Defects.

Hebrew.
MEN.
Necho—Lame.

Persian.
MEN.
Barasmones—Who squints.

Greek.

MEN.
Macer, Ischas (w.)—Thin, meagre.
Gyrtius—Bent.
Lambda (w.) (letter *L*, Λ) — Crooked legs.

Latin.

MEN.
Claudius, Claude (m. w.), Claudine (w.)—Lame.
Plautus, Plautilla (w.) — Flat-footed.
Lavinius, Lavinia (w.), Scævola —Left-handed.
Pætus—Slight squint.
Strabo—Crooked eyes.
Ravilius—Red-eyed.
Clocles—One-eyed.
Balbus, Balbina (w.) —A stammerer.

Naso—Large nose.
Grypus—Hook-nosed.
Camus—Monkey-nosed.
Calvus—Bald.
Crassus—Fat.
Flaccus—Hanging ears.
Gibbus—Hump-backed.
Curvus—Bent.
Turpilianus, Turpilia (w.)—Unsightly, ugly.

WOMEN.
Raucula—Hoarse voice.

NOTICES TO CLASS III.—PERSONAL CHARACTERISTICS.

[1] *Naaman.*—Does not the meaning of this name heighten our interest in the Bible story of Naaman the Leper? It was not only the successful general, the captain of the host of the King of Syria, upon whose arm his sovereign leant when he went to 'the house of Rimmon,' but a man distinguished also for his personal beauty, upon whom this terrible disease had fallen. The name borne by a Syrian would seem to have been a long-established Hebrew name, for we find it amongst the sons of Benjamin.

[2] *Phryne.*—This too celebrated woman owed the unpleasant name by which she was known to the extreme paleness of her complexion; but her exquisite beauty rendered her independent of colouring, and she disdained to paint like other women of her class. In the eyes of all good and wise men Corinth was disgraced, not embellished, by Phryne's statue of gold; but the disgrace went farther back, even to Corinth's acceptance of gifts from so infamous a source. By the extreme liberality of her disposition we are, however, touchingly reminded of Phryne's original name—Mnesareta, *memory of virtue*.

[3] *Paula* and *Pauline* have been here repeated under their usual Latin derivations, lest my readers should not agree with my referring them to the Greek word παῦλα, *rest*.

[4] *Cincinnatus.*—Ancient astrologers asserted that children born during the rising of the Pleiades had curly hair.

[5] *Rufus.*—The numerous Latin names (amongst which may be numbered Byrrhus, Byrrhia [*w.*], Burra [*w.*], apparently derived from the Greek *purrhos*) signifying *red hair*, which was much esteemed amongst the Romans, are in curious contrast to their lack of names significant of dark beauty, of which the Greeks had so many.

[6] *Leyla, Leila.*—Amongst the many characteristic Arabic names for which the writer has been indebted to Lane's 'Notes to the Arabian Nights,' to her regret she found untranslated this lovely name of world-wide celebrity, as the darling of all Eastern poets. Unable to rest its signification on better authority, the writer ventures to suggest that, as Leilat and Leylat sig. *nights*, it is more

than probable that Leila sig. *night*. For one of the lustrous-eyed, dark-haired daughters of the East few names could be more appropriate:—

> She walks in beauty, like the *night*
> Of cloudless climes and starry skies.

The Greeks had a name nearly synonymous, Lycoris, *beauty of twilight*.

In Ayesha, another celebrated Eastern name, it will be seen that another *suggested* signification is given in default of an authorised one. The writer supposes it to be derived from the Persian word aïsche, *happy*.

CHAPTER XIV.

Classified List—Class IV. Miscellaneous—Animals, plants, places, letters, numbers, &c.—Notices—including names principally from the Hebrew, Greek, Latin, Teutonic, Celtic, Arabic, North American Indian, &c. &c.

CLASS IV.

MISCELLANEOUS,

INCLUDING NAMES SIGNIFYING ANIMALS, PLANTS, PLACES, LETTERS, NUMBERS, ETC.

Hebrew.

MEN.

James, Jacob; *Italian*, Giacomo, Jacopo; *Spanish*, Iago, Diego, Jacqueline (*w.*), Jaquetta (*w.*)—Beguiling.

Moses; *Arabic*, Moussa, Musa, Muza—Drawn from the water.

Adam—Red earth.

Bartholomew—Son that suspends the waters.

Abijam—Father of the sea.

Eglaim—Drops of the sea.

Japhet—Hunter.

Nimrod—Leopard.

Arad—wild ass, fig. hunter of them.

Jubal—A trumpet.

Job—One who mourns.

WOMEN.

Mary,[1] Maria, Miriam, Mariamne, Marion, Minnie, Martha—Bitterness.

Greek.

MEN.

Philip, Philippa (*w.*), Philippina (*w.*), Dorippa (*w.*)—Lover of horses.

George, Georgina (*w.*)—A cultivator.

Pelagio; *Spanish*, Pelayo—The ocean, fig. a mariner.

Antiochus—For or against.
Didymus, Didyma (*w.*) — A twin.
Blaise; *Spanish*, Blas—insensate.
Iopsius—Good cheer.

WOMEN.

Penelope—A worker in cloth, or a silent worker.

Lalage—A talker.
Thetis, Thalassis—The sea.
Scione—One who lives in the shade.
Tryphena, Tryphosa — Luxurious, a lover of pleasure.
Meconium—Poppy-juice.

Latin.

MEN.

Urban—Living in the town.
Peregrine—a stranger.
Sylvester, Sylvanus, Sylvia (*w.*)—From a forest, strange, homely.
Pontius—The sea.
Pilate—a dart.

Caracalla—A garment.
Fabricius—A smith.

WOMEN.

Spanish, Dolores; *Italian*, Dolara—Sorrow.
Telega—Cloth, fig. a worker, industrious.

Teutonic.

MEN.

Ridda—A horseman.

Sholto (*s.*) (ceol)—A ship, fig. a mariner.

Celtic.

MEN.

Lear, Lyr—Sea-shore.

WOMEN.

Cordelia — Token of the flowing.
Morgiana—Lady of the sea.
Teutonic and Celtic. Nanthilda —Child of the torrent or dingle.

Persian.

MEN.

Gustasp; *Spanish*, Gaspar, Gasparine (*w.*), Caspar—A horseman.
Gour — Wild ass (hunter of them).

North American Indian.

MEN.

Wash ke mon ge—The fast dancer. | Kah beck a (*w.*)—A twin.

Vitian, Figian Islands.

MEN.

Batinisavu—Edge of a waterfall.

Plants.

Hebrew.
MEN.

Zimri—A branch. | Serug—A shoot, a tendril.

Greek.

MEN.
Smilax—A yew.

WOMEN.
Cottina—Crown of wild olive.

Daphne—Laurel.
Ipsea—Ivy.
Phillis—A reed.

Latin.

MEN.
Appius—A parsley-crown, prize of victory.
Fabian, Fabius, Fabiola (*w.*)—A bean.
Cicero—A vetch (or wart).
Papyrius—Papyrus.

Quercus—Red oak.
Sirpeius—Willow.
Vitia—A vine.
Lentulus—Lentile.
Urtia, Urticula (*w.*)—A nettle.
Pisius—A pea.

North American Indian.

MEN.
Wukmisir—Corn.
Pah ta choochee — Shooting cedar.

WOMEN.
Shako—Mint.
Shedea—Wild sage.
Layloo ah pe ai she kaw (!) — The grass, bush, and blossom.

Animals.

Hebrew.

MEN.
Gamaliel—The camel (or the recompense) of God.
Becher—Young camel.
Hamor—An ass.

Zippor, Zipporah (*w.*)—A bird.
Oreb—A raven.
Hagabah, Agabus — A grasshopper.

284 WHAT IS YOUR NAME?

Greek.

MEN.
Hippias—A horse.
Panthera—A panther.
Moschus—A calf.
Alectryon—A cock.
Corax—A raven.
Myllia—A mullet.
Batrachus—A frog.

Saurus—A lizard.
Cochlis—A snail.
Cornelius—Rook, bird of good omen.

WOMEN.
Ega, Eriphrea—A kid.
Chelidonis—A swallow.
Telligida—A little grashopper.

Latin.

MEN.
Catulus—Little dog.
Camelius—Camel.
Vitellius—Calf.
Asellus, Asinius, Asella (w.)—Ass.
Murena—Lamprey.
Mugillanus—Mullet.
Vespasian, Vespellian—Wasp.

Hircius, Caper—A goat.
Vossius—A fox.
Vulturgius—Vulture.
Passer—Sparrow.
Corvus, Corvinus—Crow.
Mergus—A sea-mew.

WOMEN.
Felicula—A kitten.
Musca—A fly.

Places.

MEN.
Tiberius, Britannicus, Germanicus, Gallus, Gaetano (Cajetano)—*modern* Khelât, &c.
Lydia, Lesbia, Elida, Melita,

WOMEN.
Nydia, Nessida, Sabina—*modern* Indiana, Vimeira, Alma.[2]

Letters.
Greek.
Beta, Delta, Epsilon, Theta—Name given to Æsop, significant of acuteness, &c.

Numbers.
Latin.

Una—1.
Secundus, Secundilla (w.)—2.
Tertius, Tertullus, Tertullian, Tertia (w.)—3.
Quartus, Quartia (w.)—4.
Quintus, Quintin, Quintillian, Quintilla (w.)—5.

Sextus, Sextina (w.) Sextilia (w.)—6.
Septimus, Septilia (w.)—7.
Octavius, Octavia (w.)—8.
Nonius, Nonia (w.)—9.
Decimus, Decima (w.)—10.

NOTICES TO CLASS IV.—MISCELLANEOUS.

¹ *Mary.*—From the sea, that vast expanse of bitter waters, the Roman Catholics have derived some of the titles they bestow on the Virgin Mary, 'Star of the sea,' 'Lady of the sea.' From the bitterness of the sea—that ever-present type to the Hebrew mind, whether for gladness or grief, the name of Miriam, as significant of the bitterness of bondage, may have been derived. In connection with this name, it is curious to notice that at the Feast of the Passover, when the overthrow of this bondage is commemorated, a cup of salt water (in remembrance of the Red Sea, it is supposed) is placed by the Jews beside the bitter herbs which are dipped into it by those who partake of the feast.

² *Alma.*—Names of places have never formed a very large or favorite class of names; a very few, therefore, have been given only as specimens. In our day, and amongst ourselves, such names are seldom met with out of one class of persons. Soldiers and sailors, wanderers over the face of the globe, not unfrequently give to their children names derived from the place of their birth. Victories, too, are commemorated in this way. It will be in the recollection of all how many a fatherless babe but a few years back was baptized in tears by the name of Alma. Almah, amongst the ancient Jews, was a word which signified a maiden.

In a churchyard where tombstones, as is their wont, were covered with records of departed worth, a little child looked up and asked, 'But where are all the wicked people buried?' Such a question might seem not irrelevant here.

A glorious array of noble and excellent qualities, epithets of dazzling beauty and exquisite grace! What, then, were the wicked and the ugly people called?

A few specimens of names of this last unfortunate class have been given, but individual names were for the most part given in *hope*, uttered with blessings by loving lips, so that by far the greater number of significations are pleasing.

Some evil-sounding names there are, which, where evil livers were there too, must have been names of evil import. The Roman name Locusta was but too terribly significant of one whose presence was a curse; a devourer of life, death and desolation following her steps. Locusta was a professed poisoner. The Greeks, too, had a Panther, and a Lycomedes, *mind of a wolf*, and *Tigris* was a woman's name! It must be confessed that we also had nearer home names of very unpleasant signification. Amongst the gentle Creiwys and Gwenwynwyns, the 'thrice fair' of the ancient Britons, moved a terrible creature Gwrvorwyn, the 'manmaid' or virago! Noble Machtildas and kindly Elgivas were no doubt often jostled aside by a Selethrytha, a *good threatener*.

But my labour of love has been to seek out for names of good not evil import. Would that in those old times these good names had *always* been lived up to; but the story of the Persian visitor to Athens is well known. The Oriental, gifted himself with a resplendent name, looked admiringly on men distinguished by such superb names as Polycletes, *the very celebrated*, Clitomachus, *the illustrious warrior*, till a better-informed friend disenchanted him by the news that his obeisances had been wasted on men whose lives were the exact opposite of their names—bestowed on them in infancy by fond and hopeful parents. But need such recollections discourage us in the ennobling task we may or ought to set before ourselves? Oh, let us not forget *we answer to Christian names*. Should we not strive truly so to do? First, in the full and wide and glorious significance of the words Christian Names; and next, in the individual graces which our respective individual names may signify.

Is the task hard? Are our Christian names so glorious that we despair of living up to them? Despair! with Heaven before us and a Saviour at our side?

'Faint yet pursuing,'
Wearied still the race renewing;
    Hold on thy way, brave heart.
In spirit strong, though limbs are failing;
Resolute, though life is paling,
    Soldier of Christ thou art!

Now may sweet Heaven send thee
Good angels to befriend thee,
    To be thy spirit's stay;
Thy faltering steps grow stronger,
Oh, yet a little longer
    Brave heart, hold on thy way.

Briar and thorn o'erleaping,
Which treacherously are creeping
        To bar the appointed road;
Through the hot noontide speeding,
The chill night-dews unheeding,
        Press forward—to thy God!

Powers of hell defeating—
In thy bright armour meeting
        Unharmed their every shock;
Thy Captain's banner o'er thee,
His blessèd Cross before thee;
        Thy refuge and thy rock.

In the straight path abiding,
Where Faith's pure star is guiding,
        Bear up, thou gallant one.
Still increasing light shall cheer thee,
When thy destined goal more near thee
        Tells that thy race is run!

See where a wreath of glory,
More bright than human story,
        Hath given to mightiest deed,
With starry light undying,
On Heaven's pure altar lying,
        Awaits the conqueror's meed!

By Him Whose mercy's never-ending,
The Saviour in Whose strength thou'rt wending
        Shall then sweet rest be given.
'Faint yet pursuing,'
Wearied—still the race pursuing,
        Speed on, brave heart, to Heaven!

ALPHABETICAL LIST OF NAMES

WITH THEIR

CLASSES AND DIVISIONS.

Notes.—A few more diminutives and varieties of form in Names are here added, which would have over-crowded the Classified List.

French terminations have occasionally been given, especially to women's names where the sound is more pleasing, as in Celestine, Hortense, Valerie, &c.

Amongst Hebrew and Greek names some will be found which were common to men and women; as with us there are a few so used by both—such as Florence, Cecil, &c.

Where the writer has been unable to decide between two significations, she has submitted both suggestions to her readers, as in Pamela, &c.

Occasionally the same name may be found in different languages, having distinct origins and significations, as the Greek and the Teutonic Ida. In some cases the meanings of such names somewhat assimilate, as the Hebrew Almah significant of a *maiden*, and the Latin Alma signifying *holy, pure*, and *fair*. Alma has, however, been placed in Class 4 amongst 'Names derived from Places,' as it is absolutely from the Russian river and its mingled memories of pride and grief that the name has become with us 'a household word.'

ALPHABETICAL LIST OF NAMES

WITH THEIR

CLASSES AND DIVISIONS.

Derivation		Class	Division	Page	Derivation		Class	Division	Page
Heb.	Aaron	2	9	258	Heb.	Adam	4		21, 281
Ar.	Abd Allah	1	2	54, 239	Grk.	Adamastus	2	7	253
,,	Abd el Ahad	1	2	239	Teu.	Adelaide	2	9	9, 50, 5
,,	Abd el Kader	1	2	239	,,	Adèle	2	9	261
,,	Abd el Kudoor	1	2	239	,,	Adelicia	2	9	261
,,	Abd el Melik	1	2	216, 239	,,	Adeline, Aline	2	9	261
,,	Abd el Meshid	1	2	239	,,	Adeliz, Adeliza	2	9	261
,,	Abd er Rahman	1	2	54, 216	,,	Adza (dim. of Adeliza)	2	9	261
,,	Abd es Selam	1	2	216, 239					
Chal.	Abd u Shems	1	2	238, 239	,,	Adeleve	2	3	246
Ar.	Abd el Wadood	1	2	239	Heb.	Adin	3	1	274
Heb.	Abdiel	1	2	236	,,	Adlai	2	3	245
Ass.	Abed Nego	1	2	92, 238	Teu.	Adolphus, Adolphine	2	6	252
Ar.	Abd ul Leyl, servant of night	4			Heb.	Adonibezek	2	9	258
					,,	Adonizedek	2	9	258
Heb.	Abel	4		24	,,	Adoram	3	1	274
Heb.	Abiel	1	2	236	,,	Adrammeleck	2	9	258
,,	Abigail	2	3	23, 245	Grk.	Adrian	2	7	253
,,	Abijam	4		281	,,	Aedonium	2	11	264
,,	Abinoam	3	1	222, 274	,,	Aelianus	2	4	247
,,	Abitub	2	2	243	,,	Aemilianus	2	11	264
,,	Abner	2	3, 4	223, 245 247	Celt.	Aeron	2	4	248
					Teu.	Afra	2	10	263
Grk.	Abra	3	1	274	Heb.	Agabus	4		283
Heb.	Abraham	2	9	91, 208	Grk.	Agapetus	2	3	245
,,	Absalom	2	3	245	,,	Agatha, Agathoina	2	2	243
Ar.	El Abtan	2	8	258					
,,	Abu 'l Fazl	2	2	244	,,	Agathenor	2	2	243
,,	Abu Noor	2	4	249	,,	Agathon	1	2	243
,,	Abu Saadat	2	12	266	,,	Agarista	2	2	243
,,	Abu 'sh Shámat	2 / 3	12 / 2	} 84, 278	,,	Aglaia	2	4	248
					Lat.	Agnes, Nancy, (Welsh) Nest	2	10	263
,,	Abu 'l Wefa	2	5	250					
Grk.	Actis	2	4	248	Heb.	Aholibamah	2	9	259
Heb.	Ada, Adah	3	1	48, 126, 274	N A.1	Ah kay ee pix en	2	7	256
Teu.	Adalbert	2	4	248	Ar.	Ahmed, Hamed	2	9	54, 261

292 ALPHABETICAL LIST OF NAMES.

Derivation	Name	Class	Division	Page	Derivation	Name	Class	Division	Page
Lat. Old Fr.	} Aignan	2	10	263	Teu.	Alphonse, Alphonsine	2	6	252
					„	Alfonzo, Ildefonzo	2	6	252
N.A.I	Akwiah, War Eagle	2	7		„	Alured	2	8	258
Ar.	Ala ed Deen (Aladdin)	1	2	239	„	Alwyn	2	3	246
					Lat.	Amadeus, Amadis	1	2	77, 237
Grk.	Alan, Aland (from Aelianus)	2	4	247	„	Amabel, Amy	2	3	245
Teu.	Alaric	2	9	260	Sans. Teu.	} Amalia	2	2	244
Lat.	Alban, Albinia, Aubyn	3	2	226, 277	„	Amalaric	2	2, 9	231, 244, 260
Teu.	Alberic, Aubrey	3	2	277					
„	Albert, Alberta, Albertine	2	4	2, 30, 205, 248	„	Amalaberga	2	2, 9	231, 244, 260
Grk.	Alcander	2	7	253	Lat.	Amand, Amanda	2	3	245
„	Alcestes	2	7	253					
Teu.	Aldegonde, Olga	2	9	261	.,	Amata	2	3	245
					Grk.	Ambrose	2	1	242
„	Aldred	2	9	260	Ar.	El Amjad	2	9	261
Grk.	Alexander, Alexandra, Alexandrina	2	6	2, 30. 102, 200, 251	Grk.	Amaranth	2	1	242
					„	Amaryllis	2	10	263
					Lat.	Amias. See Amand			
„	Alaster, Allister, Alick, Saunders	2	6	251	Heb.	Ammon, Amana	2	5	250
					Teu.	Ammie	2	6	252
„	Alcides	2	6	251	Grk.	Amelia (s.)	2	11	264
„	Alethe, Alethea	2	5	189, 250	Ar.	Amin, Amineh, Amina	1	2	230. 241,
Teu.	Alicia, Alice	2	9	261			2	5	250
„	Allix (dim. of Adelaide)	2	9	261	,,	Aminedeen	1	2	239
					Egy.	Amosis	1	2	22, 238
Grk.	Alexis, Alexia	2	6	102, 251	Grk.	Amenaïde	2	12	238, 265
Heb.	Almah	2	4	247	„	Amyntas	2	6	251
Lat.	Alma	4		284, 285	„	Ampelis, Ampelisca	3	1	275
Teu.	Alodie	2	9	261					
Teu. Old Fr.	} Aloys (from Louisa)	2	9	260	„	Anastasius, Anastasia	2	1	242
					„	Anatole, Anatolia	2	4	247
Grk.	Alectryon	4		284					
„	Alcibiades	2	7	253	Heb.	Anah	2	11	264
Ar.	Alif	3	2	276	Grk.	Anaxis, Anaxo	2	9	259
Teu.	Algar	2	7	254	„	Andrew	2	7	102, 200, 224, 253
„	Algernon (s.)	2	7	254					
„	Alfred	2	10	121, 263	„	Andronicus	2	7	253
„	Alfric	2	10	263	Celt.	Angus, Ango	2	2	49, 244
„	Almeric, Aylmer (s.)	2	9	260	Heb.	Anna, Anne, Annie	2	2, 6	2, 31, 77, 243, 251
Ar.	Almir	2	9	261	H.Sp.	Anita, Anina	2	2, 6	243
„	Alp	2	7	256	H.Fr.	Annette, Anaïs, Nanette, Nanon, Nannie, Nauina	2	2, 6	251
Pers.	Alp Arslan	2	7	256					
Teu. Sp.	} Alvarez (s.)	2	9	260					

ALPHABETICAL LIST OF NAMES.

Derivation		Class	Division	Page	Derivation		Class	Division	Page
Grk.	Angela, Angelina, Angelica	1	2	121, 151, 237	Grk.	Artemisia	1	2	235
					Celt.	Arthur	2	7	200, 255
Hin.	Ani Mutoo	2	3	247	Ar.	Asad	2	12	266
Lat.	Annunziata	1	2	237	Lat.	Asellus, Asella	4		284
Teu.	Anselm	1	2	238, 241	Fr.	Asile	2	6	191
Lat.	Anthony, Antonia, Antoninus, Antonina, Antoinette	2	7	254	Lat.	Asinius	2	6	284
					Pers.	Aslan	2	7	256
					Ar.	Assad	2	7	256
					Phœ.	Asdrubal	1	2	238
Grk.	Antiochus	4		282	Grk.	Aspasia	2	11	46, 264
„	Antenor	2	7	253	Pers.	Aspatha	1	2	238
„	Anthemia	3	1	275	Grk.	Aspidia, a shield	2	6	
Pers.	Anushirwan	2	2	244	Ital.	Assunta	1	2	
Grk.	Apelles	2	4	247	Grk.	Asteria	2	4	247
Lat.	Aper	2	7	159, 254	„	Asyncritus	2	2	243
„	Appius	4		283	Teu.	Athalric	2	9	260
„	Aquila	2	7	254	„	Athelstan	2	9	260
„	Arabella	3	1	45. 275	Grk.	Athenaïs	2	8	257
Heb.	Arad	4		281	„	Athanasius, Athanasia	2	2	129, 242
Grk.	Archeleonis	2	7	254					
„	Archelaus	2	9	72, 259	Teu.	Attala	2	9	260
„	Archebulus	2	9	259	„	Aubrey (from Alberic)	3	2	277
„	Archestrates	2	9	259					
„	Archippus	2	9	259	Lat.	Aubyn (from Alban)	3	2	277
„	Archimedes	2	8	257					
Teu.	Archibald	2	7	254	Teu.	Audrey (from Ethelreda)	2	8	258
Celt.	Ardgal	2	7	255					
Grk.	Aretas, Areta	2	2	225, 243	Lat.	Augustus, Augusta	2	9	76, 260
„	Aretaphila	2	2	243					
Heb.	Areli	2	7	253	„	Augustine, Austin	2	9	260
Grk.	Argentine	3	2	276					
„	Argyrea	3	2	276	Teu.	Audovere	2	12	246
„	Ariadne	2	11	264	„	Aulaff	2	10	51
Heb.	Ari, Arieh	2	7	253	Grk.	Aura	2	11	264
Pers.	Arisai	2	7	256	Lat.	Aurelius, Aurelian, Aurelia	3	2	277
Heb.	Ariel	2	2	236					
Pers.	Ariana, Arria	2	9	261	Grk.	Aurora	2	4	} 247, 277
„	Aristides	2	2	243			3	1	
„	Aristocles	2	2	83, 243	Lat.	Auxilius	2	6	251
„	Aristotle	2	2	243	Heb.	Ave	2	12	182, 265
„	Aristarchus	2	9	259	Teu.	Avice (Hawisa)	2	6	252
„	Aristocrates	2	2,9	185, 259	Pers.	Ayesha (s.)	2	12	266, 280
„	Aristobulus	2	6,8	251, 257	Teu.	Aylmer, Almeric	2	9	260
Teu.	Arnulph	2	7	255	Teu.	Aylward, Athelward	2	9	260
„	Armand	2	9	260					
„	Arnold	2	7	255	Heb.	} Ayub (Job)	4		281
Pers.	Arslan	2	7	256	Ar.				
„	Arslantash	2	7	255	Heb.	Azariah	1	2	92, 236
„	Arslowpe	2	7	255	„	Azrael	1	2	119
Grk.	Arsinoë	2	8	46, 257	Grk.	Azelie	2	10	263
„	Artemas, Artemis	1	2	235	Ar.	Azimuth	2	6	203
					„	Azim	2	6	252

ALPHABETICAL LIST OF NAMES.

Derivation	Name	Class	Division	Page	Derivation	Name	Class	Division	Page
Ar.	Aziz, Azeezah	2	2	244, 246	Lat.	Benvenuto	2	12	245
Heb.	Azur	2	6	251	,,	Benevolus	2	2	251
					Heb.	Benjamin	2	3	245
					Teu.	Beornhelm	2	6	252
Grk.	Bacco, Bacchis	1	2	235	,,	Beornoth	2	5	250
					Heb.	Beppo (from Giuseppe)	1	2	236
Ar.	Bahr el Kunooz	2	3	246	Ital.				
					Teu.	Berenger, Berengaria	2	7	254
Pers.	Baharam	2	7	255					
Cau.	Bajazet	1	2	238	Grk.	Berenice	2	7	253
Lat.	Balbus, Balbine	3	3	278	Teu.	Bernard, Bernarda, Bernardine	2	7	9, 255
Ass.	Balthazar	1	2	238					
Lat.	Baptist, Baptista	1	2	237	,,	Bertha	2	4	50, 248
					,,	Berthold	2	4	246, 248
Heb.	Barak	2	4	247	,,	Berthelm	2	4	248
Phœ.	Barca	2	4	247	,,	Bertrand	2	4	248
Pers.	Barasmanes	3	3	278	,,	Bertram	2	7	254
Heb.	Barjonah	2	10	262	Grk.	Beta	4		284
,,	Barnabas	2	8	257	Heb.	Bethiah	1	2	236
,,	Bartholomew	4		281	Teu.	Betstan	2	2	244
,,	Bartimeus	2	9	259	Heb.	Bettina (Elizabeth)	1	2	236
,,	Baruch	2	12	265					
Grk.	Basil, Basileus	2	9	150	Lat.	Bevis	3	1	275
,,	Basilis, Basiline, Basilica	2	9	259	,,	Bianca, Blanche	3	2	8, 277
					Heb.	Bithron	2	11	264
Celt.	Bathanal	2	7	255	Grk. Spa.	} Blaise, Blas	4		282
Teu.	Bathilde	2	2	244					
Heb.	Bathsheba	1	2	236	Lat.	Blandine	2	11	264
Vitn.	Batinasavu	4		282	Ar.	Boabdil (s.), Keeper of the gate of the heart	2	3	246
Grk.	Batrachus	4		111, 284					
Teu.	Beage, Beagestan	2	3	246					
Lat.	Beata	1	2	237	Heb.	Boaz	2	7	253
,,	Beatrice	2	12	2, 9, 30, 46, 226, 266	Celt.	Boadicea (s.)	2	7	229, 255
					Grk.	Boetius	2	6	251
Ar.	Bedr Basim	2	4	249	Celt.	Boiorigh, Brian (s.)	2	7	255
,,	Bedr er Deen	1	2	239					
,,	El Bedr el Kebeer	2	4	249	Lat.	Bona	2	2	244
					,,	Bonaventura	2	12	266
Heb.	Becher	2	3	283	,,	Boniface	2	12	266
Pers.	Behadar	2	7	255	Celt.	Botolph	2	6	252
Ar	Behadir	2	7	255	,,	Brenda, Brenna	3	2	99, 278
Hin.	Behadoor	2	7	255	,,	Brian (s.)	2	7	255
Pers.	Behras	3	1	275	Teu.	Bridget, Bride	2	6	252
Ass.	Belshazzar	1	2	238	Lat.	Britannicus	4		284
,,	Belteshazzar, Balthasar	1	2	238	Teu.	Brunehaut, Brunehilde	3	2	277
,,	Belus	1	1	235	Celt.	Budignat	2	7	255
Lat.	Benedict, Benedicta, Benoit, Benoite	1	2	9, 237, 266	Ar.	Budoor	2	4	48, 249
					Celt.	Bugega	3	2	277
					Grk.	Bulis	2	8	257

ALPHABETICAL LIST OF NAMES. 295

Derivation		Class	Division	Page	Derivation		Class	Division	Page
Celt.	Bûn	2	4	248	Lat.	Cato	2	8	258
Ar.	Bustan	3	1	275	,,	Catullus	4		284
					Teu.	Cedric (s.)	2	7	255
					Ar.	Celb, Celba	2	5	250
Grk.	Cadmus	2	8	257	Lat.	Celestinus, Celestine, Celeste	2	2	243, 263
Celt.	Cadwallader	2	7	255					
,,	Cadmar	2	7	255	Grk.	Celia, Celine, Cenie	2	9	259
Lat.	Cæcilius, Cecil, Cecilia, Cecile	3	2	277					
					Lat.	Celsus	2	9	260
Lat.	⎱ Cæsar, Cæso-	3	2	76, 277	Celt.	Ceolmund	2	6	252
San.	⎰ nia	4		75	Grk.	Cephas	2	7	253
Lat.	Caius, Caia	2	9	260	,,	Chæremon, Charimene	2	12	265
Heb.	Caleb	2	5	250					
Grk.	Calixtus, Calista	3	1	274	N.A.I	Chaheechopes	2	7	256
					Chi.	Chaonkin Lûng	2	7	256
,,	Callidora	3	1	274	Grk.	Chæremachus	2	7	253
,,	Calligenia	3	1	274	Teu.	Charles (Karl), Charlie	2	7	126, 255
,,	Callistona	3	1	274					
,,	Callimachus	2	7	253	,,	Charlotte, Carline, Lolotte, Lottie	2	7	255
,,	Callinoüs	2	8	257					
,,	Calliope	2	11	264					
,,	Callisthenia	2	7	254	,,	Caroline, Carlotta	2	7	9
,,	Calyca, Kalyca	3	2	276					
Lat.	Calvus	3	3	278	Grk.	Charis ⎰	2	3, 6	225, 245
,,	Camelius	4		284		⎱	2	11	251, 264
,,	Camillus, Camilla	2	9	260	,,	Charity	2	6	251
					,,	Charixene	2	6	251
,,	Camus	4		278	,,	Charilaus	2	12	265
,,	Candidus	3	2	277	,,	Charimene	2	12	265
Teu.	Canute	2	7	254	,,	Charmion, Charmis	2	12	265
Lat.	Caper	4		284					
Celt.	Caradoc	2	7	255	,,	Charops	2	12	265
Lat.	Caracalla	4		282	,,	Chæriphiles	2	12	265
Pers.	Carcas	2	7	255	,,	Charitoblepharos	3	1	173, 274
Lat.	Carita, Charity	2	6	252					
Teu.	⎱ Carlotta. See				N.A.I	Chee me na na quet	2	9	262
Sp.	⎰ Charles								
Lat.	Carmen (s.)	2	11	264	Grk.	Chledonis, Chledonium	4		284
Teu.	Caroline. See Charles								
Lat.	Carus, Caroline (s.), dearly loved	2	3		Heb. Ital.	⎧ Cherubino, ⎪ Angel excel- ⎨ ling in know- ⎪ ledge ⎩	1	2	
Scla.	Casimir	2	9	261	N.A.I	Chesh oo hong ha	2	8	258
Grk.	Cassiopeia	2	11	264					
Pers.	Caspar, Gaspard	4		282	Heb.	Chilion	2	2	243
					,,	Chilmah	2	8	257
Lat.	Casta	2	2	244	Lat.	Chilo	3	3	226
Grk.	Catherine. See Katharine	2	4		Teu.	Chilperic	2	6	252
					Grk.	Chione	3	2	276
Spa.	Catalina	2	4		,,	Chloe	3	1	275
Ital.	Caterina	2	4		,,	Chloris	3	2	276

ALPHABETICAL LIST OF NAMES.

Derivation		Class	Division	Page	Derivation		Class	Division	Page
Grk.	Christabel. See Christian	1	2		Celt.	Colgar	2	7	255
„	Chrestilla	2	2	243	Celt. Lat.	} Columba,	2	10	263
„	Christian, Christine	1	2	237	„	Columbus	2	10	117
					Celt.	Conan	2	9	261, 273
„	Christopher, Kitt, Kester	1	2	117, 237	Teu.	Conrad	2	8	195, 258
					Lat.	Constantine, Constantia, Constance	2	2, 5	226
„	Chrysander	2	2	243					
„	Chryseis, Chrysilla	3	2	277					
					Grk.	Cora, Kora, Corisca	2	4	248
„	Chrysostom	2	8	45, 257					
Lat.	Cincinnatus	3	2	277, 279	„	Corinne, Coralie	2	4	248
„	Cicero	4		283	„	Corax	4		284
„	Clair, Clare, Clara, Clarinda, Clarissa	2	4	130, 248	Celt.	Cordelia	4		231, 282
					Lat.	Cornelius, Cornelia, a horn	4		87
„	Claudius, Claudia	3	3	130	„	Corvus, Corvinus	4		284
„	Claude, Claudine	3	3	278	Grk.	Cosmo	2	8	257
					„	Cottina	4		283
„	Cocles	3	3	278	Lat. Fr.	} Couronne	2	9	260, 272
Grk.	Clearista	2	9	259					
„	Cleon, Cleiné	2	9	259	Grk.	Crœsus	2	9	259
„	Cleander, Clelie	2	9	259	Lat.	Crassus	3	2	278
					Grk.	Creon	2	9	259
„	Clio	2	9	259	Lat.	Crescentius, Crescens	2	9	260
„	Cleitus	2	9	259					
„	Cleodora	2	9	259	Lat.	Crispin	4		131
„	Cleogenes	2	9	259	Teu.	Cunegonde, Kunigund	4	2	260
„	Cleonice	2	9	259					
„	Cleonimia	2	9	259	Celt.	Cunobelin, Cymbeline	1	2	217, 235
„	Cleopatra	2	9	259					
„	Cleophila	2	9	259	Lat.	Curvus	4		278
„	Cleodemus	2	9	259	Teu.	Cuthbert	2	8	258
„	Cleomenes, Climene	2	8	257	„	Cuthwin	2	8	258
					Celt.	Cwenburh	2	6	50, 229, 252
„	Cleostrates	2	9	259					
„	Clinarete	2	2	243	Pers.	Cyaxares	2	7	256
„	Clorinda	2	9	259	Grk.	Cydias	2	9	259
„	Cleobulus, Cleobuline	2	8	257	„	Cyanea	3	2	276
					„	Cymopolios	3	2	226, 276
„	Cleanthe	3	1	275	„	Cyprian	4		
Lat.	Clement, Clementinus, Clemens, Clementina, Clemence	2	10	263	Grk. originally Pers.	Cyrus, Cyra, Cyril, Cyrilla, Cyrenius, Cyrene	2	4, 9	259
Grk	Clinarete	2	2	243					
Teu.	Clotilde	2	9	261					
„	Clovis (Louis)	2	9	260	Grk.	Dædalus	2	8	257
Grk.	Cochlis	4		284	Teu.	Dagmar	2	4	99, 248
Grk. Fr.	} Colette (Nicholas)	2	7	253	„	Dagobert	2	4	248
					Grk.	Damian	2	3	245

ALPHABETICAL LIST OF NAMES.

Derivation	Name	Class	Division	Page	Derivation	Name	Class	Division	Page
Heb.	Daniel	1	2	92, 236	Lat.	Donatus	1	2	237
Grk.	Daphne	4		283	Hin.	Door Dowran	2	3	247
Heb.	Darda	2	8	257	Grk.	Dorippa	4		281
,,	David	2	3	200, 245	,,	Dorothea, Doro-	1	2	2, 31, 237
,,	Deborah	2	8	257, 259		thy, Dora			
Lat.	Decimus, Decima	4		284	,,	Dorymene	2	7	254
					Scla.	Droghimir	2	9	261
Grk.	Deidamia	2	7	254	Grk.	Drosée	2	10	263
,,	Delia	2	4	248	Teu.	Dudda	2	9	260
,,	Delphine	2	3	245	,,	Dunstan	2	9	260
,,	Delta	4		284	Celt.	Dugald (s.) {	2	7	230
,,	Demetrius, Dimitri	1	2	235, 238			3	2	255, 277
,,	Demosthenes	2	7, 9	253, 259	Lat.	Dulcibella, Douce	2	10	263
Ar.	Denaneer	2	3	113, 246					
Teu.	Deorswyn, Deorswytha	2	3	246	N.A.I	Eachin chea	2	7	256
Celt.	Dermot (s.),Diarmid	2	7	202, 255	,,	Eahsapa	2	7	256
					Lat.	Eburnus	2	2	277
,,	Dervoigil	3	1	275	Teu.	Eadwolph	2	7,12	
Lat.	Desiderius, Didier, Désirée	2	3	245	,,	Edgar	2	7,12	254
					,,	Edith	2	12	2, 31, 50, 266
,,	Dévote (Fr.)	1	2	237					
		1	1	235	,,	Edmund	2	12	2, 31, 266
Grk.	Diana {	2	4	248	,,	Edward	2	12	2, 30, 121, 266
,,	Didymus, Didyma	4		282	,,	Edwin	2	3,12	246, 266
Heb.	Diego }	4		281	,,	Edwy	2	9,12	246, 266
Sp.	(James)				,,	Edma	2	8	258
Lat.	Digna, Digne	2	9	260	Heb.	Edom	3	2	276
Heb.	Dinah	2	8	257	N.A.I	Eehniskin	2	3	247
Grk.	Diodatus, Dieudonné	1	2	238	,,	Ea shah koo me	2	7	256
,,	Diocles, Dioclétian	1	1	159, 235	Grk.	Eetion	2	7	253
					,,	Ega	4		284
,,	Diochates	3	2	276	Teu.	Egbert	2	4	248, 258
,,	Diogenes	1	2	238	Grk.	Egidius, Giles, Gillian	2	6	251
,,	Diogiton	1	2	238					
,,	Dionysius, Denys, Denise	1	2	197, 238	Heb.	Eglaim	4		281
					Grk.	Elais	2	10	263
,,	Diomede	1	2	238	Heb.	Eldad	1	2	236
,,	Diphile	2	3	245	Teu.	Eldred	2	9	260
Heb.	Dishon	3	1	274	Lat.	Electa	1	2	237
,,	Dorcas	3	1	275	Grk.	Electra	3	2	277
Ar.	Doel Mekan	2	4	249	Heb.	Eli	1	2	236
Lat.	} Dolores, Dolara, Lola	1	2	182, 237, 282	,,	Eliab	1	2	236
Sp.					,,	Elimelech	1	2	236
Ital.					Grk.	Elida	4		284
,,	Domenico, Domenichina, Domingo	1	2	183, 237	Heb.	Eliezer	1	2	236
					,,	Elijah	1	2	188, 236
Lat.	Domitian	2	7	253	Grk.	Eligius. Eloy, Lo, Loo	1	2	237

ALPHABETICAL LIST OF NAMES.

Derivation	Name	Class	Division	Page	Derivation	Name	Class	Division	Page
Teu.	Eleanor, Ellinor, Ellen, Nellie	2	12	20, 266	Grk.	Erasiphron	2	11	264
					,,	Erasthenes	2	3	245
					,,	Erato, Erotium	2	3	245
Grk.	Eleutheria, Eleutherius	2	9	196, 259	Ital.	Ercole, Hercules	1	1	235
					Teu.	Eric, Erica	2	9	260
Heb.	Elisabeth, Eliza, Ellie, Elspeth, Elsie, Lizzie, Lisa, Libby, Betha, Betsy, Bessie, Bettina	1	2	2, 31, 189, 191, 236	Grk.	Erianthe	2	11	264
					,,	Eriphrea	4		284
					Teu.	Ermengarde	2	9	261
					,,	Erminia, Hermione	2	9	261
,,	Elisheba, Elia	1	2	236	,,	Ernest, Ernestine	2	8	258
Teu.	Ella	2	9	260	Heb.	Esdras	2	6	251
,,	Elgiva, Ethelgifa	2	6	50, 101, 252	,,	Eshtaol	2	7	253
					Teu.	Esmond	2	9	238
,,	Elodie	2	9	261	Lat. Fr.	} Esperance	2	12	266
Heb.	Elon	2	7	253					
Grk. Ital.	} Elma	2	3	245	Grk. Sp.	} Esteban	2	9	259
Grk.	Elpidius	2	12	265	Fr.	Etienne			
,,	Elpinice	2	7, 12	254	Celt.	Essylt, Yseult, Isolt	2	4	} 248, 275
,,	Elpis	2	12	225, 265			3	1	
Lat.	Elvira	2	7	254	Lat.	Estelle, Stella	2	4	275
Ar.	El Ward fi'l Akmann	3	2	278	Heb.	Esther, Hester	2	4	29, 35, 249
					Teu.	Ethel, Ethelinda	2	9	261
Grk.	Emilius, Emilia, Emily (s.)	2	11	2, 31, 264	,,	Ethelbert, Adalbert, Albert	2	4	2, 9, 205, 248
Lat.	Emerentia	2	2	244	,,	Ethelred, Ethelreda, Audrey	2	8, 9	227, 258, 272
Teu.	Emma	2	6	252					
Heb.	Emmanuel, Manuel, Manuela, Manuelita	1	2	77, 236	,,	Ethelwyn	2	3, 9	246
					,,	Ethelswytha	2	9	261
					,,	Ethelward, Aylward	2	9	260
Grk.	Emmeline	2	11	264					
Ar.	Enees el Jelees	2	11	265	,,	Ethelwold	2	9	260
Teu.	Engelbert	2	2, 4	244, 248	,,	Ethelwulph	2	7, 9	255
,,	Engelrain	2	2, 7	254	,,	Ethelwyne	2	3, 9	246
Heb.	Enoch	1	2	9, 223, 236	Grk.	Ethra, Ethrosyne	2	11	263
Grk.	Entimeus	2	9	259					
,,	Epaminondas	2	2	243	Teu.	Eudes	2	12	266
,,	Epaphros (Aphrodite)	1	1	235	Grk.	Eucharis	2	2, 6	46, 251
					,,	Euclid	2	9	259
Heb.	Ephraim	2	12	259	,,	Eudæmon	2	2, 12	265
Grk.	Epicharis	2	11	264	,,	Eudius	2	2, 10	262
,,	Epicurus	2	6	251	,,	Eudocia	2	8	257
,,	Epiphanius, Epiphanie, Tiphanie	1	2	183, 237, 259	,,	Eudora	2	2, 3	245
					,,	Eudoxia	2	2, 4	248
					,,	Eugene, Eugenie	2	9	259
Heb.	Ephratah	2	12	265					
Grk.	Epsilon	4		284	,,	Eulalos, Eulalie	2	2, 11	9, 46, 264
Heb.	Er	2	4	247	,,	Eumenes	2	9, 11	264
Grk. Ital.	Erasmus, Elmo	2	3	245	,,	Eunice	2	2, 7	126, 243, 253

ALPHABETICAL LIST OF NAMES. 299

Deri-vation	Name	Class	Divi-sion	Page	Deri-vation	Name	Class	Divi-sion	Page
Grk.	Euphemia, Effie, Eppie, Phemie	2	2, 11	121, 264	Lat.	Fides, Fidelis, Fidelia	2	5	250
,,	Euphrastes	2	8	83	Lat.	Felicula	4		284
,,	Euphrasia, Euphrosyne	2	12	265	,,	Felix, Felicia, Félicité, Felise	2	12	124, 266
,,	Euphron, Euphronia	2	2, 8	257	Teu.	Ferdinand (s.), (Sp.)Hernando	2	7	255
,,	Eurymenes	2	2, 8	243, 257	Pers.	Ferdusi, Feridoon	2	12	266, 273
,,	Eurydice	2	2, 8	257					
,,	Europa	3	1	275	,,	Feroz (Ar.)	2	12	266
,,	Euryone	2	2, 6	251		Ferook			
,,	Eupator	2	9	259	Grk.	Feodor, Feodora.	2	4	248
,,	Eusebius, Eusebia	2	2	243		See Phædora			
					Pers.	Ferozeshah	2	9, 12	266
,,	Eustace, Eustasia	2	2	25, 95, 243	Celt.	Fergus	2	7	201, 255
					Lat.	Fiamma (Ital.)	2	4	
,,	Euterpe	2	11	264		See Flaminius			248
,,	Euthalia	2	12	265	Celt.	Fineach	2	9	261
,,	Eutychus	2	12	156, 265	,,	Fingal (s.)	2	9	255, 261
,,	Euthynoüs	2	2, 8	243	Lat.	Firmin, Firmilianus	2	7	254
,,	Evadne	2	11	264					
,,	Evangelista, Evangeline	1	2	183, 236	,,	Flaccus	4		278
					Celt.	Flamddwyn	2	7	255
,,	Evander	2	2	243, 253	Lat.	Flaminius, Flaminia, Fiamma	2	4	248
,,	Evaristus, Evarista	2	2	243					
					,,	Flavius, Flavia	3	2	87, 277
,,	Evages	2	5	250	,,	Florus, Flora, Florian, Florinda	3	1	275
,,	Evelpis	2	2, 12	265					
,,	Evergetes	2	6	251					
,,	Evodie	2	2	243	Celt.	Flur	3	1	275
Heb.	Eva, Evelina, Eveleen, Evelyn	2	1	22, 242	,,	Foinnghuala	3	2	277
Wel.	Evan (John)	1	2	236	Grk. Ital.	} Fosco	2	4	247
Teu.	Everard (Eberard)	2	7	255	Teu.	Frank, Francis, Frances, Francesca, Fanny, (Fr.) Fanchon	2	7	9, 254
,,	Evremond	2	6, 9	260, 272					
Lat.	Expeditus	2	6	252					
,,	Extricatus	2	6	252	Lat.	Formosus, Formosa	3	1	275
Heb.	Ezekiel	1	2	236					
,,	Ezra, *a helper*	2	6		,,	Frederic, Frederica, Fritz	2	10	263
Lat.	Fabian, Fabius, Fabio, Fabiola	4		283	,,	Fulge s	2	4	248
					,,	Fulk	2	6	251
,,	Fabricius	4		282	,,	Fulvius, Fulvia, *tawny-coloured hair*	3	2	
,,	Facundus	2	8	258					
Ar.	Fadl ed Deen	1	2	239					
Celt.	Faithfaiige	3	2	278					
Pers.	Fareksavar	2	7	255	Celt.	Gael, *strong*	2	7	232
Lat.	Faustus, Fausta, Faustinus, Faustina	2	12	266	Heb.	Gabriel, Gabriela, Gabrielle	1	2	9, 236
					Lat.	Gaetano (Cajetano)	4		284
Ar.	El Feizad	2	6	252					

ALPHABETICAL LIST OF NAMES.

Derivation	Name	Class	Division	Page	Derivation	Name	Class	Division	Page
Grk.	Galatea	3	2	276	Heb.	Giuseppe, Giuseppina (Joseph)	1	2	236, 265
Lat.	Gallus	4		284	Ital.				
Celt.	Gallawyg	2	9	261					
Heb.	Gamaliel	1	2	283	Ar.	Ghanim	2	7	256
Pers.	Gaspar (Gustasp) Gasparine	4		282	Chi.	Ghiang Koo	2	3	247
					Teu.	Ghiselle, Giselle	2	3	246
Teu. Sp.	} Gaston	2	6	252	Celt.	Gladys, Gladusa	2	4	248
Lat.	Gaudentius	2	12	266	Grk.	Glaphyra	3	1	275
Ar.	Ghazaleh	3	1	275	,,	Glaucopis	3	2	276
,,	Geiran	3	1	276	,,	Glaucus	3	2	276
Grk.	Gelasia	2	12	265	,,	Glycera	2	10	263
Lat.	Gelsomina	3	1	275	Pers.	Gour	4		282
Lat. Ital.	} Gemma, *a jewel*	2	3		Teu.	Godard	2	2	244
					,,	Godfrey	1	2	2, 31, 237
Lat. Fr.	} Généreuse	2	6	252	,,	Godwin	1	2	237
					,,	Golde	3	2	277
Celt.	Geneviève, Ginevra (Gueneverr), Ganore	3	1	275	Sp.	Gomez (Gomesind)	2	2	192, 244
					Teu.	Gonda	2	7	255
Teu.	Geoffrey, Jeffrey	2	12	77, 266	,,	Gonsalvo, Gonsalez (Gunstaf), Gustavus	2	7	254
Grk.	George, Georgina	4		29,199,281					
Teu.	Gerald, Geraldine	2	7	254	N.A.I	Go to kow pah a he	2	7	256
,,	Gerard	2	7	150, 254	Celt.	Gniphon	2	7	255
,,	Germain, Germaine	2	7	254	Lat.	Gracchus	3	2	277
					,,	Grace (Gratius), Gratia, Gratianus, Gracienne, Gracieuse, Graziella, Graziosa, Engracia	2	6,11	226, 251, 264, 268
Lat.	Germanicus	4		284					
Grk.	(It.) Geronimo, (Fr.) Jérôme (Hieronymus)	1	2	237					
,,	Géronte, *an old man*	4							
Teu.	Gertrude	2	5	49,189,250					
Grk.	} Giacinta, Hyacinth	2	3		Grk.	Gregory	2	8	195
Ital.		3	1	207, 276	Teu.	Grimoald	2	7	254
Grk.	Gervase, Gerasimus, *honoured*	2	9		,,	Griselda	3	2	277
					Celt.	Grûron	2	4	250
Lat.	Gibbus	3	3	278	,,	Gryffyn, Griffith	2	7	255
Heb.	Gideon	2	7	253					
Teu.	Gilbert (Willibert)	2	4	248	Lat.	Grypus	3	3	278
					Teu.	Gudule	1	2	237
Grk.	Giles, Gillian (Egidius)	2	6	251	Pers.	Gulnare, Gullanar	3	1	48, 276
Heb. Ital.	{ Giovanni, Nanni, Giovanna. See John.				Teu.	Gunther	2	7	254
					,,	Gunthram	2	7	254
					,,	Gustavus (Gunstaf)	2	7	192, 254
Lat. Ital.	{ Giulio, Giulia, Giuletta, Julius	3	2	277	Sp.	Guzman, Guthman	2	2	244
					Fr.	Guy, Guidon	2	7	2, 31, 78

ALPHABETICAL LIST OF NAMES. 301

Derivation	Name	Class	Division	Page	Derivation	Name	Class	Division	Page
Celt.	Gwair	2	4	250	Grk.	Helena (s.),	2	4	247
„	Gwanar	2	9	261		Helen, Elena			
„	Gwen. See				„	Heloise, Eloise	2	4	247
	Gwyneth				Teu.	Henry, Henrietta, Hetty,	2	9	78, 260
Celt.	Gwendaline, Guenddolen	{2, 3}	{4, 1}	} 49, 248		Hénée, Etta, Eric, Erica,			
„	Gwenddyd	{2, 3}	{4, 1}	} 275		Harry, Harriet (Eoric)			
„	Gwenfrid	3	1	275					
„	Gwenhwyar	2	9	261	Heb.	Hephzibah	2	3	245
„	Gwenwynwyn	3	1, 2	230, 275	Teu.	Herbert	2	4	248
„	Gwyneth, Gwen	3	2	230, 277	Grk.	Hercules (Heraclius)	1	2	238
Teu.	Gyffard	2	6	252					
Grk.	Gyrtius	3	3	278	Teu.	Herman, Hermanric	2	9	260
					Teu.	Hermenegilde	2	9	261
Heb.	Hadassah	3	1	36, 264	„	Hermione, Erminia	2	9	261
Pers. Ar.	} Hafiz, Hhafiz	2	6	252	Heb.	Herod, Herodias	2	7	253
Heb.	Hagabah	4		283					
N.A.I	Hahnee	2	8	258	Ass.	) Mester, Esther	2	4	249
Grk.	Haïdee (s.)	2	11	264	Heb.	} ther			
Ar.	Hallouf	2	7	256	Grk.	Hiera	2	2	243
„	Hamed	2	9	261	„	Hippias	4		284
Heb.	Hamor	4		283	Lat.	Hilary	2	12	266
„	Hamutal	2	6	251	Teu.	Hilda	2	4	99. 248
Phœ.	Hamilcar	1	2	238	„	Hildegarde	2	6	252
Heb.	Hannah,Anna Hanani, Hananiah, &c.	{1, 2}	{2, 6}	{243, 236}	„	Hildegonde	2	7	255, 271
					„	Hildebrand	2	7	254
					? „	Hildebert	2	4	248
Ar.	Hanna (John)	1	2	236	Grk.	Hippolytus	4		158
N.A.I	Ha na tak me mauk	2	9	262	Heb.	Hiram	2	7	253
					Lat.	Hirpus	2	7	254
Teu.	Hargrim	2	7, 9	254	„	Hircius	4		284
„	Harold	2	3, 9	246	Heb.	Hobab	2	3	245
Ar.	Haroun el Rasheed	1	2	216, 239	Teu.	Holdlie {	{2, 3}	{3, 1}	} 246, 275
„	Hasna (s.) (Hos'n), beautiful	3	1		N.A.I	Hongskayde	2	9	262
					Lat.	Honorius, Honoria, Honor, Norah	2	2	226, 244
„	Hassan	3	1	275					
„	Hazut en Unfoos	2	3	246	Heb.	Hophra	1	2	238
					Pers.	Hormuz, Hormisdas, Orosmades	1	1	196, 235
Teu.	Hawisa, Avice, Heldewig (Hedwig)	2	9,12	252					
					Eng.	Hope	2	12	266
„	Heaburge	3	2	277	Grk.	Horatio, Horatia, Horace	3	1	204
Grk.	Hebe	3	1	274					
„	Hedia, Hedyla	2	11	264	Lat.	Hortense	3	1	275
„	Hector	2	7	10, 253	Teu.	Hubert	2	4	248
„	Hegemon	2	6	259	„	Hugh, Hugo, Ugolino,	2	7, 9	195, 254, 261
„	Heliodorus	2	4	238					

ALPHABETICAL LIST OF NAMES.

Derivation		Class	Division	Page	Derivation		Class	Division	Page
Celt.	Hugues (Hy Gadarn or Cadarn)	2	7, 9	217, 261	Heb.	Isaac	2	12	265
Teu.	Humbert	2	4	248	Heb. Sp.	Isabella, Isabel, Isabean, Zabillet, Bella, Tibbie, Isa (Elisabeth)	1	2	9, 236
,,	Humphrey	2	10	263					
N.A.I	Hu l' ah dee	2	2, 4	49, 249					
Ar.	Hulweh	2	11	265					
Chi.	Hwang Lûng	2	7	256	Grk.	Isaura	2	11	264
Grk.	Hyale	2	4	248, 207	,,	Ischas	3	3	278
נֹחַ	Hyacinth, Giacinta, Jacinthe	2 3	3, 11 2	207 276	Heb.	Ishmael	1	2	215, 236
					Grk.	Isidore, Isidora	1	2	238
,,	Hypatia	2	2	243	,,	Ismena	2	8	257
,,	Hymnis	2	11	264	Celt.	Isolt, Ysseult (Essylt), Isola	2 3	4 1	} 248, 275
,,	Hyperides	3	1	274					
					Heb.	Ispah	2	3	245
					,,	Israel	1	5	236
Heb. Sp.	} Iago (James)	4		281	Heb.	Jacob, Jacopo, James, (Fr.) Jacques, Jacqueline, Jacquetta	4		281
Heb.	(Gael.) Ian, (Rus.) Ivan, (Brit.) Ives (John)	1	2	236					
Grk.	Ia, Ianthe, Ione,	2	11	207, 264	,,	Jane. See John	1	2	5
	Ioessa	3	2	226, 276	Lat.	Januarius, Gennaro, Janvier, keeper of doors			
,,	Ianessa, Ianira	2	9, 10	262	Ital.				
,,	Icasie	2	8	257	Fr.		4		143
,,	Ida, Idaline	2	8	257					
Teu.	Ida (Odo)	2	12	266					
Lat.	Ignatius	2	4	77, 247	Heb.	Jael	3	1	274
Teu. Sp.	} Ildefonzo, Alfonzo	2	6		,,	Jairus	2	4	247
					.,	Japhia	2	4	247
Tur.	Ildherim	2	7	255	,,	Japhet	3	1	274
Grk.	Inachus	2	7	253	,,	Jared	2	9	258
,,	Inclyta	2	4	248	Grk	Jason	2	6	251
Pers.	Indiana	4		284	Heb.	Jedidah	2	3	245
Lat.	Immaculata	1	2	237	,,	Jedidiah	1	2	236
Grk.	Imogene (s.)	2	3	245	Ass.	Jerah	1	1	235
Lat. Sp.	} Inez (Agnes)	2	10	9, 263	Teu.	Jeffrey, Geoffrey	2	12	266
					Heb.	Jemima (Hamami)	2	10	262
Teu.	Ingeborge	2	6	252					
Lat.	Innocent, Innocentia	2	2	243	,,	Jeremiah	1	2	181, 236
					Grk.	Jerome (Hieronymus)	1	2	237
Grk.	Iphianassa	2	7, 9	259					
,,	Iphigenia	2	7	254	Heb.	Jesse, Jessie, Jessica	2	9	258
,,	Iphis	2	7	253					
,,	Iphicles	2	7, 9	253	,,	Joab	1	2	236
,,	Iphicrates	2	7, 9	253	,,	Job	4		281
,,	Ipsea	4		283	Lat.	Jocunda	2	12	266
Grk.	Irene, Irenæus, Iris	2	10	97, 262	Heb.	Jochebed	1	2	236
					,,	Joel	1	2	188, 236
Teu.	Irmentrude, Irma	2	9	261, 272	Heb.	Joachim, Joaquina	1	2	9, 240

ALPHABETICAL LIST OF NAMES. 303

Derivation	Name	Class	Division	Page	Derivation	Name	Class	Division	Page
Heb.	John, Jonathan, Joanna, Joan, Jane, Janet, Janie, Jeannette, Janina (s.), Giovanni, Giovanna, Juan, Juana, Juanita, Ivan, Ives, Ian, Owen, (Brt.) Yves,	1	2	5, 9, 236	Grk.	Katharine, Catherine, (Sco.) Katrine, (Ir.) Kathleen, (Eng.) Katie, Cattie, Kate, (Sp.) Catalina, (Russ.) Katinka, (It.) Caterina	2	2, 4	25. 135, 248
					Pers.	Kesel Arslan	2	7	256
	Yvonne, (Ar.)				,,	Kelig Aslan	2	7	256
	Hanna, (Ger.)				N.A.I	Kenen	2	7	256
	Hans, (Turk.)				Heb.	Keren happuch	2	3	245
	Ohannes				,,	Keturah	2	11	264
,,	Jonah	2	10	35, 262	,,	Kezia, Cassia	2	11	264
,,	Joseph. Josepha,	1	2	9, 236, 265	Ar.	Khadija	1	2	239
	Josephine,	2	12		Hin.	Khêlat	4		284
	Zeffie, José, Joscelyn, (It.)				Pers.	Khosrow, Kouresh	1	1	66,235,249
	Giuseppe, Giuseppina, Beppo,				,,	Korshid	2	4	65, 249
					,,	Khurdad	1	2	238
	(Sp.) Pepe,				N.A.I	Kokah	3	1	276
	Pepita, (Ar.)				,,	Komanikin	2	7	262
	Yusef				Ar.	Koot el Kuloob	2	3	246
Heb.	Joshua	1	2	41, 236	Hin.	Krishnur	1	1	235
Grk.	Jovian	1	1	235	Ar.	Kuleyb	2	5	250
Ar.	Jowareh	2	3	246	,,	Kurrat el Eyn	2	3	246
Heb	Jubal	4		281	N.A.I	Kwasind	2	7	256
,,	Judah, Judith, Giudita	1	2	188, 236	Grk.	Kyrios, Kyria, Cyrus, Cyra, Kyrillos, Cyril, Cyrilla	2	9	259
at.	Julius, Julia, Juliet, Julie, Giulio, Giuletta, Julian, Juliana	3	2	76, 277					
					Pers.	Lab	2	4	249
Lat.	Junius, Junia	3	1	226, 275	Scla.	Ladislas, Lancelot	2	9	261
,,	Justus, Justinian, Justine	2	2	244	N.A.I	Ladookea	2	7	256
					Heb.	Laish	2	7	253
					Grk.	Lalage	4		282
Ar.	Kadeeb el Ban	3	1	276	Egy.	Lalahzer	3	1	276
N.A.I	Kah beck a	4		282	Grk.	Lambda	3	3	278
,,	Kah gah gee	2	7	256	,,	Lampadius	2	4	247
Ar.	Kahraman	2	7	255	,,	Lampeto, Lampisium	2	7	248
Grk.	Kalonice	3	1	274					
,,	Kalyca, Calyca	3	2	276	Teu.	Landric	2	9	260
Ar.	Kamar es Zeman, Camaralzaman	2	4	249	,,	Laurence, Laurentius, Lorenzo, Laura, Laure, Laurette	2	9	158, 260
Teu.	Karl, Charles	2	7	255					
N.A.I	Katequa'	2	7	256					

304   ALPHABETICAL LIST OF NAMES.

Derivation		Class	Division	Page	Derivation		Class	Division	Page
Lat.	Lavinius, Lavinia	3	3	278	Teu.	Louis(Ludwig), Ludovic	2	9	260
N.A.I.	Laylooahpeai she kaw	4		283	,,	Louisa, Louis , Louison,	2	9	272
Heb.	Lazarus, Azariah, Azrael	1	2	236, 240	,,	(Rus.) Lodoiska	2	9	272
					Ar.	Looloo, Luluah	2	3, 4	146, 246
Grk.	Leander	2	7, 10	253, 262	Lat.	Lucius, Luke,	2	4	130, 162
Celt.	Lear, Lyr	4		282		Lucy, Lucie			
Heb.	Lebbeus	2	7	253	,,	Lucullus, Lucille	2	4	248
Ar.	Leila (s.) (Leyla)	3	2	278, 279	,,	Lucian, Lucienne	2	4	248
Lat.	Lenius, Lena	2	10	263					
,,	Lentulus	4		283	,,	Lucinda, Lucia	2	4	248
Teu.	Leopold, Leopoldine	2	3, 9	9, 246	Grk.	Lucifer	2	4	23
					Lat.	Luna	2	4	248
,,	Leofric	2	3	246	Chi.	Lûng So	2	7, 9	72, 256
,,	Leofstan	2	3	246	Lat.	Lupus, Loup	2	7	254
,,	Leofwyn	2	3	246	Teu.	Lutgarde	2	6	252
,,	Leonard	2	7	255	,,	Ludolf	2	6	252
,,	Leonric	2	7, 9	255	Grk.	Lycidas, Lycos	2	7	130, 253, 267
Grk.	Laena	2	7, 9	253, 270	,,	Lycostrates	2	7	253
,,	Leo, Leonidas, Lionel, Leonce	2	7, 9	253	,,	Lychnos	2	4	247
					,,	Lycoris	3	2	277
,,	Leonora, Lenore, Leonie	2	7, 9	253	,,	Lycurgus	2	4	247
					,,	Lydia	4		284
,,	Leontine	2	7, 9	253	,,	Lyra, Lyris	2	11	264
Heb.	Leczinska (Russ.) See Elisabeth				,,	Lysias, Lysander	2	6	251
Lat.	Letitia, Lettice	2	12	5, 266					
					Lat.	Mabel, May, beloved and beautiful	2	3	
Grk.	Lesbia	4		284					
,,	Leucosie	3	2	276					
,,	Leucophyra	3	2	277	Ar.	Maarout	2	6	252
Ar.	Lezzet el Dunya	2	3	246	Lat.	Macer	3	3	278
Lat.	Liberius, Liberia	2	9	260	Grk.	Machaera	2	7	253
					Celt.	Madoc	2	3, 9	246
Grk.	Ligia	2	11	264	Heb.	Magdalen, Maddalena	2	9	137
Teu.	Lina(s.)(Hlina)	2	6	252					
,,	Linda	3	1	275	,,	Madeleine, Madeline, Madge	2	9	259
Grk.	Liriope	3	2	276					
Lat.	Lilius, Lily, Lilias	2	4	248	,,	Mahala	2	11	264
					Ar.	Mahboobeh	2	3	246
,,	Lilian, Lilla	3	2	277	N.A.I	Mahsish, War Eagle	2	7	256
Celt.	Llewellyn	2	7	255					
Lat.	Locusta	4		285	,,	Mahnahbezee	3	1	276
Grk.	Lois	2	2	243	,,	Mahtohpa	3	1	256
Lat.	Longinus	3	2	226, 277	Heb.	Malachi	2	4	247
,,	Lorenzo, Laurence, Laurentia, Laura, Lauretta	2	9	158, 260	,,	Malchus, Milcah	2	9	258, 259
					Celt.	Malcolm (s.)	3	2	263
					Ar.	Malek Shah	2	9	105, 261
					Heb.	Manaen	2	6	251

ALPHABETICAL LIST OF NAMES. 305

Derivation	Name	Class	Division	Page	Derivation	Name	Class	Division	Page
Teu.	Manfred	2	10	263	N.A.I	Mee cheet a neuch	2	6	252
Heb.	Manoah	2	10	262					
Lat.	Mansuetus	2	10	263	Grk.	Medea	2	9	259
Heb.	Manuel, Emmanuel	1	2	236	„	Medora (s.)	2	3	245
					Ar.	Mehdi	2	8	258
„	Manuela, Manuelita	1		236	Heb.	Mehetabel	1	2	236
					Grk.	Megaliter	2	6	251
Lat.	Marcus, Mark, Marcia	2	7	254	„	Melander, Melanie	3	2	276
„	Marcellus, Marcella	2	7	254	„	Melanthus, Melanthusa	3	1, 2	276
„	Marcellinus, Marcelline	2	7	254	„	Melesias	2	8	257
					„	Melita	4		284
Lat.	Martin, Martine	2	7	254	Pers.	Melchior	2	9	261
Grk.	Margaret, Margarita	2	2, 4	4, 98, 198	Heb.	Melchizedek, king of righteousness	1	2	
„	Marguerite, Maggie, Meta	2	2, 4	149	Ar.	Melek el Mansour	2	7	256
„	Margery, Marjorie	2	2, 4	245, 248	Grk.	Melina (s.)	2	10	263
„	Maggie, Greta	2	2, 4		„	Melisander, Melissa, Melicerta, Melita, Millicent, Milly	2	10	262, 263
Ar.	Marjaneh	2	3	146					
		3	1	276					
Teu.	Marmaduke	2	9	260					
Grk.	Marmarium	2	4	247	Lat.	Meliora	2	2	244
Ar.	Marfain	2	7	256	Ar.	Mellaky	2	9	261
Heb.	Mary, Marie, Maria, Mara, Miriam (Ar.) Maryam, (Gael.) Morag, Marianne, Marian, Marion, Minnie, Marietta,(Sp.) Mariquita	4		9,138,212, 281, 285	Grk.	Menie (s.)	2	3	245
					„	Menelaus	2	6	251
					„	Mentor	2	7	253
					Lat.	Mergus	4		284
					„	Mercedes	2	3, 6	192, 237, 246, 252, 266, 267
					„	Mercurius	2	1	
					Celt.	Merideth	2	7	255
					„	Mervyn (Morvran)	2	7	231, 255
„	Martha, Patty	4		281					
N.A.I	Mash kee wet	2	8	258	Ar.	Mes'ood Mes'oodah	2	12	266
Grk.	Maurice,Maura, Maury, Moritz	3	2	277	„	Mesroor, happy	2	12	
Teu.	Matilda, Maude	2	7, 9	228, 255	Grk.	Metiochus	2	8	257
Heb.	Matthew, Matthias	1	2	236	„	Metrocles	2	3, 9	245, 259
					Ar.	Meymoon, Meymooneh	2	12	266
Lat.	Mathurin, Mathurine	2	2	244	Hin.	Mher ul Nica	2	2	244
„	Max, Maxima, Maximin	2	9	260	Teu.	Meyrick	2	9	254, 260
					Heb.	Michael, Michaela, Michel, Michelline	1	2	9, 92, 236
Lat. Grk.	{ Maximilian, Maximilienne	2	9, 11	231					
Teu.	May (s.) (Mai), a maiden	2	4		„	Michal	2	2	243
					Teu.	Mildred	2	10	50,190,263
Grk.	Meconium	4		282	Grk.	Miltiades, Milto	3	2	276

ALPHABETICAL LIST OF NAMES.

Derivation		Class	Division	Page	Derivation		Class	Division	Page
Grk.	Minervina	2	8	257	Heb.	Nanette (Anne, &c.)	2	2, 6	251
Teu.	Minna, Minnie	2	3	246	Lat.	Nathalie	1	2	183, 236
N.A.I	Minne ha ha	2	11	49, 265	Heb.	Nathaniel, Nathan, Neil	1	2	236
"	Minne wa wa	2	11	49, 265					
Lat.	Minutia	3	2	277	Celt. Teu.	} Nanthilde	4		231, 282
Grk.	Mitio	2	10	262					
N.A.I	Mishe mokwa, the great bear	2	7		Hin.	Narmada	2	12	266
Pers.	Mithra	1	1	235	Lat.	Naso	3	3	226, 278
"	Mithridates, Mithridad	1	2	66, 238	Ar.	Neamet Allah	1	2	239
					Heb.	Necho	3	3	278
"	Mithrabarzanes	1	2	238	Ar.	Nehar es Sena	2	4	249
Grk.	Mnechus	2	2	243	"	Nejmet es Sabak	2	4	249
"	Mnesarete	2	2	243, 279	N.A.I	Nekimé	2	7	256
Teu.	Modgudor	2	7	255, 271	Teu.	Nellie (Ellen)	2	12	266
"	Modred	2	7	255, 271	Heb.	Neri	2	4	247
Ar.	Mohammed, Mahmoud	1	2	54, 239, 261	"	Neriah	1	2	236
		2	9		Sab.	Nero	2	7	254, 270
N.A.I	Mong shong shaw	3	1	49, 276	N.A.I	Nenemoosha	2	3	247
					Grk.	Nessida	4		284
Teu.	Mona	2	4	248	"	Nestor	2	8	257
Grk.	Monica, *alone*	4			N.A.I	Netis	2	3	247
"	Monimia	2	9	259	Lat.	Nettuno	1	1	235
Hin.	Mootie	2	3, 4	247	Grk.	Nicias, Nicander, Nicanor, Nico, Nicilla, Nicium, Nicea	2	7, 9	253
Celt.	Morgiana, Morwen	4		114, 282					
"	Morhold	2	7	255					
Heb.	Moses, (Ar.) Moussa, Musa, Muza	4		281	"	Nicodemus, Nicholas, Cola, Claus, Claussen, Nicola, Nicoline, Nicolette, Colette	2	7, 9	253, 268
Grk.	Moschus	4		284					
Lat.	Mugillianus	4		284					
Celt.	Mungo	2	3	246					
N.A.I	Munne puska	2	7	94, 256	Grk.	Nicephorus	2	7	253
Celt.	Murdoch, Murtagh	2	9	261	"	Nicomedes	2	8	257
					Lat.	Nigel, Niger	3	2	277
Lat.	Muræna	4		284	Heb.	Nimrod	4		281
Grk.	Muriel	2	11	264	Sp.	Niña, Niñita	2	3	192, 246, 267
Pers.	Murwari	2	3	246					
Lat.	Musca	4		284	Ass.	Ninus	3	1	35
Ar.	Mustafa	1 2	2 3 }	239, 246	Pers.	Nisca, *a rose*	3	2	
					N.A.I	Nixwarroo	2	7	256
Grk.	Myllia	4		284	Heb.	Noah	2	10	262
"	Myrrha, Myro, Myra, Myrtale, Myrrhena	2	11	264	Ar.	Noam	2	12	266
					Lat.	Noël, Nathalie	1	2	183, 236
					Heb.	Nogah	2	4	247
					Lat.	Nonius, Nonia	4		284
					Ar.	Noor ed Deen, Noureddin	1	2	95, 239
Heb.	Naaman, Naamah, Naomi	2	11	264, 274					
		3	1	279	"	Noor et Huda	2	4	249
Vit.	Naiogabui	2	11	265	"	Noor Jehan	2	4	249
Ass.	Nana	1	1	235, 239	"	Noor Mahal	2	4	249

ALPHABETICAL LIST OF NAMES. 307

Derivation		Class	Division	Page	Derivation		Class	Division	Page
N.A.I	Not a way	2	8	258	Lat.	Palmetius, Palma, Palmyre (Fr.)	2	9	260
Grk.	Numa	2	8	257					
Lat.	Numerianus	4		284					
Ar.	Nuzhet el Fuad	2	3	246	Grk.	Pamela (s.), all sweetness, or altogether dark, a brunette	2	11	
,,	Nuzhet el Zemon	2	3	246			3	2	
Lat.	Nydia	4		284					
					Grk.	Pammenes	2	7	253
					,,	Pamphilius	2	3	245
Heb.	Obadiah	1	2	181, 236	,,	Panacea	2	6	251
Lat.	Ocella	3	3	226	,,	Panagie	2	2	243, 267
,,	Octavius, Octavian, Octavia	4		284	,,	Panarista	2	2	243
					,,	Pancrates	2	9	259
Teu.	Odo, Otho, Odalric	1	2	} 235, 266	,,	Pandora	2	12	265
		2	9, 12		,,	Pantaclea	2	9	259
,,	Odile, Odette,	2	9, 12	261	,,	Panthea	2	9	259
	Othilde, Ottilie				,,	Panthous	2	7	253
					,,	Panthera	4		284
,,	Offa	2	10	263	,,	Papyrius	4		283
,,	Olaf, Aulaff	2	10	51	,,	Parmenion	2	10	262
,,	Olga. See Aldegonde	1	2	261	,,	Parthenia	2	4	248
					,,	Parthenope	3	1	274
N.A.I	Olitipa	3	1	49, 276	,,	Pasiphila	2	3	245
Lat.	Oliver, Olivia, Olive	2	10	263	Heb.	Pasquale, Pascha	1	2	236
,,	Omobuono	2	2	244	Lat.	Passer	4		284
Grk.	Onesiphorus	2	6	251	Lat. from Grk.	} Patrick, Patricia	2	9	125, 199, 260
N.A.I	Oojeena he ha	2	7	256					
Grk.	Olympia, Olympe	2	4	248					
					Grk.	Patrocles	2	3,9	10, 245, 259
Ar.	Omar	2	2	244	,,	Paula, Pauline	2	10	263
Grk.	Ophelia	2	6	251	Lat.	Paul, Paula, Pauline	3	2	9, 277, 279
Lat.	Opportune	2	12	266					
Grk.	Orca	2	10	263	Grk.	Pausanias, one who allays sorrow	2	6	
Heb.	Oreb	4		283					
Celt.	Orkedorigh	2	9	261					
Heb.	Orpah	3	1	274	Tah.	Pauma, Pomare (s.)	2	7	257
Egy.	Osiris	1	1	235					
Teu.	Osbert	1	2	238	N.A.I	Pehta	2	7	256
,,	Osmond	1	2	238	Grk.	Peitho	2	11	264
,,	Oswald	1	2	238	,,	Pelagio, Pelagie, Pelayo	4		281
,,	Oswin	1	2	238					
N.A I	Owaissa	3	1	276	,,	Penelope	4		282
Celt.	Owen {	2	10	} 234, 236, 263	Heb.	Penninah	2	3	245
		1	2		Grk.	Pericles	2	9	225, 259
					,,	Perialla	2	2	243
					,,	Periphas	2	4	247
Lat.	Pætus	3	3	278	Lat.	Peregrine	4		282
N.A.I	Pah me cow e tah	2	8	258	,,	Perpetua, unchanging, constant	2	5	
,,	Pah too cara	2	7	256					
,,	Pah ta chooche	4		283	Hin.	Perrya Amma	2	9	262

308 ALPHABETICAL LIST OF NAMES.

Derivation	Name	Class	Division	Page	Derivation	Name	Class	Division	Page
Grk.	Perrine (Fr.). See Peter				Grk.	Polycarp	2	2	243
					"	Polydor	2	12	265
"	Petala	2	4	248	"	Polytimeus	2	2,3	245
		3	1	226	"	Polyxene	2	6	251
"	Peter (Petros),	2	7	41, 253	Lat.	Ponce	2	6	252
	Pietro, Perez,				"	Pontius	4		282
	Petrea,Pierette,				"	Poppea	3	1	275
	Petronilla, Perrine				Grk.	Porphyry	2	9	105, 259
					Lat.	Portia	2	6	252
N.A.I	Pezhekee	2	7	256	Egy.	Potiphera	1	2	238
Egy.	Pharaoh	1	1	64, 235	Lat.	Preziosa	2	3	245
Grk.	Phædra	1	1	248	"	Probus	2	2	244
"	Phædora, Feodor, Feodora	2	4	248	Grk.	Procopius	2	12	265
					Lat.	Prosper, Properzia (Ital.)	2	12	266
"	Phœbe	1	1	197, 235					
		2	4	247	"	Prudence	2	8	258
"	Phænarete	2	2,4	243	Celt.	Prûdwen, Prydain	3	1	275
"	Phaon, Phano	2	4	247					
"	Phantasia	2	8	257	N.A.I	Pshanshaw	2	11	265
"	Phenice	2	9	259	Grk.	Psyche	2	4	248
"	Phila, Phillina	2	3	245	"	Ptolemy	2	7	64
"	Philander, Philemon, Philetas	2	3	245	Lat.	Publius, Publicola	2	3	87, 245
					"	Pudens, Pudentia	2	2,10	263
"	Philalethe	2	5	250					
"	Philareta	2	2	243	"	Pulcherie	3	1	275
"	Philomela	2	11	264	Hin.	Pun Amma	2	9	262
"	Philadelphus, Philadelphia	2	3	245	Grk.	Pyrallis	3	1	275
					"	Pyrgo	2	6	251
"	Philopater, Philometer	2	3	245, 267	"	Pyrrhus, Pyrrha	3	2	276
"	Philumena, Filomena	2	3	121, 245	"	Psyllus	4		218
					"	Pythagoras	2	8	10, 257
"	Philip,Philippa, Philippine	4		281	"	Pythias	2	8	257
"	Phyllis	4		283					
"	Philyrea	3	1	275	Lat.	Quercens	4		283
"	Phintias	2	3	245	"	Quartus, Quartia	4		284
"	Phryne	4		276, 279					
Lat.	Pilate	4		282	"	Quintus, Quintillian, Quintilla	4		284
Heb.	Pinon, Peninnah	2	3	245					
Grk.	Pisander	2	11	264	"	Quietus	2	10	263
Lat.	Pisius	4		283					
Grk.	Piston, Pistus	2	5	225, 250					
Lat.	Pius, Pia	2	2	243	Ar.	Es Raad el Khasif	2	7	256
"	Placidus, Placilla	2	10	95, 263					
					Heb.	Rachel	2	10	121, 262
Grk.	Plato	3	2	83, 276	Teu.	Radegunde	2	8	258
Lat.	Plautus, Plautilla	3	3	278	Ar.	Rahab	3	2	278
					"	Rahneh	2	3	246
Grk.	Plutarch	2	12	265	Hin.	Rama	1	1	235

ALPHABETICAL LIST OF NAMES. 309

Derivation		Class	Division	Page	Derivation		Class	Division	Page
Egy.	Rameses	1	2	22	Lat.	Rosa, Rose,	3	1, 2	277
Teu.	Randolph, Ralph, Raoul	2	6	252		Rosina, Rosamond, Rosabel, Rosalba, Rosalie, Rosanne			
,,	Ranwulph	2	7	255					
Heb. Egy.	} Raphia	2	6	251	Celt.	Rowena	3	2	277
Heb.	Raphael, Raphaela	1	2	9, 236	Pers.	Roxalane (Roushen)	2	4	249
Lat.	Raucula	3	3	278	Lat.	Rufus, Rufa	3	2	277, 279
,,	Ravilius	3	3	278	,,	Rutilius, Rutilia	3	2	277
Teu.	Raymond	2	10	263					
Heb.	Rebekah, Rebecca	2	11	264	Heb.	Ruth	3	1	247, 274
Lat.	Redento, Redenta	1	2	237	Ar.	Sa'ad, Saa'deh	2	12	266
,,	Regulus, Regallianus, Regilla, Regina, Reine	2	9	7, 260	,,	Sa'ed	2	3	105, 246
					Celt.	Saidi, Sad	2	2	244
					Grk.	Sabinus, Sabina	4		284
Teu.	Reginald, Regnier	2	9	260	Teu.	Sæbald	2	7	255
					,,	Sæfreth	2	9	260
,,	Reinfred	2	10	263	,,	Sæwulph	2	7	255
Lat.	Respectus	2	9	260, 271	Ar.	Salah ed Deen, Saladin	1	2	71, 239
,,	Renatus, René	1	2	129, 237					
,,	Réséda	3	1	264	,,	Saleh	2	2	244
Teu.	Reynard	2	5	148	,,	Salem, Salameh	2	10	263
,,	Reynoid	2	3, 5	246, 268	Lat.	Sallust	2	10	266
Ar.	Reyhan	1	2	150, 239	,,	Salvator, Salvius, Salvien, Salvia, Salvina, Sage	2	6	155, 251, 266
Grk.	Rhene	2	10	263					
Celt.	Rhys, Ruiz, Ruy	2	9	261					
Teu.	Richard, Dick	2	7	199, 254	Fr.	Sage	2	8	258
,,	Ridda	4		282	Ar.	Es Samit	2	10	263
,,	Robert, Robin, Rupert, Ruperta, Robinia, Robinetta	2	8	148, 258	Heb.	Samson	2	4	247
					,,	Samuel, *asked of God*	1	2	
					Lat.	Sanchez, Sancha	1	2	244
,,	Roger, Rudiger	2	5, 8	250					
,,	Roderick, Rodriguez	2	8, 9	258	,,	Sapientia	2	8	258
					Heb.	Sapphira	2	3	245
,,	Rodolph, Rolf	2	6, 8	252	,,	Sarah	2	9	259
,,	Roland	2	6	252	,,	Sardis	2	12	265
Lat.	Romilda	2	7	254	Ar.	Sasafeh	3	1	276
Celt.	Rôs, *a rose*	3	1		Lat.	Saturnino	1	1	235, 240
Lat.	Romulus, Romola	2	7	74, 254	Heb.	Saul	2	3	245
					Grk.	Saurus	4		111, 284
Grk.	Rhoda, Rhodocella, Rhodope	3	1, 2	204, 276	Ar.	Sawab	2	5	250
					Lat.	Scævola	3	3	278
,,	Rosaura	2	11	264	,,	Scipio	2	6	88
Lat.	Rosius, Rosianus	3	2	277	Grk.	Sebastian	2	9	76, 259
					,,	Scione	4		282
Teu.	Rosamund, Rosalinda	3	1, 2	277	Lat.	Secundus, Secundilla	4		284

310 ALPHABETICAL LIST OF NAMES.

Derivation		Class	Division	Page	Derivation		Class	Division	Page
N.A.I	Seet-se-bea	2	4	249	Lat.	Simeon	2	2	243
Grk.	Seleucus	3	2	276	,,	Sirpicus	4		283
Ar.	Selim, Selimeh	2	12	266	Ass.	Sitareh, Esther, Hester	2	4	6, 249
,,	Es Semendal	2	4	249					
Grk.	Selina, Selene	2	4	235, 247	Grk.	Smilax	4		283
Ass.	Semiramis	2	10	35,127,263	N.A.I	Soangetaha	2	7	256
Heb.	Sephora	3	1	274	Grk.	Socrates	2	2	225, 243
Lat.	Septimus, Septilia	4		284	Ar.	Soem	2	3	247
					,,	Safiyeh, Sofian	2	3	69,239,246
,,	Serena	2	10	263	Tur.	Sofiyeh	2	3	69,239,246
Heb.	Seraphine, Serafina	1	2	236	Pers.	Sofi ed Deen	1	2	71, 239
					Grk.	Sophia, Sophy, Sophonie, Sofia, Sophie, Sophiele	2	8	9, 68, 134, 209, 257
,,	Serug	4		283					
Lat.	Sextus, Sextilia, Sexticia	4		284					
Ar.	Seyf ed Deen	1	2	} 239	Grk.	Sophocles	2	8, 9	257
		2	7		,,	Sophronius, Sophroniscus, Sophronia, Sophrosyne, Sophronium	2	2, 8	257
,,	Seyf ud Dowlah	2	7, 9	261			2	2, 8	243, 257
,,	Seyf el Mulook	2	7, 9	261					
N.A.I	Shako	4		283					
Ass.	Shalmaneser	1	1	235	Heb.	Solomon, Salome	2	10	24, 262
Heb.	Shallum	2	2	243					
Ar.	Shamikh	2	9	262	Grk.	Sosandra	2	6	251
Heb.	Sharai	2	9	258	,,	Sosthenes	2	2	243
Ar.	Sharaf el Benat	2	9	262	,,	Soter, Sosia	2	6	251
N.A.I	Shawondazee	2	11	265	Ass.	Sosana	2	4	209
,,	Shedea	4		283	Heb.	Susan, Susanna	3	2	191, 249, 276
Ar.	Shehr a zad, Scherezade	3	1	275					
					Ar.	Soosan	3	2	278
,,	Shejeret el Durr	2	3	48, 246	Grk.	Spiridion, Spiro	1	2	238, 241
Heb.	Shelemiah	2	2	236	Scla.	Stanislaus	2	9	261
Ar.	Shems ed Deen	1	2	239	Pers.	Statira	2	3	113, 246
,,	Shems ed Doha	2	3	249, 261	Grk.	Stephen, Stephanie, (Sp.) Esteban, (Fr.) Etienne	2	9	4, 259
,,	Shems el Mulook	2	9	261					
,,	Shems en Nehar	2	3	249					
Pers.	Shereen	2	11	98, 265	Lat.	Stella, Estelle	2	4	248
N.A.I	Shingawossa	3	1	94, 276	,,	Strabo	3	3	278
Pers.	Sher	2	7	256	,,	Sulpicius	2	6	251
,,	Sherkok	2	7	256	Grk.	Sybil, Sibyl, Sibella	1	2 }	134, 257
Ar.	Shoh	2	3	246			2	8 }	
Celt.	Sholto (s.)	4		282	,,	Syntyche	2	12	265
N.A.I	Shomecosse	2	7	256	N.A.I	Stee cha co meco	2	9	262
Phœ.	Sidonia	2	11	264					
Teu.	Sigbert	2	7	254	Lat.	Sylvester, Sylvanus, Sylvia	4		282
,,	Sigeard, Sigurd	2	7	254					
,,	Sigeric	2	7, 9	260	Teu.	Sweyn	3	2	277
,,	Sighelm	2	7	254					
,,	Sigismund	2	7	254					
,,	Sigwulph	2	7	254	Heb.	Tabitha	3	1	274
Heb.	Simon	2	2	45, 77, 243	Lat.	Tacitus, Tace	2	10	227, 263

ALPHABETICAL LIST OF NAMES. 311

Derivation		Class	Division	Page	Derivation		Class	Division	Page
N.A.I	Tai bau se gai, bursts of thunder at a distance	2	7	214	Grk.	Thetis	4		282
					,,	Theta	4		284
					Teu.	Thora, Thyra	1	2	238
					,,	Thordisa	1	2	238, 255
Ar.	Taj el Mulook	2	9	261	,,	Thorgerda	1	2	238, 255
Celt.	Taliessin	2	4	248	,,	Thorgeir	1	2	238
Heb.	Tamar	3	1	274	,,	Thorkell	1	2	238
N.A.I	Tahmiroo	3	1	49, 276	,,	Thormod	1	2	238, 271
Etr.	Tanagra	2	9	260	,,	Thorwald	1	2	238, 241
,,	Tancred (s.), Tangraid	2	9	260	Phœ.	Thomas (s.), Tom, Thomasina, (Heb.)	1	1	235, 240
,,	Tanaquil	2	7	254, 270					
Celt.	Tegid	2	10	263		Thammuz			
Grk.	Telamon	2	7	253	Grk.	Thrasymene, brave spirit	2	7	
,,	Telega	4		282					
,,	Telesia	2	2	243	,,	Thrasybulus, brave counsellor	2	7	
,,	Telligida	4		284					
Ar.	Ten'om	2	10	263					
Heb.	Terah	2	12	265	Lat.	Tiberius	4		284
Sab.	Terence, Terentia, soft, gentle	2	10	263	Grk.	Timandra	2	7	254
					,,	Timarete	2	2	243
Lat.	Tertius, Tertia, Tertullus, Tertullian	4		284	,,	Timothy, who honours God	1	2	237
					,,	Titus, Titian, Tita, venerable	2	9	
Grk.	Thaïs	3	1	274					
,,	Thalassis	4		282	Ar.	Tohfeh	2	3	246
,,	Thales, Thalia, Thallusa	2	12	265	Grk.	Topsius	4		282
					Lat.	Toussaint (French), altogether holy	1	2	
,,	Theano	2	8	257					
,,	Thekla, one who gives glory to God	2	2		Grk.	Triptolemus	2	7	253
					,,	Trismegistus	2	9	259
,,	Themistocles	2	2	243	,,	Tryphena	4		282
,,	Theodore, Theodora	1	2	237	,,	Tryphosa	4		282
					Celt.	Trystan	2	9	261
,,	Theodosius, Theodosia	1	2	237	Lat.	Tristam, sorrowful	4		
,,	Theophilus, Theophila	1	2	237	Chi.	Tsing Lûng	2	7	256
					Celt.	Tuileach	2	7	255
,,	Theophanie, Tiphaine	1	2	183,237,274	Lat.	Tullius, Tullia, Tulliola	2	2	45, 244
,,	Theophrastes	2	8	83	,,	Turpilianus, Turpilia	3	3	278
Teu.	Theodoric, Thierry	2	9	72, 260					
					N.A.I	Tunt aht oh ge	2	7	256
,,	Theodelinde, Yolande	3	1	275	Grk.	Tychicus	2	12	265
Heb.	Theresa (s.), Thérèse, Théréson, Zon, Zeno, Teresa, Thirza (Tirzah)	3	1	9, 274					
					Teu.	Udolph	2	6	252
					,,	Ulf	2	7	195, 255
					,,	Ulric, Ulrica (Odalric)	2	12	266

ALPHABETICAL LIST OF NAMES.

Derivation	Name	Class	Division	Page	Derivation	Name	Class	Division	Page
Lat.	Una	4		244, 284	Lat.	Vivian, Vivia, *life*	2	1	
,,	Ursinus, Ursinius	2	7	254	,,	Vitia	4		283
,,	Ursula, Ursina	2	7	254	Scla.	Vladimir	2	9	261, 273
Ar.	Umr Sood	2	12	266	Lat.	Volumnia	2	3	245
Grk.	Urania (Sans. Varouna)	2	8	257	,,	Vulturgius	4		284
Lat.	Urban	4		282					
Heb.	Uriel, Uriah	1	2	236	N.A.I	Wahongaskee	2	8	258
Lat.	Urtica, Urticula	4		283	,,	Wa saw me saw	2	8	256
Sp.	Urraca	4		8	,,	Washkemonge	4		282
					Teu.	Waldemar	2	9	260
					,,	Waltheof, Walter	2	9	260
Sans	Vajezatha	1	1	235	N.A.I	Weemeonka, *bending willow*	3	1	
Teu.	Vala	2	3	246					
,,	Vaen, Vanessa	3	1	275	Teu.	Wilfred	2	10	263
,,	Valborge	2	3	50, 246	,,	William, Wilhelm, Willie, Wilhelmina	2	6	29, 252
Lat.	Valentine, Valentinian	2	7	254					
,,	Valerius, Valerie	2	7	155, 254	,,	Wimund	2	2	244
					,,	Winfred, Winifred, Winnie	2	10	29, 263
Vit.	Valugaiaki	2	4	217					
Grk. Rus.	} Vasileia	2	9	259	N.A.I	Wingemund	2	3	247
					Teu.	Wistan	2	8	258
Teu.	Velleda	2	7	255	,,	Wolfgang, *gait of a wolf*	2	7	
Lat.	Verena	1	2	237					
,,	Vero, Vera, Verax, Veranius, Ver nia	2	5	189, 250	,,	Wolfheah	2	7	255
					,,	Wolfric	2	7	255
					N.A.I	Wukmisir	4		283
Lat. Grk.	} Veronica	1	2	151, 237	Teu.	Wyn	2	3	246
Celt.	Verkendorigh	2	9	261					
Lat.	Virtue	2	2		Grk.	Xerxes, (Pers.) Cyaxares	2	7	256
,,	Vespasian, Vespellian	4		155, 284	,,	Xanthe	3	2	277
Celt.	Vhir dhu Mohr	3	2	277					
Teu.	Vibert	2	4	244					
Lat.	Victor, Victoria	2	7	77, 226	Brit.	Yves, Yvonne. See John, Jane	1	2	236
,,	Victorine, Victoriola	2	7	254	Ar.	Yasimeen	3	1	48, 275
,,	Vincent, Vincentia	2	7	157, 226, 254	Teu.	Yolande (Theodelinde)	3	1	275
Lat.	Vigilius, Vigilantius	2	8	258	Celt.	Ysolt, Isolt (Essylt)	2 3	4 1	} 248, 275
Sp.	Vimeira	4		284					
Lat	Vinnulia	2	11	264	Heb.	Zadoc	2	2	243
,,	Viola, Violet, Violetta, Violante	2	11	264	,,	Zaccheus	2	4	247
					Ar.	Zaïdee	2	12	207, 266
,,	Virginius, Virginia, Virginie	2	4	248	,,	Zaïre(s.)(Zahr) *a flower*	3	1	

ALPHABETICAL LIST OF NAMES. 313

Derivation		Class	Division	Page	Derivation		Class	Division	Page
Ar.	Zahr el Bustan	3	1	275	Heb.	Zillah	2	6, 11	48, 223, 251
,,	Zahr el Naring	3	1	275	,,	Zimri	4		283
,,	Zara	2	4	207, 249	,,	Zibiah	3	1	274
,,	Zarifa	2	11	207, 275	,,	Zippor, Zippo-	4		283
Heb.	Zechariah, remembrance of God	1	2		Ar.	rah Zita	2	9	262
					Grk.	Zoë	2	1	207, 242
,,	Zeeb	2	7	253	,,	Zopyra	2	1	242
Grk.	Zelie	2	7	207, 253	,,	Zozimia	2	1	242
,,	Zenaïde	2	2	207, 243	,,	Zora	2	4	248
,,	Zeno, Zenobia	1	2	203, 224	Ar.	Zuleika(s.), Zeleekah	3	2	278
		2	1	242					
Heb.	Zephaniah	1	2	69, 236	,,	Zulma, Zuleyma, Suleyma	2	12	207
Grk.	Zephyrino, Zephyrine	1	1	196, 235, 242					
		2	1		,,	Zumurrud	2	3	48, 246

The Latin names Aper and Domitian, Class 2, Division 7, have been placed, through an oversight of the writer, amongst the Greek names of the same class and division. A similar oversight will be observed in Minutia, Class 3, Division 2, and in Macer, Class 3, Division 3, both of these names being of Latin derivation. Ignatius, rightly translated p. 77, is wrongly classed p. 247. Other oversights, doubtless, there are in upwards of 2,000 names, but, the writer trusts, not so many as may appear to a casual observer. Many names of Latin sound and appearance may be traced, it is conscientiously supposed, to a Greek origin. Argentine, born in Rome of Latin Argentum, does she not rightly claim sisterhood with Greek Argyrea, and a common descent from 'Arguros,' *silver*? Or rather let us trace back to 'Argos,' *shining, glistering*. How suggestive, then, is the doubly significant musical name of the Grecian nymph—'shining' and 'swift' as a glancing ray of light! Beyond the power of the writer's pen is it even to touch upon the wonders of scientific research regarding the undulation of light: but in the simple thought of a woman's name, Argyrea, as figurative of one whose feet were silvery and swift, there is hope for her who would fain be the bearer of even the tiniest ray of light, telling of the Light of Life—the one true Light for time and for eternity.

Errata.

Page 9, line 8, *for* Francisca *read* Francisca de Assiz (e de)
 ,,   9, ,, 10, 11, *omit* (de Assise e de)
 ,,   48, ,, 14, the reference to note should come after 'Susan,' line 12
 ,, 242, ,, 14, *for* Athenais *read* Athanasia
 ,, 281, ,, 12, *for* Japhet—Hunter *read* Japhet—Beautiful

WITHDRAWN

MAINE STATE LIBRARY
929.4 M817w, 1984
Moody, Sophy.
What is your name? A popular account of

3 5081 00088690 2

1992   1985

929.4   M817w   1984

Moody, Sophy.
                        $30.00
What is your name? A popular
  account of the meanings and
  derivations of Christian...